Jade

Jade

Fighting to the End

My Autobiography

1981–2009

JB

JOHN BLAKE

Published by John Blake Publishing Ltd,
3 Bramber Court, 2 Bramber Road,
London W14 9PB, England

www.johnblakepublishing.co.uk

First published in hardback in 2008
This edition published in paperback in 2009

ISBN: 978-1-84454-813-2

British Library Cataloguing-in-Publication Data:

A catalogue record for this book is available from the British
Library.

Design by www.envydesign.co.uk

Printed in Great Britain by CPI Bookmarque, Croydon, CR0 4TD

1 3 5 7 9 10 8 6 4 2

Papers used by John Blake Publishing are natural, recyclable
products made from wood grown in sustainable forests. The
manufacturing processes conform to the environmental regulations
of the country of origin.

Every attempt has been made to contact the relevant copyright-
holders, but some were unobtainable. We would be grateful if the
appropriate people could contact us.

Contents

Acknowledgements

Thanks to my mum for loving me unconditionally. You have as many great things about you as you have faults and it's because of what I've been through that I've become the strong person that I am today. I love you to bits.

Thank you to Sean O'Brien for taking me under his wing when no one else would.

Thanks to Danny Hayward and Simon Bridger for being good friends, and also to Lucie Cave for helping me write another brilliant book.

Finally, thank you to Bobby and Freddy, my beautiful boys, for helping me get through the tough times and making me smile every single day.

Jade's Final Chapter –
by Lucie Cave

'Life is for laughing'
Jade Goody, February 2009

This is the second of Jade Goody's books about her life – something, even before she was fatefully diagnosed with cancer in August 2008, she had always planned as a precious record for her two beloved sons Bobby and Freddy. Jade brought me on board as her ghost-writer to help her pen an honest account of her colourful upbringing – to show her boys just how much their mum had achieved and to serve as an inspirational reminder that success can be built on hard work, persistence and inner strength.

The Jade I got to know was more open, honest and candid than any celebrity I'd ever met (and probably ever will again). Unique, strong, brave, big-hearted and extremely vulnerable, Jade wore her heart firmly on her sleeve in a way no-one else, especially those in the public eye, would dare. And despite the fact that by the time we embarked on her first book in 2006 she was one of the most famous people in the UK (with three reality TV shows under her belt and having sold more perfumes than J-Lo and David Beckham) there was never an ounce of the diva about her.

Most celebs want things done on their terms or not at all. But rather than making me trek all the way to her place in Essex whenever we worked on her autobiography, Jade insisted on driving herself to my house. Of course, Jade being Jade she was usually late – and I'd get the inevitable phone call telling me that the sat nav in her car had sent her 'the wrong way' (this happened to her a lot – she was stopped by police for driving the wrong direction down Oxford Street once) or that she'd spent the afternoon searching for a missing budgie that Jack had bought her as a present (turned out she'd left the window of her conservatory open). One evening I got a knock on my door and opened it to see her standing there in fits of giggles because she couldn't park her car so we had to leave it in the middle of my road and hope none of my neighbours needed to go anywhere. But no matter what time she eventually arrived, Jade was always full of apologies and would stay working with me for hours (in between making calls to her babysitter – mum Jackiey or ex-boyfriend Jeff – to check that her little boys had brushed their teeth and gone to bed on time).

She might have been known for having a big mouth, but Jade was super-polite at all times. Manners were of utmost importance to her – something she instilled in her sons. She would always say 'please' and 'thank you' and would courteously ask if it was okay for her to use my bathroom when she needed the loo. Jade visited my house loads, but wouldn't ever accept anything other than a glass of water

– this was typical of Jade, she didn't want to be a burden.

When Jade was around you certainly always knew about it and my flatmates would chuckle to themselves whenever she poked her head round the door with her trademark grin. At the time of writing the first book together, *Jade: My Autobiography*, she had just opened her salon, 'Ugly's' in Essex, which meant she often turned up in her beautician's uniform. This was way too short (and tight) for her but somehow she pulled it off. Working with so many beauty treatments meant Jade was a guinea pig for new products – and regularly appeared with different-coloured skin or excitedly pointing to a 'wrinkle-free' patch on her forehead. Once she turned up with extremely unusual eyebrows – 'I've had them tattooed!' she cackled. But Jade could get away with it. One of the enduring things about her – and the thing most people remarked on when they met her – was how very pretty she was in the flesh. Flawless skin and jaw-dropping features made her incredible to look at, and when she lost all her hair from chemo she still looked arrestingly beautiful.

Jade's life story was so eventful – a film-maker couldn't have dreamed it up. She'd sit on my bed recalling the things that had happened to her – growing up with a drug addict dad who was in and out of prison, Jade was then forced to care for her mum after an accident left her paralysed. But Jade still managed to find a funny side. 'I remember when I first got pubes. I was so proud of them. Then my mum leant over the bath with a razor and shaved them into a heart shape!' As with her later years, nothing was without drama. Jade sold her bed to a neighbour for £25 aged seven and was arrested for shoplifting in Selfridges when she was a teenager (she got caught because she went back to ask for carrier bags for her stolen goods). Then the ups and downs just kept on coming – a drug addict boyfriend, being sent into foster care, buying her first designer outfit ('I got this white Moschino outfit with little stick men and women all over it. I thought it was the nuts.') It was only in 2002 that her colourful existence became part of our world too. And if she hadn't been saved in the first week of *Big Brother* (she was up against Lynn in the public vote but was chosen by her fellow housemates to stay) we would never have experienced the delights of this unique breed of celebrity.

Sitting in my bedroom reliving her experiences, she was a floodgate of emotions. Hiding behind a pillow and shrieking at the mention of the 'BJ with PJ' under the sheets in *Big Brother 3*, tears streaming down her face when recalling stories from her childhood, beaming with pride when talking of her sons, giggling when I pointed out that she was saying words wrong (she spoke about drinking Absinthe and called it 'Absiss') and nervously picking the buttons off my duvet when approaching a subject that made her feel uncomfortable, like having to defend her mum's unconventional behaviour. One of the sweetest things about Jade was what a complete prude she was – she would go all red whenever I asked her about sex and revealed she was one of the last girls at her school to lose her virginity. Jade would never dream of flaunting her sexuality and she was always a one-man woman. All her boyfriends (of which there were only a few) had to woo Jade like a proper lady – because that's what she was.

She also had a brilliant singing voice – something I still can't quite get my head around. The fact that she won *Celebrity Stars in Their Eyes* in 2006 somehow went under the showbiz radar – but for Jade it was one of her proudest achievements. 'People in the audience were cheering and clapping, I couldn't believe I'd won!' Jade was also immensely chuffed when she created her perfumes – 'Ssh' and 'Controversial' – because it was something she'd genuinely put her heart and soul into. 'Some people thought I'd had it all done for me. But I worked so hard getting it right,' she told me at the time. 'The most amazing thing was when I smelt people walking past me in the supermarket and they were wearing my perfume. The scent of Jade Goody. Who'd have thought it?!'

Jade had so many obstacles in her life but she tackled everything head on, with courage and honesty. The day after her eviction from *Celebrity Big Brother* in 2007, she called me in tears (I was shopping at the time and couldn't work out who was on the phone at first because she was so hysterical). Despite what many accused her of afterwards, Jade's primary concern was, as always, her two boys. She was distraught about what might happen to them if she became a national hate figure. As was trademark Jade, she'd acted first and thought later, and immediately wanted to apologise for any offence she'd caused. It would have been far easier for her to hide away and hope the furore would die down, but Jade never did take the easy route.

In her 27 short years Jade Goody experienced more ups and downs than a rollercoaster at Southend – yet no matter how low she was she always managed to see the funny side. It's the memory of her beaming smile and that familiar ripple of infectious laughter that I, like most people, will remember forever.

When this book concludes, at the end of 2008, she was still looking, as she always did, on the bright side. No one – not least Jade herself – could have imagined that the cancer would spread in such an aggressive way and that this young woman, who'd fought against the odds and won so many times before, would be robbed of her life at only 27 years old.

'I'm fighting for my life,' she told the *Sun* newspaper in August 2008. 'I am going to fight the damn thing every step of the way because I have two beautiful boys who are my world. But I have to be realistic and face the possibility that I may not live to see them grow up.' She was determined to shield Bobby and Freddy from the horrors of what she called 'the C word' – a resolution she maintained throughout most of her illness. 'I can't face telling my boys because they are so young' she said, 'They think mummy has tadpoles in her tummy.'

A few weeks later, Jade underwent a gruelling eight-hour operation involving a radical hysterectomy to remove her womb, meaning the mother-of-two would be unable to have any more children. She was left in tears after doctors told her that her cancer had spread to the sac around her abdominal organs. But in typical Jade style she resolutely told reporters: 'My odds of surviving are 50/50...but I'm clinging on by my fingernails!'

As if Jade hadn't been dealt enough of a blow, in September 2008 her 21-year-old boyfriend Jack Tweed was sentenced to 18 months in prison for attacking a teenager with a golf club back in December 2006. Jade told a friend: 'This couldn't have come at a worse time. I'm in bits. I'm devastated. Jack is my rock.'

No matter what Jade was going through, her utmost

priority remained to shelter her beloved sons from the harshness of the real world. She told them Jack had gone to Africa with Tarzan 'saving the lions and tigers'. And as always, she even managed to find some amusement in her visits to see Jack in prison. 'The funniest thing is that everyone in there either knows me or my mother personally!' she laughed in a magazine interview. 'He said to me, "Thank God the top dog in here used to go to school with you". And he told me the man dishing up the food was a friend of my dad's!'

In October 2008, painfully aware that she was going to lose her hair to chemotherapy, Jade bit the bullet and chopped off her long locks. 'I'm preparing myself for the day it falls out,' she shrugged bravely. 'But I'm not going to wear a wig. I'm going to look like an egg head soon – and if everyone knows I'm bald, what's the point?' In a magazine photoshoot showing off her 'new look' she joked, 'I look like Henry the hedgehog'.

Three weeks into her first six-week bout of treatment, Jade was clearly suffering – but she still did her damndest to look on the bright side. A text sent to me on 21st October was written with characteristic humour:

'Thanks for your text, not been that well, it is all catching up on me. On my third week now and I feel shit, on top of all the treatment I am going through my change – fifty year olds go through this. I cant sleep, waking up soking [sic] wet. I am a mess. Being put on HRT tablet til I am 50 ha ha got to laugh, hope you are ok xx'

Despite being separated from Jack, Jade insisted she was

standing by her man, but joked that her only complaint was his fading tan. 'Jack looks a bit pasty!' she remarked when asked about him in an interview. 'He likes using sun beds and there aren't any in prison.' Jade then made a permanent declaration of her love by tattooing his name on her wrist.

As December drew close Jade was determined to ensure her two young sons remembered what could be their last Christmas together. Beaming from ear to ear, she took five-year-old Bobby and four-year-old Freddy to Hyde Park's Winter Wonderland for ice-skating, fair rides and a trip to meet Father Christmas. As onlookers gawped, Jade laughed, joked and pulled funny faces to amuse her sons, hiding any sign of the trauma going on in her life. 'I appreciate everything I have so much more now,' she said afterwards. 'I need to live'.

It was only during an emotional TV interview on *This Morning* that it became clear just how unprepared Jade was for what lay ahead. Jade told presenter Philip Schofield that she preferred to stay in the dark about the exact details of her illness. 'I haven't done any research or anything and I don't want to know,' she said. 'I only know what I need to know, which is "this is my medication and this is that, this is when I get better". I don't want to know the ins and outs because it's too much for my brain to take it in. It really is.' She also confessed that as always, she was finding it hard to ask for help. 'I have always been the person who is the "looker afterer" so to ask people to help me is very difficult,' she told TV viewers. And when asked about Jack, she replied: 'He's my rock. I just want a cuddle.'

Loyal Jade was also intent on trying to honour her

agreement to appear in pantomine in Lincoln. But despite dutifully attending rehearsals as the Wicked Queen in *Snow White and the Seven Dwarves*, Jade wasn't able to appear on stage after all. Unable to shake off a flu virus, she spent part of New Year's Eve in hospital. 'I was only in hospital for a few hours,' she valiantly insisted afterwards. 'I felt well enough to see in the New Year with my sons and my friend Kevin Adams and his family. We had food, had a singsong, then watched Elton John's gig on TV.'

But by the start of 2009, Jade was forced to face the harsh reality of her illness. In a heart-wrenching interview she told the *Daily Mirror* how she screamed when she noticed her hair had begun to fall out – and that in three days it was virtually gone. 'I stood there screaming until my mum came running. When she saw the hair on the floor, she gave me a cuddle and started rubbing my head the way she did when I was a baby. All of a sudden handfuls more hair was peeling off in her hands. I was wailing and screaming. It was awful.'

And although she tried desperately to hide the hair loss from Bobby and Freddy, one morning she rushed downstairs without her headscarf and they saw her bald head. 'When Bobby saw me he said "What's happened Mum?" He looked so worried and started crying. It was devastating but I waited until he wasn't around and then I broke down myself.'

As usual, Jade's attitude was to pick herself back up and get on with it. 'I don't want kids to be embarrassed by my baldness,' she announced, 'I don't want them to think that if you're bald you need to hide away.' So Jade decided that rather than face 'people staring at me in Tesco' she would go public with her baldness and courageously unveiled her new appearance, alongside a moving piece written in the *News of the World* by her former *CBB* housemate, journalist Carole Malone. Carole wrote: 'I tell her she looks lovely and she laughs nervously: "Do I really?" It's bad enough that this disease can kill you, but it eats away at your confidence, your looks and your sexuality as well.'

With searing honesty, Jade told the *News of the World*: 'I've lost my hair, chucked up every single night. I'm on four bags of medication, and I can't even walk upstairs anymore,' before adding, 'I've been through so much without Jack and I'm nervous that when he comes out he won't be able to handle it.'

But when the time came to show her boyfriend Jack what she looked like without hair, Jade was as matter of fact as ever. 'I let him have a little peek at my bald head and he welled up,' she recalled. 'He told me it was the first time I have actually looked ill. No matter what kind of bloke you are with, every woman wants their man to fancy them. And of course, that worries me. I think "There's no way he's going to fancy me like this, no way!"'

Jack later said, 'It was a shock. I just wanted to hold her and make sure she was alright. But she's always the same Jade, just with no hair. It still feels the same when I kiss her, I still fancy her. There's nothing different.'

Much to their delight it was reported that Jack was set for early release, but Jade still insisted he continued to keep up appearances with her little boys. She told a newspaper, 'He's been on the phone to them from prison pretending he's in Africa fighting lions and tigers. He doesn't care that there are seven lags behind him in the queue taking the mickey. He does sweet things for the boys – and me. On Mother's Day he buys presents for me and says they're from them. Their own dad has never even done that.'

On the prospect of seeing him again, Jade said, 'We're both going through the hardest times of our lives, but we're doing it on our own. So if this doesn't make us stronger and work as a couple, nothing will. Maybe we'll be like Angelina and Brad!'

Determined not to let her illness get the better of her, in January 2009 Jade took her mum Jackiey and sons Bobby and Freddy for a short break in the sunshine before her chemotherapy sessions resumed. But while she managed a smile, self-conscious Jade, who usually wears a bikini on holiday, covered up in a swimsuit and Fifties-style swimming hat to cover her bald head. When her mum spoke out about her feelings in a Sunday newspaper, the distress of Jade's illness seemed all the more real. Tearful Jackiey broke down and said: 'Please don't let her die', sobbing that when she looked at Jade, she wondered how she became so brave. 'She's like a tigress protecting her babies,' she told the *People* newspaper. 'She's fighting this cancer so hard because she doesn't want to leave those two little boys.'

On 28th January 2009 Jade finally received some good news – Jack Tweed was released from prison and their passionate reunion was watched gleefully by the nation's press. Speaking excitedly afterwards she said: 'It was fantastic to see Jack. We went straight to Toys R Us and Jack bought a monkey for Freddy and a crocodile for Bobby – the animals he told the boys he's been looking after in Africa – then we picked them up from school together. They were so pleased to see him!'

Sadly, the couple's reunion was to be short-lived – as a condition of his early release, Jack was tagged and required to stay at home with his mother after 7p.m. Not before topping up his tan first, though. 'He spent his first full day out of jail at a tanning shop', laughed Jade.

And for Jade, things were to get increasingly worse. After suffering extreme pain in her bowel, on February 3rd 2009 the 27-year-old was rushed to hospital in an attempt to ease the pain. It was then that doctors delivered the devastating news that her cervical cancer had spread and was now incurable. Jade said later: 'I couldn't breathe when they told me. I just screamed and cried and said, "Can't anyone do anything to help me!" Because a few weeks ago when they first told me the chemo hadn't worked they said it didn't have to be the end. I know they've done everything they can to help me and I'm grateful. But I really thought I might be OK.'

In an interview a few weeks after the news, Jade touchingly described about how Jack took the prognosis. 'He was just sobbing; we laid on the bed together. He said he couldn't believe it and that he would find all these remedies for me. He's been on the computer ever since looking for all these medicines I can take. But I don't want them. He even wanted me to go to America to take them but I don't want to do it. I don't want to spend too much time away from Jack and my children. If the treatment out there didn't work and I died I'd have lost that time.'

Her mum Jackiey told reporters: 'No mum wants to bury her daughter and I'm determined it's not going to happen. Jade and I are praying for a miracle.'

It wasn't quite the proposal he'd planned (Jade said, 'When I visited Jack in jail he'd told me he had a fantastic idea for a way to propose. He said he wanted to take me to the seven wonders of the world and ask me to marry him at each of them') but on the eve of Valentine's Day, Jack Tweed popped the question to his girlfriend at her hospital bedside. A day later, they exchanged rings by the Thames in London. Jack got down on one knee, as his frail fiancée looked on happily from her wheelchair. Jade told friends, 'I was over the moon. I love Jack with all my heart and I want to be his wife more than anything in the world. And I will be. He's devastated but he's really trying to hold it together for me. But as soon as he found out I was going to die he just said, "Right then, we're getting married. You're a special woman, I love you and I would be honoured to call you my wife. And I don't care if it's just for a few weeks."'

In spite of her weak condition, Jade's wedding dress was now her top priority. On Sunday 15th February 2009 a gaunt but happy Jade Goody – her fiance Jack devotedly pushing her in her wheelchair – visited Harrods in London's Knightsbridge where she found what she described as 'the most beautiful dress.' The gown – a cream and ivory exclusive Uranio dress from the Pronovias 2009 collection by Manuel Mota – was made of silk mikado and had a classic design with a high neckline, a V-back and a full skirt with box pleating. On hearing that Jade was in his store, Harrods boss Mohamed Al Fayed announced, 'That's my wedding present to you two.'

Wasting no time, Jade summoned her five closest friends to her bedside to plan the wedding she'd always wanted. Jade's best friend Kate Jackson recalled: 'Jade said to us: "I'm getting married and I want you to be bridesmaids". Then she started flinging out random orders about what we had to do for the preparations.' Kate told the *Mirror*: 'Jade always says "Don't worry, everything will be all right". Some days she is in incredible pain, but her first thought is to comfort others. There are so many people who want to see her but whenever they break down she just tries to make them feel better.'

Jade said: 'I'm so looking forward to being a bride. And I want to walk towards my groom, just like any other young woman would on what is meant to be the best day of their lives.' With that, the Goody/Tweed wedding machine was in full motion. Undeterred by her illness, Jade spent the next few days sending out instructions from her hospital bed, using her laptop to ensure everything was going to be perfect, right down to the last detail.

Husband-to-be Jack spoke publicly for the first time about her condition and quietly remarked: 'I would chop both my arms off just to make her okay again.' Jade, as usual, continued to try and make light of her situation. 'The operation has left me with a massive scar,' she told readers of one magazine. 'It goes from my lady bits, right up to my bra. It makes me look like I've got two belly buttons!'

The media was in overdrive anticipating what was to be the most talked about wedding of the decade. Jade's story had touched even the coldest of hearts – and ironically, in her final few weeks, she became more famous than she could ever have imagined. US talk show hosts Oprah Winfrey and Larry King began a bidding war for Jade's first overseas interview, while newspapers, magazines and TV companies in the UK threw thousands of pounds into the pot in a bid to feature the wedding. Jade's aim, as it had always been, was to earn as much money as possible to provide for her two sons. More focused than ever, she carefully calculated that she would be able to build up enough funds to ensure that Bobby and Freddy would remain at their private school until they are 18. Jade said defiantly, 'I know people think I'm betraying my roots by sending them to a private school, but I want them to have the very best chance in life. And that's what my money is for. What's the point of everything if I can't do that for them?'

The drama and tension around Jade's big day was building by the minute, with newspapers reporting on her heartache over the fact that due to her fiance's prison tag and curfew, her wedding night would be spent alone. But a day later it was announced that, like everyone else in the country, the government was also moved by this sad event. Justice Minister Jack Straw intervened, lifting a curfew on Jack Tweed so the couple could stay together for one night after the ceremony. Mr Straw said it was an exceptional case. 'It is crucial that offenders are treated equally within the rules regardless of the publicity surrounding their case but I was satisfied that it was reasonable to allow this.' Prime Minister Gordon Brown welcomed the decision, saying: 'I think everybody is sad at the tragedy that's befallen Jade Goody. Everyone who suffers cancer has the thoughts of me and I think the whole country over what they've got to go through.'

Jade and Jack were over the moon. Something Jack, on a trip to the tailor with his mates to be fitted for wedding suits, seemed to take a bit too literally – when he was photographed mooning at paparazzi. 'I was so embarrassed when I saw those pictures,' snapped Jade in an interview just before the wedding – illustrating that her relationship with Jack was still as feisty as it had ever been. 'It wasn't the right circumstances for him to be doing that, there I was lying in hospital and he was flashing his bum with his mates at the tailor's. It was ridiculous, he's 21, nearly a husband – was I flashing my tits at 21?' But Jack retorted good-naturedly, 'Hey, what about you on *Big Brother*? You got your kebab out!' At which Jade couldn't help but laugh.

Jack's mates had further plans to embarrass him. Dressed in a white bra and women's underpants, a sheepish Jack Tweed was snapped leaving his mother's house on the morning of his stag do. He was joined by friends who were also dressed in women's underwear, as they made their way to the Down Hall Country House Hotel where the wedding was to take place. Meanwhile, a giggling Jade stepped out with her bridesmaids, all of whom were wearing bald caps on their heads – 'We're all egg heads now!' she laughed.

On Sunday, February 22nd Jade sat in her suite at Down Hall having her makeup carefully applied while barking orders to people around her about what needed to be done. She was resigned to the fact that she would be in constant pain – even the smallest movements caused her to flinch – but this was her day and she wasn't going to let anyone spoil it. Having flown in on a helicopter the night before ('It's something I've always wanted since I was a little girl') her wedding dress was fitted with painkillers so that the brave bride could walk down the aisle.

200 guests, including Antony Costa from Blue, Jamelia and husband, Davina McCall and Richard and Judy had all been gathering since 11.45a.m. marvelling at the flower arrangements that had been provided by Sir Elton John's florist. They might have planned the wedding in only nine

days but Jade and Jack had been flooded with offers of help and financial assistance from well wishers. At 12.45p.m. harpists signalled the start of ceremony and Jade, escorted by her 70-year-old granddad John Craddock, beamed as she walked down the aisle while guests tried their best to fight back tears. In typical Jade style the ceremony was full of laughter and when Jack was asked if he would take her as his wife, Jade joked 'Are you sure?'

Repeating words movingly crafted by Bishop Jonathan Blake, Jade told Jack, 'I love you forever and without reserve. When I see you I feel well again', before turning and telling the congregation that she had to take off her Christian Louboutin shoes because her feet hurt. As Jack put the ring on her finger she giggled nervously. 'You're clumsy and funny but I love you and I want to marry you', Jack said. The pair then made a pledge to light a candle every year on this day – him on earth and her in heaven – before Jade's two little boys ran over and flung their arms around their mum's neck. The boys helped carry their mother's train as she and her new husband made their way out of the church to a standing ovation.

At the reception, Jade welled up as she read out a letter five-year-old Bobby had written – 'Mummy and Jack, you both look lovely and Mummy you are the best Mummy in the whole wide world. Congratulations on your best day ever, love Bobby and Freddy.' Before the ceremony Jade had given her sons friendship bracelets, telling them gently, 'You should never take them off and if you're sad, missing Mummy or upset, rub them and think of me.' The boys were also delighted to receive two signed AC Milan shirts from their hero David Beckham – who said that he and Victoria wanted to help in any way they could.

The brave star somehow danced through her pain as pop trio Sugababes played live at her wedding reception. Her proud grandfather John told the *Daily Mirror*: 'You should have seen her dancing with all those dolly birds. She was jumping up and down dancing like a jive bunny. It was brilliant. She had a wild time.'

Jade also enjoyed her first dance with Jack as husband and wife to Aerosmith's wedding classic 'Don't Want To Miss A Thing' and the loved-up pair fell into a passionate kiss as the crowd cheered wildly. Jade said 'That last kiss felt like we were in heaven' before reluctantly agreeing to go to bed at 10.30p.m. after just managing to stay awake for the fireworks display.

The nation was desperate to know how the wedding had gone, so Jade gave her consent for Jade's bridesmaid Kelly Reading to speak on ITV's *This Morning*. Kelly told Fern Britton and Philip Schofield that the Jade had given each member of her bridal party a ring engraved with the message 'With you always' and brought along a few slices of wedding cake as a gift from Jade.

The exertion of the wedding had taken its toll on poor Jade, and a few days later she left her home to go to a nearby hospice after suffering from hallucinations. Sucking on a pain relief stick and dressed in a loose white sweatshirt and trousers, Jade told photographers she would be 'going away for a few days'. Her publicist Max Clifford told the waiting press she needed to get her pain medication adjusted. 'She was in a very frail state,' he said. The terrifying hallucinations, caused by her medication, left her 'shaking like a leaf' and asking 'Where am I?' But he stressed Jade had not gone into the hospice to die and was expected to return to her Essex home.

Despite her thoughts being now firmly on a christening for her young sons – 'I want them to know about god so they can be close to me when I die' – Jade faced yet another setback. In crippling agony she was rushed to hospital on March 2nd for an emergency operation to help relieve the 'terrible pain' in her stomach. Her publicist Max Clifford sadly told the press, 'Her prognosis is two to four weeks – but there are worries she won't make it to the weekend.'

On 25th February, Jade had gathered friends and advisors together to discuss her final chapter. Yet even then, the down-to-earth star was trying to continue life as normally as possible and she served up spaghetti Bolognese for everyone to eat. She told her confidantes that they needed to start planning her funeral – and when they protested she insisted, 'No, we NEED to sort things out, I want to tell you what I want'.

Jade was also delicately planning how she would finally tell her boys. 'I have a book that the hospital gave me. It's about a badger that's dying and it explains about heaven and where people go,' she said. 'So I have been reading that to my boys. I think my boys know that I am dying. Yeah, I think they do now. I'm going to read the book to them so they know what happens when I'm gone.'

Even in her last days, her friends told how they were astonished by her bravery. 'Jade seems to be comforting us', said her friend Jennifer Smith. 'I was breaking down and she said "life's for laughing, don't get upset."'

Even at her lowest ebb, Jade was determined to see the funny side of life. Throughout her illness, although she was really suffering, Jade found strength in her humour.

Speaking about her death she told friends to look in the sky 'not for the brightest star – but the fattest one. That'll be me.'

Lucie Cave
March 2009

'You could never be neutral about Jade Goody – when she first applied for *Big Brother* she provoked a mixed reaction amongst the team. Whatever anyone thought, the fundamental truth was that Jade was, in herself, hugely interesting and entertaining. Sure enough, when the show went on air she appalled and enthralled people in equal measure. I was the man who made the phone call that changed Jade's life forever. When I called to say she was in the house I was met with a barrage of screams and the sound of her dropping the phone. As viewers, our relationship with Jade was as complicated as she was herself – we loved her in her vulnerable moments and loathed her when she puffed herself up to release some of the vitriol she was capable of. But through it all the overriding thing I remember about Jade is her courage. She wasn't afraid to be who she was and, in the end, she faced her awful disease with characteristic bravery. She was a comet that shot through the dull, over PR-ed celebrity firmament and I will really, really miss her.'

Phil Edgar Jones
Executive producer, *Big Brother*

'As a GP I have had a surge of women attending for smears. Some of these women have come up to nine years late for their smears and I have asked them "what led you to attend after all this time?" Most of them have talked about Jade. These women have not attended previously as they have been anxious about the procedure, and it has been a source of great satisfaction to me that they have felt a sense of relief at getting it over and done with and have realised it's not such a big deal. The national screening programme for cervical cancer is a proven and effective way to prevent cancer and its essential that women take it up when offered. It is clear that Jade's tragic story has touched many thousands of women in the UK in a very positive way and will almost certainly have a real impact on women's health for many years to come.'

Dr Emma Naylor, General Practitioner

The 'Jade Goody' effect saw a massive increase in the number of women going for cervical screening, according to cancer specialists. A university in south-east London recorded 21 per cent more women coming for smear tests since Jade was diagnosed with cervical cancer in August 2008. For more information about coping with cancer, go to www.macmillan.org.uk

Prologue

'It's just a heavy period – nothing to worry about.'

That was what the doctors had said to me when I was rushed into hospital after collapsing from severe bleeding (for the fourth time in as many years).

I still have those words ringing in my ears now. Ringing, banging, screaming, SHOUTING in my ears. Because that turned out not to be the case.

I was actually suffering from the aggravated stage (i.e. very dangerous) of cervical cancer. What's more, I'd been carrying the nasty disease around with me for at least the last two years.

And, despite all the tests I'd had, it hadn't been detected.

I was now being told that, if nothing had been done about it, I'd have been dead within three months. I've had some things thrown at me in my time but this took the bloody biscuit. Was there *anything* more that could happen to me?

Just like everything else in my life, the news that I had cancer was played out in the most public way possible – on live TV. In a weird twist of fate I was now a housemate on *Bigg Boss* – the Indian version of *Celebrity Big Brother*. And it was here, in the familiar surroundings of a diary room chair, that I was once again told my fate. Only this time I wasn't being told that I should put on some clothes or be quiet; I wasn't being told that the public wanted me out; I was being told something much more serious, and something that I had absolutely no control over.

I had cancer.

And I needed to go back to the UK for treatment immediately.

The night before I flew home I lay in the bath in my hotel room for what seemed like hours. I felt numb. How had it come to this? Why hadn't it been detected before? Was I going to die? What would my boys do if something happened to me? Does this mean I can never have kids again? If I stay in this bath any longer am I going to turn into a prune?

Ironically, what upset me most of all at that time was the fact that I had to leave India just as I was starting to redeem myself for all that had happened ...

The Voice of
Big Brother

Normal human behaviour in the *Big Brother* house includes the participants rowing and making up. And what even many of the show's biggest fans cannot believe is that such events are unplanned. The manipulative, all-seeing producers must have chosen Jade and Shilpa in order to provoke racial conflict. They do not understand that *Big Brother* is 12 characters in search of a story. The producers put this group together, but the cast wrote the script. And no one knew in advance what that script would be. With 35 cameras, 20 security staff and a production team of 200, it is carefully managed. There are rules which the housemates must abide by, including prohibitions on violent or threatening behaviour. Of course they fall out and take sides from time to time, but the production team finds that the housemates usually resolve their differences, as happened on this occasion when Jade and Shilpa made up. All sorts of things occur in the house, but it is absurd to claim that this series was designed to serve up racism as entertainment. Indeed, was racism involved at all?

No doubt about it, according to the *Sun*, the *Mirror* and the *News of the World* ('Vile racist', 'Vile Jade Goody'). But the many columnists who debated the issue were evenly split between racism, bullying and class as the motive for the fallout. The complaints to Channel 4 were also divided. The point is that you cannot be certain about a person's motives. So this was never an open-and-shut case. As it happens, I know Jade Goody and I do not believe her to be remotely racist. Her father [was] mixed race. She spent nine weeks in the *Big Brother* house in 2002 with three black people without the hint of a racist attitude. She had a blazing row with one of them, Adele, but that was about verrucas.

Jade certainly has a temper and may be prone to bullying – not an attractive trait, but not a crime either.

Peter Bazalgette, chief creative officer of Endemol,
Prospect magazine, March 2007

Introduction

December 2006

'John, it's going to kill me off. Going back on *Big Brother* will be the death of me. I just have this feeling.'

'Don't be a fucking idiot,' he laughed. John Noel, the agent I'd been with ever since I emerged from the *Big Brother* house in 2002, wasn't one to mince his words. 'Come on, Jade, get your head out of your arse. What have you got to lose? You're going to make money out of it; and you're hardly in there for any time at all. The worst that can happen is that you don't win it. It's a great opportunity. What can go wrong?'

5 January 2007

Time to face the crowd. Wow! What an over-whelming experience.

I have never had such a reception in my life. It sounded like the entire audience huddled outside the *Celebrity Big Brother* house were cheering my name. 'Jade, we love you!' 'Jade, you look great!' 'Jade to win *Celeb Big*

Brother!' They were shouting for Jack too, and I could see how chuffed he was to be recognised in his own right. It was like we were some sort of golden couple – I don't think even Posh and Becks would have got a better reaction. People were going properly mental for us. It was all the more surreal because this was exactly where I stood when I went into the same house (well, except for a few changes of furniture) five years ago. Yet back then no one had the foggiest idea who I was, or cared for that matter. On that occasion they'd just had the pleasure of seeing my stupid audition video on which I spoke faster and louder than anyone on the planet and had for some reason decided to demonstrate my party trick, which consisted of climbing through an elastic band (nope, me neither).

But now here I was, a national home-grown celebrity, about to return to the very show that had got me where I was today. And it's the reason I've been able to afford to get a nice house, expensive cars and keep my kids in a manner I could never have dreamed of when I was young. I waved to the crowd with a big grin on my face and held Jack's arm as we walked into the house. It was such a nice feeling, knowing that all these people genuinely liked me and wanted me to do well.

Perhaps John Noel was right. Maybe this was a good thing to do. After all, what could I possibly have to lose?

29 January 2007

I lay on the bed in the dark and sobbed. I was too scared to take off my coat because it felt like if I did it meant I had to stay in this unfamiliar place for good. And being here – in 'rehab' – frightened the living hell out of me. It was as if I was in that film *One Flew Over the Cuckoo's*

Nest. Was that what it had come to? Was I mad? How was I here? How could I have fucked up so royally?

I was in The Priory, under doctor's orders.

For the past week I'd been on the front page of every newspaper and magazine in the country, alongside words like 'racist pig' or 'vile bully'. The nation hated me. My life was crumbling beneath me.

Every five minutes or so someone would gently prise open my door, peer silently into my room and shine a torch in my face to see that I was OK. It was a really traumatic time for me. In the end I must've cried myself to sleep because the next thing it was morning and the doctor was calmly informing me that he was upping the dose of my depression tablets.

Depression tablets? I never ever dreamed I'd need them in my life. Was I depressed? Was that what was wrong with me? Was that why I couldn't eat and couldn't stop crying? Was that why I didn't know who I was any more?

A few minutes later a lady came in and explained what kind of treatments I would be having while I was in The Priory. I was going to have to confront some of the issues from my past. I was going to have to talk about my mum and address stuff that I'd never dared to tell anyone before. Things that had been buried so far back in my mind that I thought I might never be able to find them again. Because I didn't want to find them – the memories hurt too much.

I sat in this small, characterless room listening to the therapist coaxing me through what I needed to do. I was just staring blankly at the wall, willing myself to forget. But slowly she began to prise my brain open, asking me to recall the things that upset me the most. I started talking and talking. And all of a sudden the floodgates opened and it was like it was never going to end. As I spoke I could feel my heart aching. I talked about my relationship with my mum: how I'd looked after her; how I'd acted as her carer after the horrific motorbike accident she had when I was five years old when she was paralysed on one side of her body and lost all use of one arm.

I described how since as early as I could remember I'd spent my whole life trying to protect my mum – frantically hiding the stolen chequebooks she used to have lying around the house when the police barged in on one of their raids; desperately denying to the teachers at school that she'd hit me for fear of being sent to social services (which I still was – and foster care was one of the worst experiences of my life). I told the therapist that my main concern and fear had always been making sure my mum would never become like my dad – ending up in prison, doing drugs or having to leave me – and how for so long I'd succeeded in keeping her safe. For the best part of my teenage years she stayed out of trouble. But it all changed when I was 18. And at that point in my life, when I needed her most, it felt like my whole world had come crashing down.

This was my pain. More painful than anything I've ever felt in my life before or since. And this was what I was being forced to talk about. Something I'd never admitted until that day in rehab. I glossed over it in my last book – I'd been too frightened to tell a living soul. You see, I didn't want to hurt my mum – as usual, I wanted to protect her – and I hadn't been able to cope with what opening up these memories would do to me emotionally.

It still cuts me like a knife just speaking about it now. But, as I discovered in The Priory, it's one of the reasons I'm so fucked up to this day.

I've always told people, 'Mum's not like my dad was. She'd never get involved in hard drugs. Her only vice was weed, and she smoked it because it kept her mellow.' And for most of my life that was true. I accepted her doing puff, and I'd had a bit of a period with the old 'erb myself in my teenage years – hardly surprising considering she taught me to roll my first spliff aged four, then captured the whole proud event by taking a photo. But this was different. When I was 18 my mum fell into the trap I had spent my whole life fearing. She was hanging around with a group of people who I knew to be into crack cocaine, and possibly other even nastier drugs, and I was petrified she would end up the same way as my dad.

For those of you who don't know, my dad was a heroin addict, a smack head or a scag head, as it's known in the back alleys. He was in and out of jail all my young life. He spent the entire time lying to me about whether or not he was using; and once he even made me take a urine test and pretend it was his because he and his heroin addict of a girlfriend had had a baby and they wanted to pretend to the hospital that they were clean. Pretty heavy stuff for a young girl to have to deal with, I'm sure you'll agree. My dad's dead now, and it's all because of his relationship with drugs. He was found overdosed in the toilet of a Kentucky Fried Chicken restaurant – which must go down as one of the classiest exits in history.

Of course my mum knew all this. Like me, she'd seen first-hand what drugs could do to a person. And she'd always been adamant that she would rather lose the use of both arms than get involved in that world. She knew how shit scared I was about her ever doing crack or heroin. But one day, just as I feared, she gave in to the temptation. And from then on, for around three years (until I went into the *Big Brother* house in 2002), she lied to me. She told me I was wrong, that she wasn't on the stuff and that I was being delusional (which I still pronounce 'deluged'). Lies, lies, lies.

Day in day out she would say to me, 'I'm not doing what you think, Jade. I wouldn't do that to you.'

Every evening when I came home from whatever shitty shop job I was managing to hold down at the time I'd walk through the door, scared of what I might find, and I'd confront her and demand to know if she was doing crack – but every time she would deny it. I wasn't stupid (OK, I wasn't completely stupid). I could see the signs. She was erratic, scatty, nervy – and high. I was convinced I was about to lose my mum for ever and that meant my own life might as well be over. It wasn't worth living. She meant everything to me, and what's more I'd given up everything to look after her. I'd sacrificed my whole childhood. I'd acted like I was *her* bloody mum, for God's sake, and I felt kicked in the stomach that this was how she was repaying me.

You might think I'm a wuss, but tears are streaming down my cheeks just knowing I have to talk about my mum in this way in the pages of this book. I can't deal with it. I can't bear to talk about it. The memories are so raw; too raw. I can't face the fact that she lied to me for so long. But at the same time I don't want you to judge her for it.

In the end the therapist at The Priory actually had to stop me because she could see it was far too much for me to be able to deal with at that time.

My mum's lies have haunted me ever since. Now, whenever anyone hides the truth from me – even if it's just a tiny insignificant little thing – I get angry and I see red.

Liar, liar. That's all I can see …

1
Low Life

It actually took me a few months to fathom that Mum's new group of friends were wrong 'uns and that thanks to them she was getting hooked on drugs. At the very beginning of her friendship with those nasty addicts I didn't know what she was doing. I didn't realise at first that they were even on the stuff. Or perhaps I just chose to block it out. Mum just seemed happy (funny that), which was all that mattered to me. Also, I was content that I'd found some new friends because of her. Mum had been seeing a woman – let's call her Janet (I won't reveal her true identity just in case she doesn't want to be outed as a lesbian by this book) – and I became mates with one of Janet's sisters. I'll call her sister Shelly, because she certainly won't want me to tell you her real name – you'll understand why in a minute.

Shelly was a few years older than me, about 21, she was really pretty and had blonde hair. I wasn't overly impressed by her age because I was used to hanging out with people above my age group, but I was excited by the world she lived in and the parties she used to go to. It was the time when House and Garage music was the scene to be in, and every weekend she and her mates would invite me out clubbing. We'd get really dressed up – me in an over-the-top Moschino outfit that I used to call my pride and joy and thought was the nuts. It consisted of a white skirt and a white shirt with little black stick-men and women all over it. I wore it everywhere. What the hell was I thinking? Or another number that was covered in the designer's logo to the point that you probably couldn't even see the dress itself. I might as well have had 'D&G' tattooed on my face, I was so eager to prove I was cool. It pains me now to admit that I've since realised I was actually a chav before they were given a name. We'd go to Bagleys, Camden Palace, warehouse parties in Old Street – the lot. My shoes would be all scuffed when I got out of the club – these were proper full-on, dirty raves. And I loved them.

The girls would all take pills when they went out – which was something I never wanted to do. I'd only ever smoked weed and that was enough for me, besides I'd seen what drugs had done to my dad. It used to freak me out to see him when he was high on heroin. I was around drugs so much that I even learnt to differentiate between the types of drug people were on. You can tell the difference between someone who smokes crack and a scag head because crack makes you all scatty, whereas a heroin addict will be really fussy, not with-it, and they won't be able to get their words out properly. I used to have lots of conversations with my dad where he'd look at me and pull all these faces like he was really out of it, and it frightened the life out of me. And because of this I was petrified that I could end up the same

2

way if I went down that road – even if it was just ecstasy and not the harder stuff. I thought, that's how it starts.

None of the girls questioned the fact that I wasn't into it. I was never frowned upon or pressurised to do it, so it was no problem for us to all go out together. Anyway, I could dance like a nutter without alcohol even. And the sort of faces I pulled on the dance floor probably made people think I was on the strongest drug imaginable – I would look like I was properly gurning. (I can't help my face, that's just the way I was born.) I'd never been around this sort of thing before – people on ecstasy – and it was a completely different atmosphere to the potheads I was used to. Everyone went crazy, hugging each other and dancing like manic things for a billion hours non-stop. I loved the music at these clubs; everyone seemed so happy and full of beans all the time.

I hung out with them for months, and we had loads of mad nights out together, but then one I night I realised just how different I really was to those other girls. On the way home Shelly spotted one of those little Jamaican corner shops that are open all night and announced that she wanted to get some chicken. 'Oooh, I want some curried goat and rice,' I said, famished. She went in and came out again with my food, but nothing for herself. I thought it was a bit odd, but didn't question it. Then she went to another shop and bought a bottle of water, a ballpoint pen and an elastic band. Again, weird. There were about five of us in the car, including a guy Shelly was seeing at the time, and it was decided that we'd all go round to his house for a bit. Once we got into the lounge my heart sank and I felt that familiar sick feeling. I knew from their faces they were about to do hard drugs. It was the look of greed my dad used to have before he jacked up.

Shelly's boyfriend poured the water out of the bottle, dismantled the pen and stuck it through a hole in the top – then got some silver foil, put it on the rim of the bottle and fixed it with the elastic band. He had made a crack pipe.

I felt so alone. I wanted nothing more than to get out of there. I watched them pass the pipe around, inhaling deeply and gazing at each other in their dreamy state. They offered it to me but I shook my head and looked at the floor. I didn't know these people any more. How could they do this? I didn't dare say anything though. At that point I was too scared to move. I wanted to cry but I managed to hold it in somehow. They became all erratic and scatty, talking and laughing while passing the pipe round for more and more hits. It felt like I was there forever. When they finally called it a night I couldn't stand up fast enough. I hadn't touched my curried goat (funnily enough).

I shared a cab home with Shelly's mate, and as I closed my front door I knew that was the last time I was ever going to see them. And I was going to come clean to Mum. Not that she could say anything, because she was hanging round with an even worse crowd – crack addicts, to be precise. Only until now I'd tried my hardest to pretend she wasn't one of them.

I knew my mum was easily influenced and, for some awful reason that I just couldn't fathom for the life of me, she'd started befriending these parasites who wanted to hang out with her (simply so they had company when they got their next hit). My biggest fear was that she'd start taking drugs herself and would turn out like my dad. After all we'd been through with him, I couldn't work out why she'd want to be friends with people like that. At first I believed her when she said she hadn't tried crack herself, but after a while it became obvious she was doing it too. And it broke my heart. I've never been able to deal with it and until recently I've never even told anyone about it. I've just buried my head in the sand and tried to deal with it myself. I was my mum's carer. I was all she had, and vice versa. So to me that meant I would have to be the one to get her through this.

But every day when I came home from work (which by now was as a nurse in a dental practice) I'd have this empty feeling in my stomach, not knowing what I was going to find.

To this day there are two smells that I cannot stomach. One is the smell of dirty ashtrays. For some reason, when crack addicts make a pipe they always light a cigarette and let the ash burn right down. I don't know why they leave it there, but they do, and without fail, if you go into a room where someone has been doing crack, you'll find ashtrays full of burnt-down cigarettes, full to the brim with ash.

The second smell I can't abide is matches. When I was just a few years old, if I wasn't watching my dad injecting himself with heroin, I would see him burning the stuff on tin foil with a spoon – what they call 'chasing the dragon'. The smell of matches makes me feel like I'm going to throw up. I used to see pieces of tin foil all over my dad's house, burnt with the residue from the heroin. And now that I've finally got a home of my own I still find it incredibly hard to have tin foil in the house because it gives me the creeps and makes me feel dirty.

It was tin foil that gave away that my mum was doing drugs herself. I'd already discovered at Shelly's boyfriend's house that crack addicts use it to put on top of the bottle to make a crack pipe. So, when I first suspected Mum of smoking crack (I knew she would never touch heroin because of what had happened to my dad, but to her for some reason crack was different), I'd rush into the kitchen and hunt for the roll of tin foil in the drawer to see if any squares had been cut out for the pipe.

'I know you've done it,' I would scream, as the lies just came flying out of Mum's mouth denying all knowledge.

I wouldn't say she was scared of me, but the nature of our relationship while I was growing up means that I've always been the figure of authority, the one who calls the shots or who says what's acceptable and what isn't. So when I accused her of doing crack she just behaved like a child being told off, desperate to cover her tracks in case she was going to get a smacked bum.

It all began when she brought home a new boyfriend, I'll call him Peter. (For those who don't know Jackiey's background, she regularly chopped and changed from men to women. As a rule she was bisexual, which as far as she was concerned just meant she could pick and choose.) This Peter was a recovering heroin addict and Mum seemed to be intent on helping him through it. Never once did I think she'd turn to heroin, because of my dad, so I was OK with it to start with. But I did wonder what the hell she saw in him, because it was clear he'd been through the mill. In fact, he looked bloody rough. And, after her relationship with my dad, I thought she'd learnt her lesson.

Peter seemed like quite a nice bloke. But my mum is very easily persuaded, and unbeknown to me Peter had introduced her to a crowd of people who were his 'mates'. And these so-called friends were all into crack. Peter was on it too (what's the point of coming off heroin only to get hooked on something just as bad?) and before long Mum was becoming part of that world.

When I found out he'd got her on crack I wanted to stab him.

I remember the first time I came home and realised what was going on. I walked in and noticed my mum was all sweaty and seemed preoccupied and scatty. Straight away I had a hunch.

'It stinks in here,' I said, turning up my nose. And it did, although back then I didn't recognise the stench of crack. Now I can smell it a mile off.

Mum suddenly looked a bit worried and started tidying up. Then I noticed some ashtrays that had been washed up. There were loads of them. I was used to Mum smoking a bit of puff, but she would never have ashtrays all over the place. Something didn't fit.

'Why did you wash the ashtrays up? They're not dirty.'

'Oh, I don't know,' she mumbled. She was so nervous, it was obvious. 'I, er, I need to go out, Jade. See you in a bit.' And with that she was gone. She literally fled out the door – and she didn't come home for about two days. By which time she was acting as if nothing had happened.

Once Peter had introduced her to crack, it didn't take long before Mum had a whole heap of new 'friends' feeding off her addiction. One of these was a woman called Mel. (I mentioned her briefly in my last book, but didn't quite fill you in on the extent of her influence on my mum.) She was a nasty, ugly, dirty user of a woman. And I hated the sight of her.

Mum must've been using for about three years. In that time all her usual priorities just started disappearing. I'd get home and the fridge would have nothing in it apart from maybe a bottle of milk – if I was lucky. Not that Mum has ever been one to have a fridge packed full of groceries (now I'm older I always have to have the fridge crammed, because I never had that when I was growing up), but she'd always buy what she could with her disability allowance. That was, until drugs became more important than food. During that time she lost all sense of normal, acceptable behaviour. She stopped caring about anyone apart from herself.

Mum knew perfectly well I was on to her. I ended up taking lots of time off work because I was too worried about leaving her alone for fear of what she'd get up to. I was always especially scared on the day she got her disability allowance, because that was money – drug money.

This is the kind of low life that Mel was: Mum would go to the Post Office and tell me she'd be back in a few minutes. Meanwhile, Mel would be lingering at the Post Office ready to pounce on my weakling of a mum and tempt her away to buy drugs before she could so much as protest. As a result, I'd be sitting indoors waiting for my mum to come home, but she'd be gone for hours, sometimes even days, blowing her allowance on drugs.

I didn't want to tell any of my friends, though. I was too scared and embarrassed. In those days I was going out with a guy called Danny who was heavily into coke and liked to beat me up in his spare time. So back then I didn't really have a great deal to choose from. Neither option was very appealing. All I could do most nights was hide in my bedroom and hope it would all go away. You always want people to think you've got the perfect mum and the perfect dad, don't you? Well, all my mates already knew my dad didn't fit into that category, so I was desperate for them to believe that my mum was amazing. And for the most part she was. But to have to admit to my friends that Mum was a drug addict! They would think she was dirty, and I couldn't stand that. So I hid the truth. And I didn't tell one single person.

Mum actually won the lottery once, believe it or not. She and one of her 'mates' got something in the region of £15,000, which they split between them. It embarrasses me to talk about it now, and you can guess why. She blew the lot on drugs – all £7,500 of it. Oh, except for one present she bought for me – a light-green plastic mac from Mark One that cost about £6.99. She'd even tried to keep her winnings a secret from me to start with because she knew I'd want to know what she was going to spend it on.

Every night I would go home and frantically search for evidence of my mum's drug use. Would she be on crack? Would she even be alive? I used to argue and argue with her, and I hated it. In the end we were fighting like cat and dog.

Mel was still on the scene and it made me feel violently ill just to think of her. Ultimately, one day she made me feel plain violent.

Mel lived near to my nan and granddad, the two cutest and gentlest people on earth. I mentioned in my last book that I raised a hand to Mel because one day she walked past them on the landing and muttered under her breath to my granddad, 'You bastard.'

Well, that wasn't the half of it.

I was always telling my nan and granddad that Mel was bad news and that Mum was getting involved with her, but they didn't like to interfere where Mum was concerned. They've always known Jackiey has a mind of her own and I think they feel better just staying out of things and leaving her to her own devices. But at the same time they could see how much it was all upsetting me. And that hurt them.

I remember one afternoon I was round at their house eating lunch – my granddad makes the best sandwiches, 'doorsteps' he calls them, and that day he'd made me a ham and cheese one – and all of a sudden there was a banging on the front door. My nan went to see who it was and scuttled back after a few moments and said to my granddad, 'John, it's that Mel woman.'

My ears pricked up instantly and I dropped the doorstep sandwich in my lap. 'Who?' I stood up. 'What does she want, Nan?'

'She asked me for some money.'

That scavenging, disgusting drug addict of a woman had so little shame that she had actually asked my little nan for money so she could buy drugs! That was it. I was at the door in a second. 'Do yourself a favour, Mel, and get away from the door now.'

Her face was pulling all sorts of contorted shapes, she was so bloody out of it.

'Oh, Jade – where's your mum? Come on, lend us 20 quid, will ya?'

I am not proud of what I did next. And anyone who already thinks I've got a bad temper will just think they're being proved right after hearing this. But put yourself in my shoes and imagine what you'd want to do to the person who was encouraging your mum to take drugs.

I pulled Mel by the hair, then shut the door, dragged her outside and proceeded to hit her uncontrollably.

'How dare you bring your dirty self to my nan and granddad's and ask them for their pension so you can buy more crack!'

Above left: At home, just after my cancer diagnosis in August 2008. I was devastated but determined to fight it all the way. © *Lynn Hilton/Rex Features*

Above right: The first couple of months were a whirlwind of hospital visits, with so much information to take in. © *Rex Features*

Below left: In December 2008 I had something to celebrate – a signing for the hardback edition of my book. © *David Fisher/Rex Features*

Below right: With my personal trainer Kevin Adams, who has given me massive support throughout my illness. © *Frank Doran/Rex Features*

Above: Bald and proud!

© *Peter Lawson/Rex Features*

Below: Jack being in prison was so tough – and I was overjoyed when he
was finally released.

© *Peter Lawson/Rex Features*

Above left: Out with Jack, shopping for my dream wedding dress.

© *Peter Lawson/Rex Features*

Above right: Mohammed Al Fayed kindly gave me a beautiful dress to wear for my big day – all the way from Harrods!

© *Marco Secchi/Rex Features*

Left: My mum and nan out shopping before the wedding.

© *Martin Stenning/Rex Features*

Jack and I did a little photoshoot for the press before the wedding.
That kiss was all over the papers!

Rex Features

Above: With my friends before the wedding – I made them all wear 'bald' caps!

© *Rex Features*

Below left: Off to make myself look beautiful for the big day!

© *Rex Features*

Below right: Jack and his mates decided to wear bras and pants for their journey to the wedding venue at Down Hall!

© *Rex Features*

Above: The wedding cars outside Jack's mum's house on our wedding day, 22nd February 2009.

Below: Arriving in style!

Above: The gorgeous Down Hall in Essex, where Jack and I got married.
© *Stefan Rousseau/PA Wire/PA Photos*

Below: Our wedding was beautiful – we even had a banner across the sky!
© *Carl Court/PA Wire/PA Photos*

Above: Jack and Kevin with my gorgeous boys on their way to school.

© *Martin Rose/Eastnews/Rex Features*

I was livid. I hit her over and over again until physically I couldn't fight any more. When my mum appeared round the corner I turned on her as well. 'Take your fucking scummy friend away. You're welcome to each other. I don't want to see you again. You make me feel sick. Go and fuck off to your crack den!'

Of course, it wasn't long before she was back home wanting more money from me. The worst thing was, I couldn't not give it to her, otherwise she'd just go and beg it from someone else. Towards the end of her using she didn't even bother going to other people's houses to do her drugs. She'd do it at home, while I sat in my bedroom knowing what she was up to but not having the strength to stop her. I knew full well that those drugs had more influence on her than I ever could.

My mum didn't have a door on her bedroom, and for a while I didn't dare walk past it in case I caught a glimpse of her smoking crack. I couldn't handle seeing her at it with my own eyes.

But I couldn't leave the house and go to see one of my mates either, because I knew I would break down, and I didn't want them having any idea what was going on. People think I'm a strong person, but under the surface I'm far from it. I can put a front on for a little while, but it soon crumbles. At that time in my life my bedroom was the only place I could express my true feelings. And most of the time that meant sobbing myself to sleep.

Then one day I sat in my room and thought, I'm never going to beat the drugs. They're always going to win. And I can't believe I'm admitting this but a voice in my head said to me, 'I might as well do a bit of crack myself. I might as well go the same way as her. At least then we'd be together.'

Of course I knew I could never do that. But I wanted her to see what her behaviour was doing to me.

I'll never forget what happened next. I wiped the tears from my face and walked out of my bedroom to the lounge, where she was smoking crack. I kept telling myself, 'Be brave, Jade,' as I approached her in deadly earnest.

'Right then, hand it over.'

'What are you talking about, Jade?'

'The crack. The drugs. Come on, Mum – if it's good enough for you, it's good enough for me.'

'No, Jade! You can't ever do that!'

'Well, you've always taught me to follow your example, to listen to you. So that's what I'm doing now. I'd like some, please.'

'No, you're not having any.'

'Don't tell me I can't have something when you ask me for money so you can buy it.'

And there and then, to prove a point, I decided to show her how nasty and heartbreaking it was to see a member of your family, your own flesh and blood, killing themselves in front of your very eyes. I took some of her crack, put it in a Rizla paper to make a joint and I smoked it.

I felt dirty and disgusting.

'How does it make you feel watching me do this?' I asked.

'You can't do that, you're my baby daughter!'

'And this is how you treat your baby daughter, is it?'

All the time I had tears streaming down my face. I was willing her to stop me and to promise me she'd never do it again. But she didn't. I'd foolishly thought that if she could see what it looked like – and if she thought that her own daughter was about to go to the same dark place she was – she'd put a stop to it.

12

I couldn't even smoke it all, it made me feel too ill. I ran to the toilet, stuck my fingers down my throat and made myself sick, and sick, and sick. I was shaking and crying. Then I ran into my room and shut the door.

And moments after I'd gone into my room? I heard her at it again.

I felt like utter shit. As I lay on my bed I even started hitting myself, somehow trying to take the pain away. I've never self-harmed or anything like that – I couldn't properly cut myself anyway because I'm too squeamish about blood – but if I wasn't such a wimp I could've easily got a knife and stabbed myself. Instead I bashed my head repeatedly against the wall as hard as I could, I pulled my hair out of my head until my scalp was red raw and I pinched my skin until it went purple. I was so frustrated. I didn't come out of my room for two whole days. During which time my mum continued to smoke crack.

Eventually, though, it got too much and my tears turned to anger – and hatred. Mum didn't understand how I felt. It was like a knife going through my heart and shattering all my good thoughts about her.

Finally I cracked. I got up off my bed, opened the door and stormed out into the lounge. I rushed over to where Mum was, grabbed her by the throat and pushed her hard up against the wall. 'You make me feel physically sick!' I shrieked. I was nearly choking her, but I didn't care. I was swinging her around the lounge like she was a little rag doll – she was so weak from all the drugs. I just couldn't stop myself. The build-up and the upset had become too much. I was shouting, 'After everything I've given up for you, everything I've done for you! You've just thrown it all back in my face.'

Mum was crying. I was crying. But the rage I had was awful. I was at boiling point. And although I wanted to stop I couldn't. At that moment I felt like fighting with her was the only way to get through to her.

Finally she found some strength and started to retaliate – and we began to have a proper full-blown fight. She punched me and I whacked her back. It must've gone on for about half an hour. I had a big black eye and cuts all over my face and so did she. But of course, afterwards, rather than her feeling remorseful, it was still me who was the one that felt bad. I'd lost all respect for myself because I'd hit my own mother. It had got to the point where I'd asked her to either choose me or the crack and she'd chosen the crack. And that killed me. Because my dad had chosen drugs over me too.

I couldn't deal with it back then, and to be honest it still makes me sick to the stomach talking about it now. After that fight I moved out of our home for a time, but ended up having to come back not long after because I couldn't afford my rent.

But now you know the real reason I applied for *Big Brother 3*. I had to find an escape from my mum. I also had to get away from my boyfriend Danny (who, as I've said, was nearly as much of a dodgy character as Mel was). Everywhere I turned there were people doing drugs – even my other friends were doing pills in clubs. I couldn't get away from it.

So when I saw the advert for *Big Brother* it felt like I'd been offered a lifeline. And I honestly think that's what it was. It was as if I was being offered the chance to be a kid again. Like I was in a holiday camp or being allowed to go back to school.

2
Best-laid Plans ...

What was it about me? I always wanted to be a good girl, but no matter what I did I somehow ended up on the wrong side of the tracks. When I was at school I dreamed of being head girl. I wanted to get straight As and be told by the teachers that I was going to amount to something. Well, I fucked that up, didn't I? At my school, when you did well in something you got a letter of merit, but if you did badly you got a demerit.

I must've held the record for the most demerits in existence.

Somehow, though, I did manage to blag myself the title of Games Captain, which meant I got to wear the special badge on my uniform. I bribed everyone in my class to vote for me to the point that they had no choice if they wanted any chance of peace and quiet. That badge was my pride and joy. I also had a 'School Committee' badge that I wore each day, even though I was never actually on the committee. That one I nicked. But the cream of the crop, the absolute best badge of honour, was the Gold Lion badge. You only got awarded one of those if you reached 1000 merits, and I had about as much hope of that as of Prince Charles knocking on my door and asking me to be his queen. So the only way I could get one was to cheat. To prove you deserved a Gold Lion you had to show the head teacher a certificate saying you'd gained 1000 merits. I asked one of the clever girls in my class if I could have her certificate. Somehow I persuaded her that she could just tell the teacher she'd lost it and ask for another one.

Then I went home and set about my mission: forgery. I must've been up most of the night. Mum poked her head round the door and thought I'd been hit over the head and had something wrong with me. What else could explain this sudden desire to do my homework? First I delicately rubbed out the girl's name, then I put the certificate in my typewriter and spent ages making sure I had the paper lined up right so that I could type my name in its place. Once I was finished I smiled contentedly to myself. It looked just like the real deal.

When I proudly marched into class the next morning and presented my merit certificate to my form tutor it looked so convincing that he couldn't question me – although he did nearly fall off his chair.

And that was how I got my Gold Lion badge.

I wanted to be a prefect too – not to do anything like telling younger kids off and being all superior, but just to have the badge. Believe it or not, my dream nearly came true when I was on holiday in Marbella recently. Two fellas came up to me as I sat by the pool and said, 'We think you're brilliant, girl. And we just wanted to give you this.' They handed me a case with a badge in it that said 'Prefect Girl'.

I was so chuffed. 'I'm a prefect at last!' I shrieked.

The boys just laughed. 'No, Jade,' one of them corrected me. 'Take it out of the box. It says "Perfect Girl"!'

What a dipstick.

I still loved it, though, and I refused to take it off for the rest of the holiday. I even wore it on my bikini.

There was a teacher at our school that we used to call 'The Witch' because she only ever wore one type of shoe. (Kids are so nice, aren't they?) I was obsessed with looking at her feet every time she came into the classroom. She didn't seem like any other regular teacher and after a while we became convinced that she had wooden toes. So one lunchtime I decided to find out whether this was true. Me and a couple of my mates made sure we sat opposite her at the dinner table. I pretended to drop something on the floor, then crawled underneath and stabbed her foot with my fork. And she didn't flinch! I was so excited that I shouted, 'Oh my God, it's true!' and banged my head on the table. For that I got sent to the headmaster. But it was worth it.

At another of my schools there was a supply teacher who had fuzzy grey hair. He used to touch the girls in a not very appropriate way and pat their bums. One time he patted me on the tush and I said, 'Get your fucking hands off me!' I was having none of it. You may have gathered by now that I became a bit of a ringleader in my teenage years. So when this supply teacher was covering one of my next classes I whispered to everyone not to do any work and they sat there with their arms folded for the entire lesson while I pinged pieces of paper at him. He instantly sent me to the headmistress's office (I might as well have moved into that place I was there so much) and I had no qualms about reporting to her that he was a pervert. Not long afterwards it was discovered that he'd received complaints at the private school he was teaching at previously. So he got kicked out. See, sometimes it's actually worth being the mouthy one.

But it was hardly surprising I was the way I was. I didn't have the most conventional home life. With all the scams my mum was up to it was nothing unusual to go home from school and see a police car outside. We got raided all the time. Most kids would arrive home from school to the sight of their mum hanging out the washing or cooking the dinner. I'd come round the corner with my face in my hands, hoping I wouldn't see another police car race up with its sirens blaring. I'd get off the bus from school and my heart would sink. What's she done now? I'd think. Then I'd go into a cold sweat, and panic with the fear that they could take her away from me. I was always worrying. I'd often walk in to see policemen ripping up the carpet and pulling things apart in my bedroom. I'd shout, 'Put that back! It's in my room! I've just tidied up!' Still, they never used to find anything – mainly because I'd done a bloody good job of hiding things inside chip packets in the freezer or some other unlikely place.

Trouble and Jade Goody just go hand in hand, it seems. I've even nicked hubcaps off cars in the middle of the night! Not for no reason, of course, and not just for fun. Whenever I do something bad it's usually as a result of someone spurring me on. And in this instance it was my ex-boyfriend Danny (you know the one – coke head, girlfriend basher). He used to have a blue Peugeot 206 and because he lived in a dodgy area he'd often come home and find one of his hubcaps had gone missing or the car had been scratched by kids. So we'd drive out to a Peugeot garage – his idea, not mine, honest! – in the middle of the night to get a replacement one. I was paranoid that there were cameras everywhere and that whoever got caught would have to run really fast – something I decided he was incapable of because he was so fat. So I nominated myself to do it instead of him. Which I did quite successfully on numerous occasions, much to Danny's delight. (If anyone from Peugeot is reading this, please don't sue me. It was Danny's idea and I've never ever done it since.)

Another random fact for you: I was actually taught to look after myself by one of the most hardened and notorious gangsters in the country. When I was about 11 I used to do kick boxing in this gym in Greenwich and one of the guys who trained there took a liking to my mum and me. Not in a creepy way – he just seemed to warm to the fact that we both told it like it was and were no nonsense. He trained me to box for months and months and I actually got quite good at it (don't laugh). After that I never saw him again. But it wasn't until years later that I found out who he actually was. Mum rang me and said, 'Remember years ago when you got taught boxing by some big fella called Lenny?'

'Yeah, vaguely.'

'Well, he's died. It was on the news.'

'Why was it on the news?'

'Because his name was Lenny McLean – and apparently he was one of the hardest men in Britain!'

Wow. Imagine if he was alive now – I'd never need to worry about having problems ever again!

3
Re-re-wind

Of course there have been plenty of things in my life that I wouldn't class as 'problems'. The most important of which are my beautiful little sons, Bobby and Freddy. And I would never have had them if it hadn't been for my relationship with their dad, Jeff Brazier.

For those who don't know I'll give a brief potted history of me and Mr Brazier (so you can skip this chapter if you already know the ins and outs).

I met Jeff the year I came out of the *Big Brother* house in 2002 (I came fourth and emerged dressed like Miss Piggy on acid). He was living with Kevin Adams – the guy my agent John Noel had hired to be my personal trainer (and, believe me, I needed one). I can honestly say that when I clapped eyes on Jeff it felt like love at first sight. I thought he was beautiful and fancied the pants off him. In fact, I think he was only wearing pants at the time (well, a football kit anyway). I didn't let him see I liked him, though, and pretty quickly we became friends – friends who flirted and bickered and made it pretty damn obvious we were falling in love to everyone except ourselves.

Once we finally got together properly it wasn't long before I fell pregnant with our first child, Bobby Jack. Finding out I was pregnant was a complete surprise. I still don't know how it happened, because I was on the pill. I'd been getting pains in my stomach, so I went to the doctor. I was supposed to be going to work that day – to rehearse for the fitness video I was making (which got to number one, thank you very much) – but I couldn't go anywhere. I was in utter shock and I burst out crying. I remember begging the doctor not to tell anyone, because my biggest fear was the papers finding out. Fucking hell, I thought, I can't believe this has happened to me. Straight away I rang Jeff, who was at work. I was sobbing, 'Jeff ... Jeff ...' I could hardly get the words out. 'I'm pregnant.'

There was a silence, then he just said, 'What?' I was crying and crying. Jeff didn't hesitate. 'I'm coming straight home,' he said. I didn't even register what his reaction was because I was too wrapped up in myself. I found out later that after he got off the phone he leapt out of his seat and was screaming, 'Yes!' because he was so happy. But I wasn't at first. I didn't like it. I remember I even phoned my friend Charlene and told her, 'I want to stab my belly! I want to get rid of it! I want to make myself fall over!' It was a horrific thing to say, but I was only 21 at the time and I was just frightened.

Jeff came through the front door and gave me a massive hug and said, 'Babe, I'm with you all the way – if you want to get rid of it, you can, and I'll support your decision. But if you decide to keep it, I'm a hundred per cent there for you.'

And it was then that I realised how much he wanted to keep the baby, and deep down that I did too. It was our baby and from the start I was determined to give my child a proper family, a nice home and two parents who loved it. I think the media and the public were a bit shocked that I'd want to have a kid when I seemed to have so much other stuff going for me. But once we'd come to terms with it we were over the moon and I knew Jeff would make a fantastic dad – which he has.

Fast forward a few months and we were both still accepting jobs that had been offered to us. For me it was panto (as the Wicked Queen in *Snow White and the Seven Dwarfs* – very appropriately named 'Dumplina', which explained the fact that my dress was bursting at the seams) and as a fat heffalump trying to work out what to do behind the wheel of Comic Relief's *Celebrity Driving School*. Jeff was the host for a new T4 show called *Dirty Laundry* with June Sarpong. While this was good for our bank balance, it wasn't quite so good for our relationship, so inevitably the strain began to show and we started rowing (fighting, that is, not sitting in a boat).

To be fair, I think most of the fighting was down to me and my hormones. They were all over the place. I felt so fat and ugly. I couldn't even do my shoelaces up, for God's sake!

Jeff used to come home from work and I'd be lying in the bath, in complete darkness except for a few candles flickering around me. Mariah Carey would be blaring from the stereo and I'd be bawling my eyes out. Jeff would look at me and say, 'Why are you crying?' I'd stare at him for a few seconds, then blub, 'I don't know!' I definitely wasn't the easiest person to live with at that time. Jeff would be out at the shops or doing some TV work, and I'd be on the phone to him saying, 'You're leaving me, aren't you? I'm pregnant and you don't care!' I became jealous of everything he did, and in the end I think that's what drove him further and further away from me. I became a horrible person. I'd never felt this insecure before and I didn't know how to deal with it.

So then, just to show the nation how many problems we were having, we stupidly agreed to take part in Channel 4's *Celebrity Wife Swap* (great idea that one) with Charles and Diana Ingram (the ones accused of the big coughing scam on *Who Wants To Be A Millionaire?*). Ironically, living with Major Ingram actually made me realise what a good thing I had with Jeff, and for a few weeks things got a bit better. I had Bobby four weeks early – brought on by a spicy curry, would you believe! He weighed 5lb 7oz at birth, so he wasn't a big baby, but it was the most painful thing I had ever experienced. Jeff and I fell in love with him in an instant.

Pretty soon I'd lost the baby weight, done another fitness video and smartened up my look. By which time it was Jeff's turn to feel insecure and paranoid about me, so the problems and the rows reared their ugly head once more. It was also during this time that I developed an eating disorder. I was making myself sick to keep my weight down, and when I wasn't doing that I was developing a serious (and very secret) addiction to slimming pills. The more people said how good I looked – I had long dark hair extensions at the time and I nearly combusted on the spot when I read that one newspaper thought I looked like Liz Hurley – the more pressure I felt to maintain it. Slimming pills just seemed like the easy answer to keep the weight off. That was largely because I'd had to confess to Jeff and my mum about making myself sick, which meant it wasn't very easy for me to hang out near the porcelain pot as often as I wanted to. Pills offered me a sneaky way of doing the same job. I got well and truly hooked on them. Soon I was taking more pills than I should, at up to £230 a bottle, and buying packets of stronger ones off the internet. At one stage I even took a £2,000 trip to America, pretending to be on holiday, just so I could buy the stronger pills. I don't know what the hell I was thinking.

The sad thing is that slimming pills seem to be sold everywhere and are so easy to get hold of. It worries me how many other girls are out there now doing what I was.

One night I accidentally drank alcohol at a party after I'd taken a slimming pill, completely forgetting that you're not meant to drink when you're on them. I don't think I've ever been so out of it in my life. My heart was racing so fast I thought it was going to jump out of my chest. I actually thought I might have a heart attack. It was frightening. I thought I was being buried alive and that night I couldn't sleep a wink. I'm a good mother and my addiction never affected Bobby – or Freddy when he came on to the scene – but pills like these are dangerous enough without alcohol.

Still, I carried on popping pills on and off, refusing to talk about it. Even worse, I wasn't aware at that time how much damage I was doing to my insides. My body is still paying the price now and will be for the rest of my life.

Jeff and I were fighting a lot, but we still loved each other. And then, unexpectedly, we discovered I was pregnant with our second child while I was in the middle of filming a reality show for Channel 5 called *Back To Reality*. I fainted on TV and was rushed to hospital, where it was confirmed. Even though Jeff's attitude towards the pregnancy was so positive, our relationship was still a mess, and I spent the following week seriously thinking about whether or not to keep the baby. It was a really difficult time because I didn't have a clear idea of what I wanted to do. But I kept these feelings from Jeff and took some time out to think about things. I honestly think that, if I hadn't already had Bobby, I might've had an abortion. Once you are a mother, though, things change. I could never deny Bobby the chance of having a brother or sister. I simply couldn't do it. So that was it.

Then, while I was pregnant, Jeff and I had a huge great whopper of a row which involved me battering him with a spatula and anything else I could lay my hands on. The next day it was all over the papers. After that we split for good and I gave birth to Freddy as a single mum – although Jeff was present when he was born and, looking back, I'm so glad about that. But the birth was incredibly traumatic – I lost an untold amount of blood and had to have a transfusion (which I've since learnt is something to do with the mess my body is in from the slimming pills).

After Jeff I dated a footballer called Ryan Amoo for about two years. He turned out to be a complete psycho who turned on me one day and kept me a virtual prisoner in my own home. I was petrified he was going to kill me. He might have looked to the general public like a skinny little weed but that day he was one seriously scary motherfucker.

Then, towards the end of 2005, I got back with Jeff again – are you keeping up here? – and we really thought we'd be able to make a go of it the second time around. But in the long run we just weren't right for each other. We'd been through so much from such a young age, but we had to accept that perhaps it was too much and we could never go back to square one.

So by 2006 I was a single girl again – and I was ready to find a nice handsome young man.

4
Jack the Lad

I didn't have very long as a singleton because very soon there was another man in my life – Jack Tweed.

Only he was actually more of a *boy*. But we'll get to that part in a bit.

I first met Jack in a nightclub in 2005, just before the time Jeff and I began trying to patch things up (unsuccessfully, as it turned out). Back then I thought it was just one of those encounters that nothing came of. I don't remember much about that evening, only that I couldn't help noticing how good-looking he was (but that was the extent of my lust – honest, Jeff!). All my mates were eyeing him up that evening, so he became quite the topic of conversation. Jack and I kept catching each other's eye, which made me go a bit shy, believe it or not. Then Jen decided to go over and talk to him and give him my phone number. I was mortified because I could see them both talking about me and looking over. I hate stuff

29

like that, it makes me cringe. So I legged it out of the club because I couldn't stand to watch them.

But I still wanted to know what he'd said about me. When Jen came out she told me he thought I was 'fit' and had asked for my number, which she put in his phone. She didn't get his for me, but I thought it was better that way because at least then if he called I'd know he was keen. The next day I let it go out of my mind, convinced I wouldn't hear from him. After that Jeff and I started growing closer, so I forgot about Jack completely.

Then, at the V Festival in 2005, just before I heard the shocking news about my dad's death, I got a text from Jack. Jeff and I were still not officially an item at this point, but things were definitely heading that way. But when I got the text, even though it only said, 'Where are you?', I have to admit I got butterflies. I was a bit drunk (OK – I was plastered), so I decided to ring him back. I don't think I would've been able to type a reply that made sense anyway. He answered, 'Hello?' and I said, 'Who's this?'

'It's Jack,' came the reply.

Of course I already knew it was him, plus I didn't know any other Jacks.

Then he suddenly said, 'Oh, I'm going to have to ring you back 'cos I'm at a football game.'

Fine, I thought, and forgot about it because I was focused on Jeff.

After things finally ended with Jeff, I met Jack again, in the same club as before – 195. I ignored him all night because I was embarrassed. He kept looking at me but I didn't know what his game was because he hadn't called me back after V. Jen was with me again and insisted on going over to speak to him. Well, I wasn't going to stand there on the other side of the room again like a lemon, so I went with her. I mumbled, 'All right?' and he immediately replied, 'You're with Jeff, aren't you?', so I explained that we'd tried to make a go of things but it hadn't worked out. It turned out that Jack had read about us being together at V and that's why he hadn't called again. So once again we attempted to swap numbers. All I knew was that I really fancied him. But even then I wasn't sure what was going to happen. And I certainly didn't know he was six years younger than me. Jack told me he was 22, and a football agent. I didn't think to question him.

We went on a few dates after that and things started progressing. Then one day Jen called me up and said, 'I've been doing my research and on the internet someone's written, "Jade Goody's dating Jack Tweed and he's only 18."' Saying, 'He's a liar!', she ordered me to ring him up pronto.

So I did as I was told – I called and confronted him.

There was no hesitation. 'I don't know what you're talking about, it's total rubbish,' Jack answered.

I wanted to believe him, so that was it, I was convinced.

I'd say our first proper date was a few days after that. Jack booked us a room in the Sanderson Hotel in the West End, and it was on this night that we first had sex. I hadn't expected to be treated to a fancy hotel – I'm used to paying for most things with guys – so I thought it was really sweet. We went on one of those funny rickshaws round town, then to a club, and spent most of the evening laughing and joking.

About two months into our relationship my PR,

Katherine Lister, told me she'd had a phone call from the *News of the World*. They were going to run a story revealing Jack's real age. The headline was something to the tune of 'Jade's toyboy lover – 18'. I felt sick. It meant that all this time he'd been lying to me.

And I hate liars.

I rang him up, shaking. I tried to be as calm as possible, though. 'Before I ring my publicist and tell her she's got her facts wrong,' I said, 'you need to answer me one question: how old are you, Jack?'

Silence.

Please don't say you're 18, I kept thinking. Please don't say you're 18! The problem was, in true me style, I then went and got my words muddled up. Instead of saying, 'Swear on my life that you're not 18', I said, 'Swear on my life that you're 18.'

There was a pause. Then came the confused reply, 'Er, what?'

So I said it again. 'Swear on my life that you're 18.'

He of course answered, 'Jade, I am. I'm 18.'

I screamed a bit, then put the phone down. I was mortified. Not to mention shocked. I found out later that his mum Mary had been telling him for weeks that he needed to confess. She knew it was only a matter of time before I found out. Maybe I should've sussed myself, but he acted so much older and I didn't have any reason to suspect he'd lie.

After a few minutes Jack called me back and tried to explain (although it took me a while before I actually stopped yelling and started to listen). He just kept saying, if it worked for Cameron and Justin (they were together at the time), why not for us? Age was just a number, he said,

and I acted younger than him most of the time anyway. He
had a point. But I still couldn't get my head round it. I kept
thinking, When I was on *Big Brother* Jack was still at
school. When I was giving PJ a blow job he was doing his
homework! Eventually I calmed down a bit and he
explained that he'd wanted to tell me for ages but was too
scared. He said he didn't think we'd have lasted as long as
we had and that when things started getting serious he
didn't want to ruin it.

Somewhere along the way he'd also told me he was half-
Italian and adopted. Why he said he was adopted I don't
know – nor does he. How he thought that little admission
was going to woo me is beyond comprehension. But the
Italian thing I could understand. It's just a shame he's so
shit at covering his tracks. He rolled over in bed one night
and I saw his bum was completely white.

'You're not half-Italian at all!' I laughed. 'You got that
from sunbeds!'

Only once we'd got to the truth of everything could we
begin with a proper relationship. And after that, for a long
while, the age thing was never a problem.

And Jack was pretty special too. Even before I knew
how good he was with my children I'd fallen for him.
Yes, he's good-looking and, yes (I'm running the risk of
sounding like Jordan here), he's got a lot of stamina –
there are some bonuses to being young! He made me feel
happy and alive. We laughed loads and rarely argued.
Besides, I was a mother of two – which meant he'd
taken on far more than I had. The best thing was that he
genuinely wasn't interested in the fame game at all,
which drew me to him even more. Jack was only young
but he was more content sitting in at home with me and

watching telly than he was hanging out with his mates. Plus he was better with my kids than I could ever possibly imagine. I think it was because he was so carefree himself. I remember falling asleep one afternoon and waking up to see him and Bobby at the foot of the bed dressed in matching Superman outfits. I loved it.

Jeff's way of dealing with it all was to do a magazine interview. In it he said something along the lines of 'I don't know why Jade's with Jack, maybe it's because she's young herself. I feel like his father.'

I thought it was all quite bitter at the time, especially as he'd moved on himself and had another girlfriend. I told him afterwards he should just be happy for me and pleased that our children have got someone they feel comfortable with. Luckily he seemed to see sense and it's never been awkward between Jeff and Jack since. They were never best friends but we all hung out together when the children were involved, because that was when it was important to be grown up about things.

Jack and I were first properly papped when we went to the Bahamas on holiday. We had such a laugh there. That's when he laid down the law about my wobbly bits. He suddenly announced, 'Now I'm your boyfriend, no more tits out.'

I nearly choked on my pina colada. 'But when I'm sunbathing I don't want to get white triangles!' I argued.

But he was adamant. And my boobs didn't get to see the light of day after that. In a way I liked the fact that he didn't want other men looking at me that way. I respected him for it.

My first Christmas with Jack was amazing. *OK!* magazine flew the two of us and the boys to Lapland for a magazine shoot. It was so magical there – the kids loved it. I'd always wanted to go, but I have to admit I was disappointed by Santa because he was wearing a green outfit, not a red one. Someone told me afterwards that it was meant to be green in the first place and it was only because of some Coca-Cola advert back in the 1930s that Santa's costume turned red. But I didn't believe them. The trip wasn't the most romantic, though, as there was no adult time, and because it was the start of our relationship Jack and me were gagging for it (time alone, that is, not what you think). So one night when the kids were asleep I suggested we went out for a naked run in the snow. If anyone had seen us they'd have had a heart attack. We were throwing snowballs at each other and doing stupid poses. It was hilarious. And cold.

In typical cheesy fashion, the day I realised I actually loved Jack was Valentine's Day. We'd planned a big romantic evening. He was paying for the hotel and I was treating us to dinner at Gordon Ramsay at Claridges. He did offer to pay for everything but I knew that would mean he'd be skint for the rest of his life. And I could afford it. Obviously I'd left it until the last minute to get his present, though, and was still rushing around Selfridges at four that afternoon trying to find him something. In the end I settled on a lovely pair of designer shoes. They were really cool. I didn't have time to wrap them up, so I plonked them on the bed in the hotel, still in the bag from the shop.

We decided to leave the present-giving until after dinner so that we had something to look forward to. The restaurant was amazing, and soooo posh! When we walked in I saw Jimmy Carr and his missus, who said hi and smiled, and a few tables away there was Jonathan Ross and his wife. Jonathan's always so lovely to me and that night was no different, although I'm sure he must secretly have thought, Bloody hell, we come in here to get away from the likes of her!

Jack was more overwhelmed and nervous than impressed. And I found that really sweet. The food was gorgeous (well done, Gordon) and we felt a bit tipsy by the time we got back to the hotel. Which was just as well, because I had to gear myself up for giving Jack a special treat. Earlier in the week I'd bought myself a load of saucy underwear from Agent Provocateur and was going to surprise him with it later. Not that I had it on under my dress already, of course. That would have made far too much sense. It was all still in a carrier bag under the hotel bed, so I was going to have to sneak off and change somehow. But first it was present time.

The hotel, in Kensington, was gorgeous. I'd always wanted to stay at the Baglioni because that's where Mariah Carey stays (and if you know me you'll know what a massive fan of hers I am). When we were back in our room, which was all dark and mysterious-looking, Jack pulled out a bag and got out these beautifully wrapped presents and carefully placed them on the bed. He'd gone to so much trouble – they were red and all had individual ribbons round them. I looked at my effort – a pair of shoes dumped in a Selfridges bag. Oops.

I opened mine first. The first thing I unwrapped was a little dainty necklace that I'd seen Victoria Beckham wearing – it was a bronze-coloured solid heart with a little ribbon and a pearl round it. I was really taken aback and touched.

Next was a brown velvet clutch bag with a big clasp at the front, which I fell in love with immediately. Then I got the Arctic Monkeys CD that I really wanted. Finally I opened the last present – a belt.

It was vile. It had the biggest buckle on it I've ever seen and my immediate reaction was: 'What do you want me to do with this then? If I put it round my waist my trousers will fall down, it's so heavy!'

Jack laughed and started trying to pretend his mum had chosen it, which I knew was a lie. Bless him.

'OK – where's mine then?' he grinned and I sheepishly handed him the carrier bag apologising for my lack of wrapping paper. He opened it up and pulled out the shoes. There was a long pause as he looked at them.

'Jade?'

'Yeah?'

'I'm 18 – not 80.'

'What the fuck do you mean?' I said, laughing. 'They're nice shoes!'

'For a granddad maybe. Look at them!'

I tried to persuade him they were designer and cool but in the end we had to agree to disagree. He hated them. We both started cracking up.

Then it was time for my surprise. I put the telly on and switched it to MTV to divert him, then sneakily grabbed the bag with my lingerie in.

'I'm just going to the bathroom – won't be long.'

God, I didn't realise how fiddly this saucy underwear lark was. It took me for ever to do the suspenders up. I had a black frilly basque, crotchless knickers, stockings ...

the works. But I was so long in there Jack started shouting, 'Jade! What the fuck are you doing in there? Hurry up!'

'I'll be out in a minute!'

I wanted to make sure the stocking seams were straight but they kept going all twisted. I should've known it was a catastrophe waiting to happen. I hadn't thought about how I was going to do the big reveal. What was I thinking? Should I just throw open the door and say, 'Ta da!' or what? What if he just laughs? I should've waited until I was more drunk.

I grabbed the door handle. Gulp. I felt like a right tit. I couldn't have picked a worse moment. There I was standing in the entrance trying to do my best seductive pose and Jack was glued to the TV set, dancing wildly in his little white pants and singing along to George Michael.

I closed the door again.

He must've heard the slam. 'Jade – what are you doing in there?' he asked.

So I took a deep breath and I walked out, still to the tune of 'You gotta have faith, faith, faith'. Jack stopped in his tracks and we both pissed ourselves laughing.

'I feel like such a plonker!' I laughed. Tears were streaming down our cheeks, it was so funny.

Eventually we calmed down and lay on the bed. One of Beyonce's slow songs was playing in the background, and we started kissing. Suddenly I gave way to the urge to blurt out, 'I love you,' and I started crying. It was so emotional. Jack looked at me and smiled, 'I love you too, Jade.'

It might've been a messy beginning but it couldn't have ended more perfectly.

For ages after that night, whenever we heard the song 'Faith' we pissed ourselves laughing.

The boys were falling in love with Jack too. Bobby was also falling in love with the colour pink for a while, which was slightly worrying. Until he was about two I let his hair grow long, so he looked like a little girl at the best of times, but then he began wanting me to put it up in bunches or ponytails. And he was constantly picking up Hoovers and brooms like a little housewife. He even asked for a doll at one point, to which I replied, 'B, can't you have an action man?' He's a very sweet and sensitive little boy and I wouldn't change the way he is for the world, but I did begin to wonder how he might turn out. His girlie phase was short-lived, though. As soon as I cut his hair short he turned into a proper little boy. His speech came on miles and he started digging up holes and playing soldier games. Phew.

Jack was like a big kid himself really. And he seemed to have a thing for buying me animals as presents. No matter how many times I told him that I couldn't stand a messy house, he seemed intent on ignoring me. Not long after we were first going out I came home one day and he met me at the front door with a broad grin. 'I've got you a surprise!'

'What is it?'

I walked inside and there was a budgie screeching in a cage.

'The boys love him. We've named him Jimmy,' said Jack.

Not only was it bloody noisy but it seemed to be spitting birdseed out and making a mess all over my conservatory.

'You're responsible for cleaning it up,' I said.

A few days later I was tidying the house and had the

windows open. How was I to know that Jimmy's cage wasn't locked? He flew out. Oops.

Jack was convinced I'd done it on purpose. 'You've let him into the wild. He's going to die. You've killed him!' he moaned.

In my old house we also had a pond and I'd bought some pike to go in there. One was called Custard and Bobby loved him. But I was told when I got them that no other fish or water creatures were allowed to go in the pond with them, as it would upset the balance or something. I made sure Jack knew this full well. Or so I thought.

Until I got back from the shops one day.

'Surprise!'

'Jack, what have you done?'

He'd bought me two terrapins and put them in the pond.

The next morning I went down to the pond to find the fish dead and this terrapin floating on the surface with stuff leaking out of it like something out of a horror movie. The whole pond had been contaminated.

A slightly nicer present came in the form of Batman. A little dachshund that Jack bought me for Valentine's one year. Even he nearly ended up with one paw missing – but I'll tell you about that later.

5
Kiss and Don't Tell Me Again

Not long into our relationship, one of the tabloids got hold of a picture of Jack with his arm round another girl. So the speculation began. And Jack got his first taste of fame. What the reporters didn't find out of course was that it was his cousin Jess. Then he got a call from a magazine asking him how he felt about me and what was going on in our relationship, and he replied, 'It's nothing serious.' Which of course I *loved* and had an argument with him about. He protested, 'You always told me to downplay it if anyone asks!' And I had, but that didn't mean I liked it when I saw it in print.

That was the first story about Jack and another girl. But it certainly wasn't the last. After that there were so bloody many I lost count. The girls even started to merge into each other. So much so that I didn't know what to believe any more.

The first real kiss-and-tell (although Jack still denies

every single one to this day) was a girl called Anna who claimed he'd snogged her down an alley near Faces and had been begging her for sex. I didn't know what to think. But I made him pay for it. When the story came out I flipped and kicked him out of the house. He was adamant nothing had gone on between them and begged me to believe him. But I was fuming. How could he? And how could he be so fucking stupid to think no one would find out? I was so confused and upset. My kids had grown to love and adore Jack – he'd become a big part of their life by now – but now that he'd done something like this I was starting to question what that all meant and how long he was going to be around if he couldn't be trusted.

I wanted to believe him. I wanted to think he wouldn't do that to me. And I wanted to be with him. So, eventually, I forgave him.

But these things never completely go away, do they? A few weeks later we were on a night out in London at my favourite club, Embassy, and Jack disappeared off to the loo. After about half an hour I went to look for him because he hadn't come back – and I saw him standing by the wall talking to the same bloody Anna bird who'd sold her story. What's more, he had his hand on her arse! I marched over and pushed him as hard as I could.

'What the fuck do you think you're doing?'

'We were just having a chat, that's all.'

'Are you having a laugh?'

I was fuming. I stormed out to the car park and he followed.

'How dare you mug me off like that, Jack!'

'I wasn't doing anything wrong, I promise.' He was slurring his words, he was so pissed.

'I saw it with my own eyes, Jack!' And with that I punched him in the face. He then pushed me away and I fell to the floor. So I got up and I kicked him as hard as I could. I didn't know at the time but my stiletto went right into his side and punctured the skin. We only realised the next day when he woke up in agony. I can't remember what else happened that night – it all became such a blur. All I know is that Jack insisted on coming home with me, then we passed out and woke with raging headaches (plus, for him, the bonus of a hole in his side).

I've come to realise that Jack's a completely different person when he's had a drink. It's like he is that Jekyll and Clyde character (someone told me the other day it's actually 'Hyde' but I think 'Clyde' sounds more like a name myself). He turns mad and seems to do everything he can to provoke a reaction from me.

Another prime example was the photo of him and a topless girl in his bed on holiday not long after – dutifully printed for all to see in the *People* newspaper. And although there was pretty damning evidence against Jack, what readers didn't know at the time was that I was there on that very same trip. We'd gone to Marbella with separate groups of friends. I was on a hen do and he'd booked a lads' holiday not long after. Even though we were dating, we still didn't want to spend the whole time together because it wasn't fair on our mates. So we stayed in separate hotels, did our own thing and arranged to meet up only occasionally.

It all seemed to be working, well until one night I felt tipsy and wanted to go and surprise him in his room. I went to reception and asked for his room key, which they gave to me, and I opened the door. Admittedly, there was a tiny part of me that thought, Oh my God, what am I going to find in here? But I carried on anyway. He was sharing the room with one of his mates, so I could instantly see there were two single beds. But when I looked in the room I saw Jack lying in one bed, naked with a sheet draped over him, and beside him was a girl with blonde hair, sprawled out on the other bed fast asleep. One of his mates was asleep on the floor by the window.

I immediately saw red, pulled the sheet off Jack and slapped him round the head.

'What the fuck? What are you doing in the room naked with a naked girl next to you?'

He was half-asleep and drowsy. 'Jade? What are you talking about?'

'That's it. I've had enough of you Jack! I never want to talk to you again,' I said before marching out of his room and slamming the door.

And I didn't. Well, not for the rest of the holiday anyway. And boy, did it do his head in. Each day after that he would see me on the beach with my mates and come over trying to explain his way out of the bedroom-and-girl situation, and I would turn my head and ignore him. Each night he'd see me in a club talking to a group of boys and come over all jealous, shouting, 'You make me sick!'

I just blanked him and walked off.

Then one evening he got into such a frustrated rage that he kicked my door down. It was about 2am and I was sitting in my hotel room on my own after coming back from one of the clubs. How the hell Jack managed to batter the whole door down I'll never know – he's not exactly a big bloke. But he did it, then started ranting his head off at me, accusing me of being with another bloke.

Er, excuse me! Was he deluded? I wasn't the one naked in a room with another person! He was knocking things all over the place – I just remember all my Gina shoes flying about everywhere – and he kept pushing me against the wall. Then my mate Gemma came out of the lift with a guy she'd pulled (hoping to have some time alone together) and saw us through the kicked-in door.

'Jade! What's going on?'

Gemma and the guy ended up pushing Jack out of the hotel and forcing him to pay for the door in the process. I was so bloody embarrassed.

Afterwards my mates were livid. 'Why are you still with him, Jade? You can do so much better than that.'

'But he's good with my kids ...'

'If that's the only reason, you're really fooling yourself.'

So I decided I had no choice but to dump him.

And I did – until we got back to England and he begged and begged for my forgiveness. I know, I was weak, but I couldn't resist him at the time.

A few days later a reporter knocked on my door brandishing a picture of Jack and the blonde girl in the same bed together! I didn't say anything in front of the journalist – I just shrugged and said, 'It's Jack's business, not mine.' But as soon as I'd closed the door I turned round to see Jack's sheepish face staring back at me. And I slapped it. Hard.

What woman wouldn't?

He started protesting that he'd been set up. It turned out his mate who was in the room with them has a friend at the *People* and had sold the story. I felt a right mug.

Someone was watching my back, though. Jack got death threats from a guy in prison. It was addressed to 'Jade

Goody, Big Brother, Essex' and it got to my house! There were a few letters saying similar things. 'I'm sick and tired of that fella cheating on you, Jade, if he ever cheats again don't worry cos I'm in here for murder and I'll have him up the arse.' Jack was petrified. But I told him it was his own fault for reading my post in the first place.

After my 25th birthday party – which had a Tarts and Vicars theme (I thought I looked great, Jack thought I looked like a slut) – the press started speculating even more that things were going wrong between us because they said it looked like he'd been sulking all night. But the fact was, Jack just liked to sit back and leave me to it. He wasn't one to be prancing around in front of the cameras, whereas I was. I do think Jack found me a bit annoying that night because I was so hammered and loud, but I know there's a part that also thought it was amusing. And anyway, it was just me, so he had to deal with it.

Danielle Lloyd was at that birthday party. It was strange because it was before *Celebrity Big Brother* so I didn't know who she was at that stage. I just remember this pretty girl coming over to me while I was throwing myself around the dance floor like a pissed idiot. She'd turned up with her mum and they were both dressed as tarts. She said to me, 'Oh, Jade, I'd love to be walking out of a club to all those photographers like you,' and I just smiled.

The kiss-and-tells with Jack just kept on coming. And I was getting sick to the stomach having to defend him. *Heat* and other magazines were running big articles with titles like 'Five Reasons Why Jade Should Dump Jack' and when I read them I had to agree – there was so much evidence against him. What the heck was I doing?

Once I even ended up having to defend him to Jonathan Ross. I was a guest on Jonathan's show and was sitting in the make-up room when he came over to me and told me I could do so much better than Jack. And for someone of his status to actually care enough that he had to speak to me about it was really saying something. Why would a grown man, who's really successful, be that bothered unless he could see something I couldn't? I felt quite pathetic, but still, for some reason, I stuck up for him.

When it came to it, I was too pathetic to leave Jack. At that point anyway.

Actually, if you believe what the papers were saying, I was more in love with Kate Moss than I ever was with any boyfriend. I first met her on a flight to LA (we were both in first class and she kept turning round and chatting to me – which nearly made me choke on my champagne) and since then I've seen her at a few events and each time we've said hi. But rumours about our 'friendship' really surfaced after the O₂ Wireless festival in the summer of 2005. She was there with her mates (remember those pictures of her in the shorts and red ankle boots?) and I was with mine. After one of the bands had finished she came over and said, 'I *love* your programme, Jade.' (I was on Living TV at the time, I'd just filmed *Jade's Salon* and there was a new one called *Just Jade* in which I was trying to find the right scent to launch my own perfume.) 'I watch it all the time,' she continued. 'It's hilarious!' Then she started quoting back to me things I'd said! By the time she walked off I had my mouth open in awe.

I know people say Kate has done bad things in her private life but I still look up to her. I think she's amazing. I even had arguments with Jack about her because he said

47

he thought she was a bad role model. I still love her. At the end of that festival she asked me back to her house, saying she was having a party. It was mad. She was pleading, 'Please come!' But I didn't. I told her I was with too many other people and it wouldn't be fair. If I'm honest, though, the real reason was because I would've felt so out of my depth. I would've been with all these famous people and I wouldn't have had a clue what to say to them. And then if they had started taking you-know-what I would've felt uncomfortable – it's just not my scene. I know what Kate Moss has done and I've read the stories about it in the papers. But I've never seen her do it myself and I admire her. I think I was worried that whatever I saw might change my opinion about her.

Nevertheless, the fact that she invited me to her house? Wow!

That same day I had people like Natalie Imbruglia and Bob Geldof coming over to me, also saying they watched my show. It was madness. And amazing. Jack just kept looking at me and telling me how proud he felt. He said that whenever things like that happened or when he saw me on TV he got goose pimples – because he felt so full of pride that I was his girlfriend.

6
Running Scared

In April 2006 I did the London Marathon. The dreaded 26.2 miles.

Why, oh why, oh why?

The previous year I'd mentioned to my agent, Sally at John Noel Management, that I wanted to do it. But of course I had no idea whatsoever how far it was. I didn't have the foggiest how much training I needed to do. As always, I was clueless. I was so busy filming for my TV show and working at the salon that before I knew it the weeks were passing me by and I hadn't done *any* exercise. By the time 23 April came I'd done, oooh, all of four hours' training. I think I'd just about managed 20 minutes on the treadmill. I was eating curries one week and on holiday the next. Jack used to be a runner himself, so he knew what he was talking about when he looked at me a few days beforehand and said, 'You're going to kill yourself, Jade.'

I don't really like running trainers. I think they make your feet look funny. So I thought I'd wear the Nike ones I usually wore to netball. Because they had air bubbles, I thought they would be OK. Oh yes, and I decided to accessorise with a Gucci bum bag. My excuse was that I had to have a microphone pack in there with me for the Living TV show. I also had my mobile phone, some make-up and a mirror. Good job I had the make-up really because I looked *so* well groomed by the time I'd finished (that's a joke – did you see me?). Gordon Ramsay was being interviewed alongside where I was hovering about at the starting track and he clearly didn't like what he saw. He runs marathons all the time and he made it pretty plain he didn't think I was taking it seriously. 'You're wearing tennis shoes!' he said, and kept giving me odd looks. I'd like to think it was because he feared I might steal the show off him when we were on camera. Or maybe he thought I might beat him!

As soon as the whistle blew I had a sinking feeling in the pit of my belly and the full realisation of what I had in front of me hit home. All I could see was a mass of people passing me by. First there was Sophie Anderton, then Rebecca Loos, then Jeff (he'd been training properly and laughed as he went past) – and so the sea of fit bodies went on.

I would never attempt to run it again but I can understand why people do. The atmosphere was out of this world. Just amazing. No one seems to think I did any running – because all the pictures in the press afterwards were of me walking – but that was because that's the only time they could snap me. I managed 21 miles in five hours, which is pretty good going. So, believe it or not, I did actually run. Then walk. Then run. Then hobble. Then jog. Then cry. Then collapse.

The bit that really got to me was when I got to whichever

bridge was around the halfway mark. When I reached it I burst into tears. At first I was just overwhelmed at the sight of all those people cheering and the feeling I got from hearing their chants of support. But as I got over the bridge I saw everyone running back the other way and realised with a sinking feeling that the circuit doubles back on itself. That's when my exhilaration suddenly turned into despair. By then I was in such pain my right leg had started twitching and the muscle just seemed to seize up like a rock. I've never felt anything like it. It was excruciating. And then to see all those people running back the other way. *No!* I thought. I didn't believe I could carry on.

I would've stopped then and there if it weren't for these two amazing women I met. They kept encouraging me and walking with me or running, depending on what I could manage. But I got to 21 miles and saw this ambulance parked on the side of the road ahead of us. My body had packed up. All I could see was black. I could taste blood in my throat, I felt sick and I was shaking. The two ladies were begging me not to stop because I only had a few miles left but I just couldn't go any further. I hobbled into the ambulance, cried, 'Please help me!' and collapsed. The paramedics gave me gas and air and said I needed to go the hospital, but all I wanted was to go home.

Meanwhile, Jack was at the finishing line waiting for me. They were all there with him – my mum, the boys and my mate Carly. I was gutted I didn't make it but I knew my body couldn't take any more. In the end a police car took me to a Salvation Army place where I had to wait for a cab because, with the surrounding roads blocked off, no cars could get near the course. The Salvation Army were holding a day specifically for recovering drug addicts. And there I was screaming for painkillers. Not the best idea I've ever had.

Jack was so proud of me afterwards. He knew how upset I was that I never got a medal, so he gave me the one he'd been awarded for some running event he'd once done. I was really touched. That's what he was like back then, always doing sweet things. I eventually got my own medal on my next birthday, because my mates wrote to the Marathon's organisers and asked if I could have one. Luckily they thought I still deserved it. Unlike most of the press – the week following the event I was criticised left, right and bloody centre. All these columnists were laying into me.

Ulrika Johnson said in the *News of the World*, 'I'm a bit of a runner myself – not a brilliant one, but I do 15 to 20 miles a week. So I found watching that lazy lump of lard Jade Goody attempt the London Marathon on a regime of curry and no training an insult to all runners. Places are hard enough to come by. The one she wasted for the sake of getting her mug in the papers could have gone to someone raising decent money for charity.'

Some columnist in the *Sun* wrote, 'Jade Goody trades on having the brains of a baboon, but she's brilliant at self-publicity. Her London Marathon stunt was totally irresponsible, though ... she tried to run 26 miles having done no training apart from stuffing herself with curry. Medics with better things to do had to waste their time treating her before she was carted off to hospital, where she wasted the time of more doctors and nurses. Time you grew up, girl.'

I just sat there reading these things (still nursing the sorest legs I've ever had in my life) and thought, You fucking fuckers, bollocks to you! I still raised money for my charity and I got to 21 miles. I raised cash for the NSPCC, so up your bums – the lot of you!

There was one columnist who was surprisingly nice about me, and I was told she usually had quite a nasty tongue on her. Her name was Carole Malone and she wrote in the *Sunday Mirror*. She wrote that I was a 'Plodder with a bit of a pluck' and 'It's always been a great source of angst to me that a woman with tumbleweed for brains and who has all the charm of your average slug manages to earn £1 million a year.'

OK, so that wasn't the nice bit, but somewhere in there there's a compliment:

'However, the fact that before she collapsed Jade Goody managed to run 18 miles in last week's London Marathon with no training and carrying two extra stone is pretty impressive. Of course, the reason she attempted it in the first place is because she's as thick as a brick outhouse and has no concept of what that kind of run could have done to her body. Even so ... hats off to her!'

Thanks, Carole (I think). I later went on to become friends with Ms Malone in the *Celebrity Big Brother* house, so perhaps this was her subconscious way of sowing the seeds of love for me – or something.

Anyway, looking back on my Marathon experience I think I did well. I got as far as I bloody could. Twenty-one miles is quite an achievement in my book. Of course, that doesn't change the fact that I am never ever going to do anything like that again.

Ever.

I wasn't much better behaved when I was behind the wheel than I was on two legs. Jack and I went to T4 on the beach that summer and I decided to drive. Problem was, it was all the way out in Weston-super-Mare, and the journey home took for ever. I was stuck in traffic for most of the time and I remember texting my mum (she was looking after the kids) to say I was going to be late. At that moment a fella in the car next to us shouted, 'Jade, can I have a picture?'

'Of course you can!' I said, and smiled.

The next week that very picture was in *Heat*, which pointed out that I was breaking the law by texting while driving.

Bugger!

You can't say I never get my comeuppance for bad behaviour, though. Bad luck seems to follow me like a bad smell. For example, when I discovered a family friend had robbed me of over £12,000. My mum had made friends with a guy called Luke who lived next door to us in my old house in Essex. He had a nice family and used to take his little niece out to play in the park with my boys. We became quite close to him and after a while it seemed a normal thing to do for him to babysit the kids occasionally. We trusted him.

One day I got a phone call from my financial adviser. 'Have you been betting, Jade?'

'What? I don't bet!'

'Online betting, I mean, on the computer. You've actually won quite a bit by the look of things.'

'What?'

It turned out that Luke had been setting up paypal accounts using my name. Not only that, but when I went to the bank about it they started quizzing me about certain cheque numbers and when I looked for the stubs in the book they were missing. They'd been razor-bladed out.

Luke had been forging my signature for months, and putting money from my bank into his account with these cheques. Thankfully, even though I was a stupid twerp for not having paid enough attention to my finances, the bank had to pay me all the funds back because they were at fault as the signatures he'd forged were nothing like mine. We had to take it to court, and when I faced Luke in the dock I felt sick. It was the ultimate betrayal. Not only had he wormed his way in with my mum, but he'd also used my kids to get to my money. And I'd let this evil creature look after my children.

Drama after drama ...

When I look back at some of the stuff that's happened to me I can hardly believe it. I sometimes wonder whether I bring all this on myself. I know I should probably think more before I do things, but I doubt I'll ever change. One other thing I wish I'd done later that year was to make sure I got into the right taxi. Perhaps then I wouldn't have been kidnapped. Which was without doubt the most frightening thing I've ever experienced.

I was at Embassy with Jack and a few friends, and when we wanted to leave I ordered a car from the company I've been using for years. With them I don't even need to tell the driver where I'm going because the company has all my details. On this occasion I was a bit drunk and saw a man waiting outside who, when I asked if he was for me, instantly said yes. That was my first mistake. It's quite a drive from the West End to my home and I usually end up falling asleep on the journey. So Jack and I were dozing for what must have been about 40 minutes when all of a sudden we woke up – in the middle of nowhere. The driver had stopped, it was pitch dark and all I could see were what looked like forests all around us. At this stage I didn't have reason to suspect anything apart from the fact that maybe the driver was in a bad mood, so I said politely, 'Is there a problem?'

He replied in this gruff voice, 'I'm not driving any more.'

I said, 'What do you mean? Just drive the car! Where are we? I'm sorry I fell asleep, I can direct you from here.'

With that he got out of the car, opened the door and started confronting Jack. Jack then climbed out too and before I knew it they were squaring up to each other – it was all getting pretty aggressive. Jack's not exactly a big guy, so I followed and started trying to calm things down. Then the driver got back in the front of the car, I climbed in the back and Jack went to get in the other side. But before he reached the door, the driver sped off! It was the most horrible thing I have ever been through. As I looked out of the back all I could see was Jack getting smaller and smaller in the distance. I was petrified. Luckily I still had my phone with me and had the car company I use on speed dial, so I rang them. Screaming down the phone, I demanded to know what was going on. The controller said, 'Jade, this isn't the car you were meant to be in. The driver waited at Embassy for ages for you.'

Shit. So who was this man?

My heart was beating fast, my mouth got drier and drier. I couldn't breathe. Jack was out of sight. I didn't know what to do. Instinct then kicked in – and it was to grab the driver's head and begin hitting him as hard as I could. I pulled on the gear stick, tried everything. What do I do? I was thinking. Jump out of the car and do a roly-poly down the road? Then I leant across, yanked the handbrake and it stopped. I could see Jack was running up towards me and I opened the door and headed for him as fast as I could, yelling at the top of my voice. I was hysterical. When we reached each other Jack hugged me tight and said, 'It's all right, I've got you,' and we both turned to see where the driver was.

But he'd gone.

All that was left was his car, in the middle of the road, the doors still open, lights still on. Without thinking we started walking back along the road, not knowing at all where we were going. There was nothing but trees around us. By now it must have been about 3.30am, and we were scared shitless. It sounds stupid, but I didn't even call the police because I didn't know where we were.

Then, in the distance, we saw a guy coming towards us walking his dog. It was one of those spotty dogs like in *101 Dalmatians*. He had a torch in his hand and when he reached us he just said, 'You all right? I heard some screaming from where I live.' Then he turned and said, 'Come with me, I'll take you home.' Still shaken, we walked along with him for just a few seconds until we got to this old-fashioned gate, the kind where you have to lift the latch to open. I remember thinking how weird it was that he didn't ask what had happened. But I was so relieved to be there I didn't dare say anything.

We reached his car, which had the back seats down, presumably for the dog. We got in and he drove us home. It wasn't until I was in my house, replaying things in my mind, that I realised he'd left the dog behind. Why would he have done that? He'd hardly said a word to us on the journey home, and when we'd arrived I gave him about £100 in cash to say thank you. But, looking back, his sudden appearance didn't add up either. Nothing from that night did. Surely any normal person in his position would have said, 'Come into my house, I'll ring the police for you and let them know exactly where you are,' wouldn't they? Also, if he'd been that kind and caring he would never have taken the money. Weird. It still sends a chill down my spine even thinking about it.

I didn't think there was any chance the police would find the first driver if I reported him, and I was sure he wouldn't go to them after the way he'd behaved towards us. But two weeks after our ordeal the police came to my house and arrested me for 'not paying a cab fare'. I knew instantly they were talking about the same night because of the way they described it. 'Are you *joking* me?' I said. I was gobsmacked. Then I relayed the whole story of that night. OK, I know I should've called them before, but stupidly I didn't think about it. But even though they seemed to believe me, my arrest would still have stood firm if it hadn't been for the fact that I'd called my car company in a hysterical state. The police managed to trace the voice recording, so I got let off. But by the time I made that call the driver had disappeared in a panic, and the police couldn't find him. They still haven't. And it scares the life out of me that he's still out there.

Nights at Embassy don't usually hold such bad memories for me. One of my favourite evenings was when I went to Leigh Francis's wife's birthday party. It was fancy dress and I decided to go as Marilyn Monroe (you can guess the comments the papers made about that one!). The party was somewhere else, but a few of us carried on and decided to take our drunken selves to the club. When we got to Embassy I clocked Tom Jones having a meal. I was so excited I bowled over (well, wobbled) and immediately launched

Me and my gorgeous boys. I can always count on them to put a smile on my face!

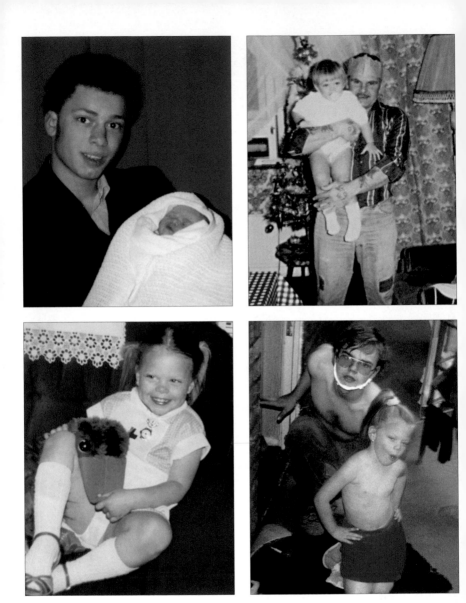

Above left: Apparently I was a total daddy's girl when I was a baby. Here I am just one day old in my dad's arms.

Above right: As a toddler, enjoying Christmas with my granddad.

Below left: Me with Emu, aged three.

Below right: What a little madam! Me with my favourite uncle, Martin, or Uncle Budgie as I knew him.

Above left: My dad, his mum and some other fella (I don't know who he is – maybe my nan's brother, or perhaps her boyfriend at the time).

Above right: Fast forward several years … Visiting my dad in prison just after I left *BB*.
Two weeks later he sold this picture to a newspaper for an absolute fortune. Bloody typical!

Below: My other nan and my granddad John. They've been together for nearly 50 years, and they're still as happy together as the day they met.

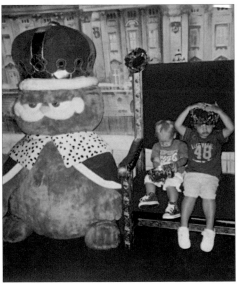 

Above left: At Adventure Island celebrating my birthday with my closest friends.

Above right: My mum and my lovely little man Bobby.

Below left: Bobby, Freddy and a giant Garfield (Bobby doesn't look too impressed does he?). This was Freddy's first premiere.

Below right: Early days with my 'toyboy lover' Jack.

Hitting the slopes in Chamonix, France.

It was all going so well … That'll teach 'em for laughing at me.

My 25th birthday party, which had a Tarts and Vicars theme. This was actually the first time I met Danielle Lloyd. She turned up at my party without an invite!

Inset: My birthday cake – isn't it fabulous?!

With Jack at my saucy birthday bash.

A couple of publicity shots for my old Living TV shows:

Above: A promotional shot for *Just Jade*.

rayburmiston.com

Left: A picture from a shoot I did with *Heat* for an article about Jade's Salon.

Nicky Johnston for Heat Magazine

I love playing the part of the sexy minx!

into my own rendition of 'You Don't Have to Be Rich to Be My Girl'. I was bopping away in front of him, but I was a mess. I had false eyelashes stuck to my eyelids, red lipstick all round my mouth. And he was scared. He was so nervous that he got his two bodyguards to sit either side of him. Luckily I know the manager of Embassy, Mark Fuller, really well, so he knew what to do with me. I heard him say to his staff, 'Get her in the VIP upstairs area now! And give her what she wants!' Which meant that all night I was given bottles of champagne, just to keep me away from poor Tom.

You'd think the kidnapping would have been enough for me to contend with for a while. But no. Not long afterwards I was picking Jack up from a night out. It was about 1am and I'd been with friends. I'd only had one glass of wine because I'm really aware of not drinking and driving. We were in my car and had the music up really loud. It was the Arctic Monkeys, which we both loved, and we were singing along at the top of our voices. I wasn't driving fast, but I wasn't exactly going like a snail either. The route to my house is full of bendy roads, so unless you know where you're going it can be a bit tricky. All of a sudden, as if from nowhere, a deer darted out into the road. I just remember thinking, A deer can kill you if it hits your windscreen. I saw a film once where two people died from that very thing. Also I thought, If I hit a deer I'll get in trouble with the Queen, because someone told me once that deers are the Queen's property. So I swerved out of the way, drove down a ditch and wrapped the car round seven trees. It was all so sudden that I didn't even have time to get scared. I just remember everything going dark and I must have passed out for a few seconds.

When I came to we were both squashed under this heap

of metal. I managed to have the sense to know we needed to get out straight away. It was easier for me, but Jack's side of the car was completely crushed. I helped him undo his seatbelt and pulled him to safety. By this time the shock was setting in and I started to panic. I was shaking like a leaf. I didn't know what to do or think. We held hands and just ran as fast as we could back to my house. We were so petrified we went to pieces. I had blood all over me, but we just sat there, huddled in my bed. I didn't phone anyone. Especially not the police. I convinced myself that if I did I'd be in massive trouble. I was so scared. And I knew that maybe I shouldn't have even drunk that one glass of wine.

At the same time somehow I knew I'd get caught. The state of the car and the noise of the crash brought the police to my front door in no time. They knocked but I just couldn't move, I was so nervous. Jack kept trying to assure me, 'You're going to be OK, it's fine,' but I kept crying, 'I'm going to go to prison ...' My door was open (will I ever learn?), so the police let themselves in and found me upstairs sobbing. They were really nice to me (they were pretty familiar with my house by now!), but said the car was a write-off and that I had to take a breath test. In the end I did it three times because it wasn't working, but thankfully I passed. I knew I wasn't over the limit but all the same I was so frightened.

The worst thing was that the police said when they saw the car they were shocked that Jack and I had come out of it alive. It was a total wreck. All I ended up with was a lump of glass in my foot and a few cuts. I feel so thankful now for how lucky I was. It has definitely made me more careful in the car, and now I'm even wary about putting music on. It can all be over so quickly. It's just not worth it.

7
Ch-ch-changes

In August 2006 I made the decision to close my salon, Ugly's. I'd set it up in 2005 as part of a show I did for Living TV called *Jade's Salon*, and I'd been really proud of my achievements. I'd learnt how to do so much – including waxing ladies' la-las (although unsurprisingly I didn't have a great many people taking me up on the offer; for that experience they preferred to book in with my co-manager, Carly) – but a year in and I was finding I had less and less time available to spend there. Despite the critics saying it was going bust, we had built up a regular client base. But in the end – as is the nature of business – it came down to money.

And circumstance. Carly and I found out that there were plans to build a nightclub in the space above us and we were asked whether we wanted to renew our lease. The rent for the building had been so expensive that there had already been times when I had to seriously question how long I could keep it going. I was paying for it out of my own money because we still hadn't quite broken even with the salon. So Carly and I sat down one evening and had a long discussion about what to do. Having a nightclub upstairs could easily mean we could come into work every Monday to find smashed windows and graffiti all over the shop. And it just wasn't worth it in the end. We knew we'd both achieved what we set out to do and were so proud we'd done it.

Carly has since branched out on her own, and I have to say she's a much happier and healthier-looking person for it. When she was managing Ugly's for me she ended up so stressed, the poor cow, that she went down to about a size zero! I think she was relieved when we decided to go our separate ways.

The salon might've closed, but thanks to another show on Living TV I found myself involved in another business venture. To make my own perfume. The programme was called *Just Jade*, and the idea was that I went in search of the perfect scent. And I can say with my hand on my heart that, my kids aside, it's my proudest achievement. I put everything into finding the right smells, the right packaging and the right look. I could easily have just put my name to it and let other people do the hard work, but I wanted the final choice to be my own. I knew I was taking a chance and that I could end up a laughing stock for being linked to the worst-ponging fragrance of all time. But I was willing to take the risk. And it paid off.

For a while I lost sight of what smelt nice and what didn't because I'd sniffed so many oils and essences. I also sniffed about a billion coffee beans because I was told that coffee clears your nose of smells after each test. Someone was probably pulling my leg, but I did it anyway. Sniff after sniff, I finally got there in the end, and the resulting fragrance was the exact perfume I wanted. My aim was for it to be distinctive and last a long time – I was fed up of putting on perfumes in the morning and by lunchtime having no smell there at all, so I wanted to be able to offer value for money.

Picking a name for it wasn't quite so easy, though. I'd have debate after debate with my mates about what it should be called.

'How about "Stench"?' one of them laughed

'Or "Stink"?' said another.

Then I was on a skiing holiday with my friends Kelly and John, and Kelly said, 'Why don't you just call it "Shut Up"? That's what people are always saying to you!'

And that's when it came to me. 'I'm going to call it "Ssh".'

During part of the TV programme I was still with Jack and he made a mini one for himself and called it 'Six Inch'. Which was very mature of him.

I can vividly recall being on a huge ladder on the big roundabout in Elephant and Castle, south London, pasting up my own billboard poster – a big picture of my face – alongside the words: '"Ssh" by Jade Goody – selling at the perfume shop'. I was so damn proud.

The show's producer, Kate Jackson, was my biggest fan. She wore it all the time so that if someone remarked, 'I like your perfume,' she could tell them and that way give me a bit of free PR. When the perfume came out all my friends went out and bought it, their mums did too and my family had it in the house by the bucketload. A few days after it landed in the Perfume Shop Kate rang me and screamed, 'You're outselling David Beckham!' My perfume had gone to number one! It wasn't just celebrity perfumes I was outselling either. I was beating Marc Jacobs, Armani, Gucci – the lot. It was madness. I was even up for a Fifi Fragrance Award – something Calvin Klein had won the year before.

To this day I can walk past a crowd of 50 people and know instantly if someone's got my perfume on. One time I was in the supermarket and I could smell it on this woman as she went past. I didn't say anything, but a few minutes later I felt a gentle tap on my shoulder. 'Hi, Jade, sorry to bother you but I just wanted to say I love your perfume. I wear it all the time.'

I beamed, 'I knew you had it on!' (Maybe I should have been hired as a sniffer dog by MI5.)

Not long after that I found myself on another TV-related quest courtesy of Living. This time it was the search for *Jade's PA*. And yes, before you ask, I definitely needed one. For example, in 12 months I'd managed to clock up around £8,000 worth of parking tickets and congestion charges. It wasn't that I was doing it on purpose – the letters just kept getting lost under the mat, then I'd be away or working. I didn't even have time to go to the post office to pay for my TV licence. So, when I finally picked Rebecca out of ten candidates, the poor girl had her work cut out. She didn't actually get to start in the end. She was due to start in January, but, because of what happened in *Big Brother*, this changed. She was still paid for a year's work though – £25,000 – which ain't too bad!

Two thousand and six was a pretty good year for the Goody family. My mum included. For ages she'd been telling me she wanted to have some surgery on her face, but she's always been too proud to take any money from me to do it. But then she got a call from a TV producer asking her if she would be interested in taking part in *Extreme Makeover* on Living TV. She'd be sent away for six weeks and her whole look would be transformed by the end of it. Mum couldn't believe her luck, and I've never seen her so focused on anything in my life. She was so dedicated to it she even stopped puffing! That's how much she wanted it.

She had a nose job, a neck lift, an eyelift, a boob job, her teeth done, her tattoos removed. It was an utter transformation. It was strange her being away, because I never usually go for very long without seeing her, but we spoke on the phone every day and she filled me in on her latest bit of surgery. I felt a bit sorry for her there all on her own, because it was a fucking painful thing to go through. Mum gets scared about operations at the best of times so with such a mammoth thing to face she got really emotional when she spoke to me, and I hated hearing her sound all weak and helpless.

On the night of the big reveal we were all invited to see the results – all Mum's friends were there and I took the kids and Jack, and my nan and granddad also came. Well, when Mum walked down those stairs my jaw fell to the floor. I didn't recognise her. All I could see was tits and teeth.

She was wearing this elegant dress (although, looking back, it was a bit over the top – all purple and diamante nonsense – I'm sure most people would have chosen a demure black number they could wear again). She was waving like royalty and she looked lovely. She properly milked the attention. All I kept saying was, 'That is not my mum!'

Her face seemed really tight, which I didn't like at first. Also, her boobs were *huge*. I thought they needed to be de-pumped a bit as they were bigger than mine and I'm a DD!

Freddy took one look at her and cried. But once he and Bobby had got used to it they started referring to her as 'Nanny McPhee the princess', because in the film *Nanny McPhee* the title character had horrible teeth. It showed how the boys felt about my mum before surgery.

Later on that evening people who worked on the show were coming up to me and saying, 'You and your mum really look alike,' which was a bit bizarre, considering she'd just had loads of fucking surgery.

I've never seen my mum behaving in such a ladylike manner, though – it was very surreal. She kept saying, 'This is fabulous!' It was all, 'Oh, thanks for the drink, it's fabulous. My teeth are fabulous, my boobs are fabulous!'

I said, '"Fabulous"? Piss off! Just because you've had your face tweaked doesn't mean you have to change the way you talk.'

Afterwards this new 'lady' climbed into a cab and went back to her poky little flat in Bermondsey. Some things never change.

But the most emotional thing for me was the positive reaction of my nan and granddad. To them, the way she looked before was just a constant horrific reminder of her accident. And coincidentally this makeover operation had come 18 years after it happened. It felt so wonderful that she could finally put the past behind her and be a new person.

Of course, this wasn't to last. Mum was soon back to her old loudmouth, lairy ways and couldn't have appeared less of a lady if she tried.

She'd booked a holiday to Jamaica with her friends. And, while she was away, every time I opened a newspaper I had a sense something was going to kick off and so I was mentally preparing myself for a story on her getting into a fight or something worse. But to my relief, and surprise, there was nothing.

That was, until she got home. I opened *Heat* to see Mum, her face contorted with anger, mouth wide open, kicking off at someone, and all I could think was that all her beauty had disappeared as if she'd never bloody had any surgery! It turned out she'd had a huge scuffle on the return flight to the UK and they'd done a news story on the incident. She and her mates had caused chaos on the journey by upsetting crew and passengers so much that she was issued with a warning to calm down or risk being removed from the flight. She was apparently so foul-mouthed and rowdy that the flight attendants threatened to divert the plane to the nearest airport unless they all calmed down. The *Heat* article even quoted one of the passengers, who said, 'She was effing and blinding about not being fed. She was so loud the whole plane was bothered. I asked to be moved four times. The supervisor was called. She was told in no uncertain terms that we would divert.'

Of course, Mum's story afterwards was slightly different. She reckoned she was pissed off with the travel company for the way they had treated her (which was just as she deserved by the sound of it!). But she still told a reporter what a wicked holiday she'd had. She always manages to look on the bright side, does Jackiey.

All this simply meant that my mum was back to her old self. Not quite the lady she had been tailored to look like.

Those poor surgeons from *Extreme Makeover* must've wondered where they'd gone wrong. She's even managed to lose one of her nice porcelain teeth.

She came round the other day and I noticed it was missing. She looked like Grotbags. Mum told me she broke it on a piece of chocolate and I raised an eyebrow.

'Are you sure you weren't gnawing on a piece of wood or something?' I asked.

Bobby took one look at her and shouted, 'Nan, stop smiling – you're looking like Nanny McPhee again.'

Saying that, I was to be in the papers for fighting a few months later. I'd gone to the cinema with Jack and sitting directly behind us, minding their own business, were two black guys and a black girl. It was the row behind them that was causing trouble. There was a woman in her sixties, her much younger date, her daughter and her daughter's date. They were being really noisy during the adverts and I could see them drinking alcopops, which as far as I was concerned meant there was definitely going to be aggro. Before long they were shouting, swearing, chucking popcorn at the people behind us and basically being fucking annoying. I bit my tongue at first because I didn't want to start anything.

But then the film began and the noise carried on. Suddenly one of the guys behind us, after being hit on the head with some popcorn, stood up, turned round and said, 'What're you doing? Can you stop that, please?'

That was it – all hell broke loose. The old woman shouted, 'Shut up, you! Get back to your own fucking country!' Then both guys stood up and a fight kicked off. The two groups were hitting each other in the aisle and in an instant it had spilt out into the foyer. This meant the poor girl sitting behind us with the two guys had been left on her own. Out of the rowdy group, the old woman was the only one still in the cinema – and she'd now turned her attentions to the girl. 'Your fucking sort!' she shouted, unprovoked.

The girl tapped me on the shoulder and whispered, 'Can I come and sit with you, please?'

I replied, 'Of course you can,' and she moved in front to our row of seats. I immediately told Jack to go outside and find out what was happening. Meanwhile, the old woman had moved out of her seat and was prodding the girl. 'Your fucking sort! Go back to your own country!'

I turned round. 'Excuse me, lady, you've been sitting in this cinema, drinking alcohol and swearing your head off. Now you're telling this girl to go back to her country! Leave it out!'

And that was when she clocked who I was. 'Oh, look who it is! It's Jade fucking Goody!'

Everyone else in the cinema had turned around by now, so I walked out into the foyer to get away, and the girl and the old woman followed.

When I got outside, a full-on scrap was in progress – with Jack on the sidelines not knowing where to look. The poor girl was only 16 and was getting really upset at seeing her two boy mates getting beaten up by these pissed thugs. All of a sudden the old woman launched across and pushed the girl towards a chair. I stood in front of her and hollered, 'Get away before you give yourself a heart attack, you old dear.' At which she punched me in the face. So I hit her right back. Before I knew it the woman's boyfriend had grabbed me and pushed me to the ground, then Jack had leapt on him shouting, 'You don't hit my fucking bird, mate. Leave my girlfriend alone!'

By now the police had been called and once they'd eventually broken up the fighting, they started questioning people. The old woman's nose was bleeding and I could see her pointing in my direction. A policeman came over and asked me, 'Are you responsible for that?'

I replied honestly, 'Yes I am, officer, but I hit her in self-defence!'

He turned and looked at me sternly. 'Yes, I know,' he said. 'They've been drinking. We've found bottles and broken glass in her bag. We've had trouble from them before.'

Thankfully, in the end we were allowed to go. The next day it was a story in the paper with the headline 'The Goody, the Bad and the Ugly'. And when I read it I smiled. Because for once I wasn't being called the ugly one – this time it was the old woman!

8
Highs and Lows

I hadn't actually admitted it to anyone yet, but my body was turning into an absolute mess because of all the damage I was doing to it. Ever since Bobby was born I'd been relying on slimming pills or laxatives to keep my weight under control. Yes, I might have exercised and, yes, I might have told certain magazines I was on some newfangled healthy-eating diet. But I was always supplementing it with tablets. During Bobby and Freddy's earlier years I'd abused my body so much that my insides were suffering big time. I couldn't even confess to the doctors, though, because I felt stupid. I'd had a series of health scares where I'd faint from losing loads of blood and have to be rushed to hospital. And the doctors just didn't know what the cause was. After one emergency a newspaper reported that it could be bowel cancer. While my mum kindly informed *Heat*, 'She's been suffering from constipation and is very worried she'd passed some blood. On Sunday night she had very bad stomach ache ...'

Cheers, Mum. A little bit too much information, thanks. Next thing I know she'll be telling them how many times a day I go for a shit.

But it was worrying. I still have problems going to the toilet now – it's painful, and that's the way it's always going to be.

By the end of 2006 I was experiencing the biggest high of my career. My perfume was selling like hotcakes and making me more money than I could ever have dreamed, my first book had become a number-one bestseller (thank you everyone who bought it) and I had three reality-TV shows under my belt, with more being talked about for the next year. I never would have thought that four years after going into the *Big Brother* house I'd still be in the public eye and people would still be interested in what I had to say or want to buy things with my blooming name on! But I was eternally grateful and never took it for granted for one second. I had achieved a lot but I was under no illusions – I knew it could all end as easily as it started.

And I was about to road-test that theory in the most public and horrendous way possible.

My agent was still the same person I'd been with since I left the *Big Brother* house in 2002, John Noel, who's known in the business for being a very straight-talking, no-nonsense northerner. He'd always done well by me and I felt I could talk to him about anything and trust him with even more. I suppose, without a father in my life, he came to represent that sort of figure for me in many ways. And to say I was pretty close to him would be an understatement.

Just before Christmas in 2006, John called me into his office for a meeting.

'I've got this project that's come up. It means going away with all your family. It's for Channel 4 and you'll be working on a farm.'

'Yeah, that sounds good,' I replied.

'The best bit is your nan and granddad will get £10,000 each, and so will your mum, you and Jack.'

'And it's just on a farm?'

'Yes.'

I didn't think to question John further. When I got home I couldn't wait to break the news to everyone, and they were so excited. My granddad kept talking about this caravan he wanted to own, my mum was talking about all the holidays she could afford (and no doubt how much weed she could buy) and Jack just started dreaming about the designer clothes and nights out he could have.

Before long I was called in for a meeting with the show's producers to discuss it in more detail.

When I arrived I was greeted by a familiar face. 'Hi, Jade, so lovely to see you again!' It was Clare, one of the producers who'd worked with me on *Big Brother* in 2002. I loved her. She was amazing to me back then and had helped me get through so much.

But what was she doing here?

As I soon discovered, John had kept a few things from me ... Me and my family were not being sent away to a farm at all – we were being sent into the *Celebrity Big Brother* house. He said he hadn't told me before because he thought I had a big mouth and the whole thing had to be top secret.

'We want you on *Celeb Big Brother* – are you in or out?' Clare said.

There was also another producer there, a guy I also knew from the last series. And I'd always liked him too. These were the people who'd got me to where I am now. Without them I'd be nothing. And they were looking at me hopefully. I felt like I was being trapped into saying yes.

'Jade, this is going to be great. It's the last *Big Brother* we're both going to work on. You made it such a hit last time and you'll make it a hit again. Please do it.'

I was put on the spot. But I had a horrible, unexplainable feeling about it. I knew it wasn't a good idea. But the problem was I'd already told my family and Jack about all this money they were going to earn, and they were beyond excited. How could I let them down now? If I was a multimillionaire like everyone thinks I am I would've turned it down then and there and offered to pay my family the same cash from my own pocket. But I'm not, and I sure wasn't then either.

But that didn't change the fact I did not want to do it.

I asked if I could have a day to think about it, and promptly called another meeting with John Noel.

'John, it's going to kill me off. Going back on *Big Brother* will be the death of me. I just have this feeling,' I told him.

He laughed. 'Don't be a fucking idiot' – John was never one to mince his words – 'What have you got to lose? You're going to make money out of it, and you're hardly in there for any time at all. The worst that can happen is that you don't win it. It's a great opportunity. What can go wrong?'

But I knew deep down I had no reason to go back into that house. Surely he could see that? I didn't realise then how much of an involvement John actually had with

Endemol – the TV company that makes *Big Brother* – and how much was at stake for him if the ratings did well.

So I was persuaded to say yes.

I broke the news to my family over Christmas dinner. Everyone had come round to mine and I'd really gone to town and bought more food (mainly from M&S, it has to be said) than should be legal. I was determined to make it the best Christmas Day ever. Then, as I dished out the turkey, I cleared my throat. 'I've got something to tell you' – blank faces all round – 'the, er, the show we're all doing isn't actually on a farm. We're going on *Celebrity Big Brother* instead.'

My granddad nearly dropped his knife and fork. 'Oh, gal, you're joking, aren't you?' The colour had drained out of him.

'Just think of the money, Granddad,' I pleaded. 'And it'll be over before we all know it!'

In the end I brought them round and that was it – we were all set to go into the *Celebrity Big Brother* house on 5 January 2007. But before that, to shield us from the outside world and make sure we didn't know who we would be on the show with, we were all sent to a house in the countryside for a week. Alongside us there were some of the *Big Brother* production team who were monitoring us.

The initial idea was that my nan and granddad would be in the *CBB* house for the same time as the rest of us. And all we knew was that we would be joining the other housemates a day after they'd first entered. I would go in with Jack, followed shortly by Mum, then Nan and Granddad. But my gran's not very well – she's got Alzheimer's and forgets loads of things – and it wasn't until we were all staying together in the country that I realised quite how bad she was. I came to realise how my nan and granddad relied on each other completely. Then one day I looked over at my nan struggling to remember what on earth she'd just crossed the room to get and I thought, What if she gets evicted first? There's no way she'll be able to survive outside without my granddad. I can't do this to them.

So I begged the producers to get them out of the show. But at the same time I didn't want them to take away their fee. Twenty grand between the two of them was a hell of a lot of money. There seemed to be no easy solution, and negotiations went on right up until the night the show was due to start. It got so close. On the night we went into the house my nan and granddad were still sitting in a holding room thinking they were going to be coming in with us. And by then I was kicking off. 'I can't put Nan and Granddad through this. I can't! I can't!' I shouted.

Clare looked at me. 'We've thought about it too, Jade. Don't worry. We've decided they're not going to come in with you.'

'But what about the money?'

'We're still going to pay them anyway. Maybe they'll come in for one day – we can't say at this stage.'

I was so relieved. But I hardly had time to catch my breath because it was time to face the crowd. And what an overwhelming experience that was.

I've never had such a reception in my life. The entire audience was cheering my name and shouting for Jack – they were going mental. It was all the more surreal because this was where I'd stood when I went into the same house five years before and no one had the foggiest idea who I was. But here was me – a national home-grown celebrity – and people actually liked me and wanted me to do well.

Perhaps John Noel was right. Maybe this was a good thing to do. After all, what could I possibly have to lose, eh?

But the minute I set foot in the *Celebrity Big Brother* house I knew it was wrong.

The doors closed behind us and I saw three people sitting in the living room.

'Hello, I'm Jade,' I said. 'And this is my boyfriend Jack.' My mum followed a few minutes afterwards, bumbling her way down the stairs.

They all looked shocked – and pretty unhappy to see us. Sitting at the table were Shilpa Shetty, a Bollywood actress (who I thought was very pretty but who instantly made me feel uneasy because of what she whispered to the others), Jermaine Jackson (Michael's brother, who I was very excited about seeing and seemed really sweet from the minute I met him) and a white-haired fella called Ken Russell (who I just thought was old).

I thought I heard Shilpa mumble, 'Jermaine, I can't believe this. It has ruined our family.' And before I could take anything in I was called into the diary room.

'Jade, this is Big Brother. Ken, Shilpa and Jermaine are now part of the Goody family. Furthermore, the other eight housemates – living next door in squalor – will become servants to the Goody family, catering for your every whim.'

'I don't want to be special!' I protested. And I didn't. This was my worst nightmare. Instantly there was a divide – and I already knew what that did to people, having lived in the rich/poor house during my *Big Brother* experience in 2002.

'Can I still brush my own teeth and that? I can't have anyone washing me!'

I felt awful.

When I met the rest of the house as they all came up from the dungeons or the cellar or whatever it was, dressed as my servants, I wanted the ground to swallow me up.

To make matters worse, Big Brother had transformed the bedroom too. It had been redecorated since last time and had new beds installed, including a four-poster for me and Jack. Shilpa said she wanted to be away from Ken because he was snoring so much so she insisted on moving her bed from its original position.

My first impressions of the other housemates varied widely. Dirk Benedict, the American actor, seemed to hate me from the minute he met me. I really liked Carole Malone, the newspaper columnist. Cleo Rocos I already knew because she was represented by my agent John Noel and she was lovely. Danielle Lloyd ran over and acted like she was my best mate even though I'd only met her once before, but I thought she was a nice enough girl. I'd always had the idea that Jo O'Meara was going to be really hard and difficult to get on with, but I really liked her a lot. Then there was Ian 'H' Watkins, who used to be in Steps. Mum started hanging around with him all the time, but I found him really irritating and thought he was laughing at her. Finally there was Leo Sayer, who was nice to me, but I found out later that he was bitching behind my back.

I was desperate to ask Jermaine about his brother Michael but wasn't sure how he'd take it. Obviously that didn't stop me though. I wanted to know if he bleached his skin and whether any of those rumours about alleged child-molesting were true. I just thought, I've got to ask, why would I not? I knew everyone else in that house wanted to, but they didn't have the balls to say anything.

As I sat down next to Jermaine my brain was ticking over. How do I approach this without offending him and without looking like I'm being a bitch? But I was genuinely curious and, to be honest, a bit confused.

'Jermaine, do you mind if I ask you something?'

'Not at all.'

So I just blurted it out, with no lead-up, no clever questioning or anything. 'You know your mum and dad, are they both black or is one black and one white?'

'They're both black, Jade.'

'I'm only asking because I'm mixed race – my dad was black – so I've had that pigmentation on my skin before that's come in little patches on my chest when I've been in the sun sometimes.'

He looked at me calmly. What the hell is this girl on? he must've been thinking.

I carried on. 'Well, obviously you're black, the famous Jackson family are all black and Michael was once black, but now he doesn't look black any more ...'

'I know, he has a skin disease.'

'But I've had pigmentation and I only get it in blotches, I didn't think you could get it all over you like he has ...'

I could see he was starting to feel really awkward. Oh fuck! I thought. But still I carried on. 'Or did Michael get patches of pigmentation at first and then the patches started joining up?'

Bless him, he kept trying to explain the skin disease.

'You don't mind me asking, do you?' I said. 'It's just because of the rumours of him having his skin bleached and stuff.'

'No. I've had the tougher questions asked of me before,' replied Jermaine.

Then I tried my next angle. 'Michael's had a tough time lately, hasn't he?'

Oh Lord. Move over Jonathan Ross.

'Was the family all supportive? What's happened exactly?'

Jermaine just replied that everything was fine. But I could see I was embarrassing him a bit and knew I should stop.

'Sixty per cent of what you hear is the media talking,' he added. 'A lot of the media and the journalists and the news media are not supposed to inject an opinion. And sometimes the producers never write the facts. With a lot of the major networks in America it's all sensationalism.'

I asked him what 'sensationalism' meant.

'Made-up things,' he replied.

'OK, Jermaine, thank you!' I said, and quickly left the room. I'd grilled him enough.

As the servant task carried on I got more and more ashamed of how they were having to behave. Who the fuck did I think I was? One of the housemates, Donny Tourette, from some weird band, had even walked because of it before I arrived, and I couldn't blame him. My mum was milking it, though. And Ken seemed to love it too. When the 'servants' came upstairs he said, 'I shall be addressed as his lordship.'

Shilpa was also used to it from her upbringing. She said quite openly that she had servants at home. She would say, 'Come on, get this, get that,' but I still just couldn't deal with it.

What I'd also never realised was how hard it would be living in that house with my mum. I got so frustrated with the situation that I kept crying all the time. She was my mum, but she was embarrassing me. Her behaviour, her language, her manners were appalling. But she was my mum. And while on the one hand I couldn't stand to watch her acting like that, on the other I didn't want to betray her. But she was going on and on. I could see how irritating her loudness was for everyone. Even worse, she just couldn't get Shilpa's name right.

'I can't understand your name,' she shouted at her one day.

'It's Shilpa. It's not a sentence, it's a frigging name.'

'Shoopa, Shoopa,' was Mum's response, making it ten times worse. What were viewers at home going to think? This was awful.

Mum started trying to get round it by calling her Princess, but Shilpa said it made her feel awkward. So Mum responded, 'You know what, I'm going to call you Nish.'

Oh my God. Could it get any worse?

'Mum,' I said, 'get her name right! She's called Shilpa. Get it right and respect it.'

I was getting so narked with Mum that I then got myself into a tizz because I felt awful that I was bad-mouthing her in the diary room. I tried to talk to Jack about it, but he just replied, 'My mum does my head in all the time – everyone's mum does.' Then he suggested, 'Every time she gets on your nerves we'll just go out in the garden.'

To make the situation even better, Mum was farting all through the night – and thinking it was hilarious. My mother was all over the place in that house. Understandable really, as she'd never been in that sort of environment before, which meant that at times it was like she was almost showing off, and it was really getting to me. I knew how people would view her on the outside world, because they'd viewed me in the same way when I'd first gone in there in 2002. And I'd behaved like a right ignorant idiot. The ironic thing was, while I was worrying about my mum, I didn't realise I was about to do it again. Only this time it would be 10,000 times worse.

Mum was emotionally unstable. One morning I remember her bursting into tears after missing out on the Eggs Benedict the servants had cooked because she was in the shower. I overheard her saying to Ian (or H from Steps as he was better known), 'I don't want to be growly at people because I'm hungry,' and he told her she should just have a sandwich later. I walked past and reminded her, 'You don't even like eggs.'

I thought Ken was quite sweet at first because he's an old man, and I feel like you should always respect old people. But then he started being all uppity and deliberately sticking his nose up at the servants. He knew that as part of the task we could only eat food they'd made and that if we made our own they could fail. But he still decided to go and help himself to cheese and crackers and that really got me mad. I ended up storming into the garden.

I just thought he was being really inconsiderate and I told him that I thought what he'd done was wrong. Regardless of what people think of me, I believe my priorities were right, and to me this was about Ken deliberately going out of his way to upset the task for the others.

We made up in the end because I felt bad about speaking

to him the way I had. I wouldn't want anyone talking to my grandfather the way I spoke to him. He didn't seem to care, saying, 'That's part of the game. It's a game, darling. I'm playing the sort of old eccentric family.' He walked soon after, though. It all got too much for him.

I spoke to Carole a lot in the house and I think she was surprised that she actually liked me. I think I shocked her a bit too, because she admitted she's always slagged me off in the past. She even said I was 'sweet' and that she'd had to completely change her perception of me. I said, 'Look, don't worry. I know I wouldn't have a job if nobody wrote about me … I'm perfectly aware this won't last for ever and, when people stop writing about me, I'm in trouble.'

'You've got your head screwed on,' she told me. 'I might have to go back on what I've written. Not a backtrack; a new road. I might have to have a rethink.' Wow!

Things were looking up for about a day. Mum and Shilpa even kissed and made up because Jackiey had finally managed to pronounce Shilpa's name properly. 'Woooh!' said Shilpa really excitedly. 'That deserves a hug!'

Then – at last – my grandparents came to dinner. I was so pleased to see them, and I knew it meant there would be no doubt about them getting their fee. It nearly brought tears to my eyes to see them together looking so cute and for a moment it actually seemed like they'd made the house bond a bit. Although they only stayed for a few hours, I was so proud of them. My mum was embarrassing, as usual, but I tried my hardest to ignore it. Shilpa couldn't believe my grandparents had been together for 46 years. She said it was wonderful 'after so many years of marriage to actually see that chemistry.'

The servant task was passed in the end, thank God. Leo

Sayer was being a bit weird throughout the whole thing. He refused to talk and was on some vow of silence as a protest to Big Brother. It was much nicer having the whole house on an equal footing, for a while at least. The problem was, with everyone together as a unit, my mum's behaviour was so much more obvious. I told Jack I was finding it hard.

'I'm just not really enjoying myself. I'd rather be at home being a mum to my kids than a mum to my mum. It's not her fault, that's just the way it's always been.' It was really tough to explain, but I felt like I was on guard the whole time, waiting for her to say something and to have to correct it.

By this time I'd started getting quite pally with Jo and Danielle. Danielle was besotted with Teddy Sheringham, her boyfriend at the time. She spoke about him every second of the day and it was clear she adored him. 'We've been through so much. We really love each other. We're going to get married,' she kept saying.

Mum was hanging out with Ian a lot (which irritated me because I was convinced he was taking the piss out of her) and the older ones, like Shilpa, Dirk and Jermaine, would stick in their groups away from the rest of us. I started getting wound up by Shilpa because she kept hogging the shopping list, though I really should've known from my past *Big Brother* experience that shopping and food are always the cause of arguments.

Jack was being pretty quiet and keeping himself to himself. There weren't really any 'lads' about for him to gel with. By the sound of things he'd have got on really well with Donny Tourette, the rocker guy who legged it when he found out he was going to have to serve me.

Then it all started kicking off between Mum and Shilpa again, in the kitchen. According to Shilpa, Mum had insulted her hair and her shawl, and said, 'If I was your mother I'd be chasing you out of here with an Indian broom.' Shilpa thought Mum was picking on her for no reason, and she probably was. But that's my mum, and I knew she spoke before she thought and honestly didn't mean it.

Then Mum was evicted.

She was the first person to leave the house and it took us all by surprise. I was distraught. It killed me.

We were all told to gather round the dining table and Mum was called to the diary room. She looked ridiculous – she had carpet burns and no shoes on her feet! We had to watch on the plasma screen as she was told she had to leave and I couldn't help myself – I burst into tears. The worst thing was that I wasn't even allowed to say goodbye to her. I just couldn't control myself after that, I was in bits. All I kept thinking was, Big Brother would never have put Jermaine, Dirk or Shilpa through the humiliation of going out there with bare feet. But they did it to my mum. There was cream all over her to soothe the burns she'd got from messing about with Ian on the carpet. And she had her top hooked up behind her, but because she only has the use of one arm she couldn't even pull it down herself. It was so degrading.

All I could think was that it would never have happened to the others. I got the impression the *Big Brother* producers jumped through hoops for Shilpa Shetty. This was magnified in my mind because she informed us of certain things in the house (obviously none of it was screened though). Of course, looking back, she may have been winding us all up, but Shilpa specifically told us all that she'd insisted on certain clauses in her contract. Apparently one was that if she went into the diary room and asked for something (within reason) she got it. I've been in the *Big Brother* house before so I know they don't just give you food and drink because you ask for it. But Shilpa would disappear into the diary room saying she was going to ask for potatoes, for instance, and emerge with two giant bags of them and a couple of chickens! I just kept thinking, this isn't the *Big Brother* I'd known, where you only got stuff if you earned it. Things like this weigh on your mind when nothing else is going on.

Jo O'Meara had told Big Brother previously that she had really bad back problems from her S Club 7 days, but that didn't make a difference to the mattress she was expected to sleep on. And when she complained Big Brother gave her painkillers. Yet there was one particular day when Shilpa told us she was going to tell BB she couldn't sleep on her mattress because it was too soft. During that day the blinds were put down in the bedroom, so no one could see in, and we later found out they had secretly given her an orthopaedic bed.

She also said she got paid a ridiculous amount of money – much more than any of the rest of us had.

Then there was one day in which we had to do a task – a VIP red-carpet assault course. We had to go across obstacles like a gunge-filled VIP Pit, a Champagne Fountain and a Crawl of Fame, among other things, with gunge everywhere. Along the way we were to collect awards. If we completed it within nine minutes we would receive a luxury-shopping budget; failure would result in basic rations. But as soon as we started Shilpa shouted,

'Stop! Stop! I need to take my contact lenses out. I need the blinds pulled up and the clock stopped!'

We were all looking at her. 'Shilpa, you can't do that now. We're going to lose the task – we're up against time!'

I thought from being in the *Big Brother* house before that BB wasn't going to care about some silly contact lenses. When I was in the house in 2002 there was a guy called Tim who had contact lenses, and when he couldn't put them in in time we failed our task.

But Shilpa carried on. 'Big Brother – open the doors!'

And with that the blinds were lifted, the doors were opened, the clock was stopped – and Shilpa went in and removed her contact lenses!

Another time they gave her a dress to wear and she didn't like it, so she was allowed to change. I know the rules of *Big Brother* are really strict, but I couldn't help feeling there was something more going on in that *Big Brother* house and that Shilpa was being treated differently to everyone else in there. I accept that when you are in an isolated condition things get totally blown out of proportion, but it all seemed really unfair to me. This is still no excuse for what followed. I just wanted to set the scene properly.

Leo Sayer was the next celebrity to walk out of his own accord. He was never going to last long anyway. But I was really upset when Carole Malone was the next to be evicted by the public. She was a really stable influence on the house and it seemed like it was all going to crumble after she went.

And crumble it did, but not before it went completely, disgustingly, downhill.

Jack decided to wank on my leg in bed. 'Stop it,' I

shrieked. 'Jack, I don't want you to mess up the bed. Go in the toilet.'

But he took no notice. 'I couldn't help it!'

'You fucking just did that all over me.' Urgh. I was disgusted. I had to clean up the bed. Admittedly, we'd had sex in the outside toilet a few days before (there were no cameras in there, which was the only reason I did it), but yuk. This was really below the belt (and the bed covers).

The house was getting more and more tense by the day. We were now arguing about the kitchen. Shilpa seemed to be hogging the cooking and one evening she brought out this chicken that wasn't cooked at all. We did moan about it behind her back, but she was starting to frustrate me. We were just very different people. And with my mum gone I just saw red. I didn't have anyone to look after now, so I seemed to let myself go more. And not in a nice way.

Then came the night to end all nights.

9
Big Mistake

I'd been having disagreements with Shilpa for a couple of days. Admittedly, looking back, it seems like I was focusing on her a little too much, but in that house it's hard not to concentrate on something. Everything gets exaggerated and turns into a far bigger deal than it might if you were in the outside world. People had been noticing that Shilpa was hogging the kitchen a lot, so I confronted her about it. And this was because I was the only one who'd say out loud what others were thinking.

'Shilpa, you're being very controlling in the kitchen. And, if we're honest, some of us don't want to eat the food you're cooking because you put a strawberry up a chicken's bum the other day, which was a bit weird. And also, we need to make sure the chicken's cooked properly otherwise we'll get ill.' (It had been put under the grill a few nights before.)

There was no denying that by that point there was a divide in the house. And I wasn't helping matters.

Then came the biggest, ugliest fight that's probably ever been seen on reality television. What's more, it was all over a bloody stock cube.

I know, how stupid. How could such a disgusting, nasty fight arise from something so small? It probably doesn't really make sense to you, but in my mind the whole horrific thing came about because Shilpa lied to me.

And I have a thing about liars. As I found out when I went into rehab, this is a massive problem for me. It's something that has plagued me and caused immense anger in my life for years. I cannot cope with lying. And it doesn't matter how small the lie is either. I have a mental block in my head.

Someone could say to me, 'I'm wearing a pink top tonight,' and then if they emerge from their bedroom wearing a blue one instead I won't be able to handle it. Instead of saying, 'How come you're in a blue top? Did you change your mind?' I'll come across really aggressive and say, 'What did you lie for?'

So much has happened in my past, which means I can't deal with liars.

Anyway, Shilpa came into the living room and demanded to know how many Oxo cubes we'd used and then, when she realised they'd run out, began to complain that they were the only things she'd ordered from the shopping list. And because I knew she was fibbing, I just flipped out. Well and truly.

'Don't lie, Shilpa. I saw you doing the shopping list. You had the shopping board for ages. That was not the only thing you ordered!'

'Yes it was!'

'No it wasn't. You're a liar!'

And so it went on. Except it became a tirade of insults about how much we disliked each other. I felt she looked down on me, and she thought I picked on her. I don't want to repeat anything that was said that night as I think the conversation has been replayed enough in people's heads. All I know for a fact is that what I said was never racially motivated. I honestly said nothing that was directed at the colour of Shilpa's skin and I never ever would. Yes, I shouted. Yes, I was nasty. And yes, I am horrified that I could behave in that way, and I wish I could take back everything that I said and did that evening. But ultimately we were fighting because we were from different classes and had different values in life. I really felt like she was looking down on me, and people who know me will know I have a chip on my shoulder about that. I don't want anyone to think they're better than me, just because they have more money or have had a more educated upbringing. I felt like, to her, I was common. And, to me, she was a posh, up-herself princess.

But it was never to do with race.

When I think of that night it's all a blur now. But, having watched the footage again, I'm terrified of the picture of me I saw. I looked like my head was going to pop off. I'm so ashamed that I reacted like that. And it's not something I ever want to repeat.

Later I was called into the diary room.

'Jade, do you think you calling Shilpa "Shilpa Poppadom" could have caused offence?'

I hadn't meant it like that. It had come out in a rage – and fallen off my tongue like every other word I seem to get wrong. Only most others, like 'East Angular', don't have quite such serious consequences.

'Well, if there was a Scottish man in here and I called him "Mr Haggis", would that cause offence?' I asked, confused.

There was a pause. 'Big Brother knows and understands what you're saying, Jade, but Big Brother would like to point out to you that you might have upset someone and that what you're saying could be construed as offensive and maybe racist.'

I was shocked. 'I'm not a racist! Please don't anyone think that!'

I couldn't quite believe what I was hearing, or what I had been seen to have done. But the penny still hadn't dropped about how seriously it was being regarded on the outside. I was fucking scared, and I was mortified that Big Brother or any of the viewers would ever think I'd meant anything racist, but deep down I believed people would know the truth: that I'm not a racist.

I had to make Shilpa realise I didn't mean to hurt her, that I didn't mean it in that way, so I immediately went out to the garden and told her what I'd said. 'Shilpa, I've referred to you as "Shilpa Poppadom", but I honestly didn't mean it in an offensive way. I've been told that my comments might be seen as racist in your culture, but I promise you I am not a racist and I am sorry if I've offended you.'

Shilpa listened to everything I said and then reached across and cuddled me. And at the time I felt we were both genuinely trying to put our differences behind us.

'As long as I'm in here I don't want anybody to have any ill feelings about me,' I said. I told her I didn't want the awkwardness any more. I didn't like it. I didn't like waking up in the morning and saying 'Good morning' to everyone but Shilpa. I'm not spiteful, and I'm not nasty on purpose. It was time to end the feud.

Shilpa and I were up for eviction that week and I knew it would be my name that Davina called. I'd been preparing myself all day. What I hadn't been training myself for was the fact that there was no crowd noise. And when I heard Davina call my name the surrounding silence made me feel sick to my stomach. 'Why is there no crowd?' I shrieked. 'What's going on?'

Big Brother called me into the diary room.

'Jade, are you OK?'

I recognised the voice. It was the producer, Clare.

'What's going on? Why is there no crowd? What is going on?'

'Some of your fans have previously had fights with some of Shilpa's fans in local pubs, so for security we're not letting any crowds in.'

'Why are they having fights? What do you mean?'

'It will all become clear when you come outside. You'll be OK, Jade. I promise you. You'll be fine and we'll get through this.'

'Clare? Get through what?'

'We will get through it.'

What the fuck was going on? I didn't have a clue what I was stepping out to. And still I was unaware of the seriousness of the situation or just how much the media had been baying for my blood.

I walked up the stairs and stepped out to the silence of the *Big Brother* compound. It was eerie. There was no noise. I saw Davina looking at me stony-faced. When I'd stood on these steps five years ago, I remembered, she'd grabbed me and given me a huge hug. She'd whispered in my ear, 'You were brilliant, absolutely fabulous. Enjoy this. Just take it all in ... I wanted you to win. Be wise with your money and get that house you've always wanted.'

But this time her words couldn't have been more different. 'Jade, what have you done?'

She took me into the studio. I was all over the place.

What had I done?

'I've got two things to show you,' she began.

'OK ...'

One of the clips was going to be of the argument, I knew that. And I thought maybe there would be a bit of footage showing me being bitchy. Which I regretted.

But what I saw next on the television screen nearly floored me: there were the chimes from ITV's *News at 10*. The news? I've been on the fucking news? What the hell? Racist ...? Complaints ...? Uproar ...? It was all such a blur. I was on the news? Oh my God. Gordon Brown was talking about me ... I was on *Newsnight* ... People in India were burning things to do with *Big Brother* ... It was like something out of a film. A horror film.

Fuck.

What the ...?

Shit ...

Then Davina showed me the argument. And I've never seen such a vicious-looking face in my life. 'The face of hate' I think I was called in one newspaper, and they were right. I was disgusted to look at myself.

I can't really remember what Davina said to me after that, but I just said what came from my gut. 'With my hand on my heart I apologise to anyone that I have offended ... It was not meant to sound the way it did. I meant no hate. I can't justify myself when I look back at that – what I watched was nasty. Yes, I said those things and they are nasty, but I am not a racist ... I shouldn't have done that ... This made my career and it will end it.'

Davina asked me about my 'Shilpa Poppadom' comment, and by now I was so distressed. 'It's being interpreted as a racist comment, but it wasn't,' I said. 'Shilpa doesn't think I'm a racist, but everyone else does. I don't know what to do. I'm scared. I am not a racist and I will stand my ground until everyone knows that. I can see why people think I am, though. I look like a complete and utter small person. When I said that I didn't mean it in a racist way.'

I have never been more frightened in my life.

The whole feeling of being rejected petrified the hell out of me.

I was hated four years ago, but it was different this time. In the past I had been named the most hated person next to Osama bin Laden. I had been called a fat troll. And people had waved banners saying 'Burn that pig'. But back then I didn't have anything to lose; now I had so much. I didn't want to go through that crap again. If everyone thought what I said was meant in a racist way, I knew I didn't stand a chance. I would never judge anybody by the colour of his or her skin. My dad was mixed race – that's why I look like I do and have big lips. Bloody hell, my mum refused to let me go to one school because she said the people in the area were racist! I'm not racist, but that's not what other people thought. I didn't know how it had got to this.

But it had, somehow.

All I could think was that I'd let my two kids down. I

understood why people didn't like me any more. If this is my punishment, I thought, then it's my fault for the way I am. I'm so upset with myself. If that's the end of my career, I only have myself to blame. I deserve everything that's coming to me.

My head was whirring. All those years ago my ex Danny used to come round and hit whatever got in his way, usually me. I would sit alone in the dark, nursing my bruises, rocking back and forth. I used to think I'd be better off dead. I thought I had turned my life around since then. Now this? How did I let myself end up in this dark place again?

10
Trial and Error

I used to love having an argument and feeling like I was the winner in a fight, but I know that's not the answer now. I can see how wrong I was in many ways. Arguing is just damaging and it stresses me out. It makes me feel drained and exhausted. And at the end of the day there's nothing ever gained except negativity. I know people know me as big-mouthed Jade Goody who attacks everyone. And that's fine, people can have an opinion of me but I'm honestly not a raving lunatic. Saying that, everyone knows I've got a temper, so it would be silly for me to sit here and pretend to be sweet and innocent.

When the cameras stopped rolling and my eviction interview was over, I looked around the audience sheepishly. There was a mixed crowd of people, with a group of Asians directly placed in front of where I'd been sitting. I'd been vaguely aware of them booing when I'd come in, but I'd been too stunned to take much of it in.

Yet now, as I looked at them, they screamed, 'Jade, we love you. Don't worry!'

Had they been told to boo by the producers? Why were they being all nice now the cameras weren't on them?

I forced a smile and said, 'Thank you. I'm really so sorry if I've offended you. I didn't mean to.'

Davina didn't talk to me again. She just walked off. It was like she didn't even know me and it was the worst feeling ever.

I was taken to a room to see a psychiatrist and shown a huge pile of my press cuttings.

In the room were the counsellor, me, John and Katherine Lister, my PR. All everyone kept saying was, 'You'll be OK, Jade. You'll be fine.' But even then, no matter how horrendous the situation clearly appeared to everyone surrounding me, all these articles branding me a racist and a bully were just swimming before my eyes as if in a dream. None of it connected. None of it meant anything. Nothing truly hit me until the next day.

John told me he'd stopped the press conference, which meant nothing to me at the time. I'd only ever done a press conference when I came out of *Big Brother* the first time, and that was a blur. At this point I didn't know that the reason for stopping it was because I would never have been able to cope with the questions and the hatred from the media. Instead I was told I was doing one newspaper interview, with the *News of the World*, and that was happening tomorrow.

I just accepted it. John knew what he was doing.

I was taken to a hotel near the *Big Brother* house. It's the same hotel all the housemates go to each year after their eviction, so it wasn't exactly difficult for paparazzi and reporters to know where I was. And there were swarms of them everywhere. I had two bodyguards, Mick and Tony, the same guys who'd looked after me the first time I came out of *Big Brother*. So I just accepted it. I was quickly whisked to my room, no telly allowed, nothing to read and told to get some rest. I lay on my bed staring at the ceiling. I don't know how long I was like that for, but before I drifted off I remember hearing one of the bodyguards – I think it was Mick – saying to Tony, 'Get those paps away – they're just causing trouble.' I found out later that one of the paparazzi had ordered an Indian takeaway to be delivered to the hotel in my name in the hope that I'd come to the door so they could get a shot of it.

I knew I'd done wrong in the house, but until the *News of the World* interview it still hadn't quite sunk in how much I was hated. My head was full of questions about what was going on, but I couldn't work out how to say them, or what I wanted to ask. My brain felt like one of those globes on a stand, just spinning and spinning. On the way to the interview the next day I wasn't even trying to prepare myself because I'd done so many in the past and I'd always just chatted and been honest with the journalists, usually having a bit of a laugh. I knew this one wouldn't be a laugh, of course, but I thought if I spoke from the heart I would be able to convince people I hadn't meant to offend. Little did I know quite how much it would affect me. It was the most tense, daunting, horrific interview I have ever done in my life.

The interviewer was Jules Stenson. Katherine was with me throughout. I already knew that I wasn't getting paid for it – the money was going to charity, and there was no way on earth I wanted it myself. Katherine had also told me that we didn't have any sway over what was printed. For the first time in five years my agent didn't have copy approval. Most magazines and newspapers refuse to give this sort of thing anyway (unless they are getting Madonna!) but that's what I'd been used to with John Noel Management, who always demand it – and it works. Damage limitation, I guess you'd call it. But there was no way I was going to be given the liberty of that. Besides, by that stage it was far too late for me to repair any damage.

All Katherine said to me beforehand was: 'Be honest and say what you need to say.' Which of course I did. I've never been 'briefed' for an interview, and I'd be rubbish if I was. If someone told me what I should and shouldn't say I'd cock it up anyway and you'd be able to tell instantly that I wasn't being myself.

The tape recorder was switched on and also there was someone filming the interview for the *News of the World* website. I didn't think anything of it because I'd seen before I went into the house that more and more celebrities were being filmed as well as being papped, so I just assumed this was what always happened now.

I was nervous, though. I didn't know or understand what was going on or why everything had turned so bad. And then the interviewer just started firing question after question after question. He was reading quotes back to me of things that I'd said – and they were truly horrendous. I broke down and sobbed. I couldn't help it – the seriousness of the situation and the consequence of what I'd done in that house had now, finally, truly, hit me – like a juggernaut. From the minute the interview started to the second it finished I was in floods of tears. At one point I couldn't even breathe because I was crying so much. Even the interviewer seemed shocked at my reaction – I could tell he was taken aback and he said, 'I'm sorry, Jade, but I have to be harsh with you. These questions need asking.'

Apparently, Davina had been perceived as being too soft on me, which meant that from now on every journalist who spoke to me was going to be determined to make sure I got what I deserved.

The whole thing is such a blur to me now I can hardly remember a thing that was written. But I've read over it since, and it's still uncomfortable to look at in print even now:

Are you a racist?
No, I'm not a racist, but I accept I made racist comments. I don't see people for the colour that they are, or where they come from.

I'm mixed race myself and I speak to everyone of every colour, background and nationality. I don't care about where people are from.
How do you justify the comments you made to Shilpa?
I'm not going to justify my actions because they were wrong. I was shocked to see how I behaved. I was shocked and disgusted at myself. I don't know why I said those things to her or why those words came into my head. I wasn't thinking in my head a nasty thought. I'm not making excuses because I know that it's wrong. I now know that it's offensive. Maybe I'm just really stupid and nasty at heart. But I really don't think I am.

During the Oxo cube row you shouted at Shilpa: 'You're a f***ing loser and a liar, you need a day in the slums!'

I said: 'You are a f***ing loser and a liar!' and I did say that.

I know that Shilpa doesn't live in the slums, because I took the time to get to know her. The slums is a word that Shilpa would have told me. I can't justify my actions for that. It wasn't meant as a racist comment.

You told her: 'Shut the f*** up! Who the f*** are you? You aren't some princess in Neverland, you're a normal housemate like everyone else.'

I remember saying that and it's wrong, but it's not a racial comment. In my rage of anger that's why I said she wasn't a princess and not a god, she's a normal f***ing person.

You also referred to her as 'Shilpa F***awallah, Shilpa Durupa, Shilpa Poppadom'.

I remember saying Shilpa F*** something.

Does it shock you that you said those things?

My anger when I watched it on the screen shocked me. I didn't like it. I didn't know that my presence could be so intimidating or bullying.

I don't want that, but I don't know any other way to argue.

I've never blamed my past for anything I've done, but I don't know any other way. My only way to argue is to shout – to get louder and louder so that I can't hear what they're saying.

It's the way I am. I didn't know it was a problem until I watched it. I don't want people to be scared of me, or think that I'm intimidating.

You can see why 'Shilpa F***awallah' is racist?
It is. Because I now know that in Shilpa's religion anything to do with swearing or the 'f' word is seen as hurtful and racist. For me it's normal to say effing this and effing that. I didn't think that these words would cause offence.

Do you accept that those comments and comments like it are racist?
I hold my hand up to my comments and to people reading them or hearing them and thinking I'm a racist. I can understand why those words would look racist because I didn't get on particularly well with Shilpa. It's offensive to her and her culture. I didn't think 'poppadom' was a racist word. I now know that things that I may not think are racist can actually be racist. It's my own fault for not knowing enough about other people's cultures.

How does that make you feel?
I feel sh*t. I hate myself right now. The first time I was on *Big Brother* it was like a holiday camp but I've now got people out there who look up to me. I didn't want to get evicted for the wrong reasons. Evict me because I'm loud or annoying, but not because I'm a racist, because I'm not.

You ganged up with Jo and Danielle against Shilpa.
You sometimes click with people more than others. I clicked with Danielle and Jo because they are the same age, we live in the same area and we had things in common.

After the Oxo cube row Danielle said: 'That was f***ing fantastic. I loved it, I think she should f*** off home' – a blatantly racist comment.

Yes it is, but that didn't come from me. I didn't say anything as I was too angry.

You were there when Jo then said: 'That's made me feel better. I must say, it's made my day.'

I wasn't taking any notice of what they were saying. I was so angry at the time. I was angry with me.

Danielle then said about Shilpa: 'She can't even speak English properly.'

I feel ashamed about that. I'm ashamed about everything.

Katherine couldn't look me in the eye. She had never been in that situation with me before. She'd only ever sat in on interviews when I was having a giggle and being silly, but this was far from that. I could see that she was upset at seeing me in such a state.

By the end I was a total mess. I sat there like a shell, shaking and crying. Katherine called John and told him to come and see me because I was in such a bad way.

When John arrived he was like a father figure to me. My own dad wasn't here any more, and even when he had been he was never a dad. As a young girl I'd sit and daydream about him taking me to playgrounds and fairs and on nice family holidays, but the reality was quite different. OK, so he'd come and visit me once or twice a year, but that would be on the rare occasions he was out of prison. He was behind bars his whole life: 54 convictions, or something like that, I think he had.

I had such a close relationship with John, but even then he was so hard to read. You'd never be able to tell when he was happy because he was so deadpan. I'd always know when he was angry, though. I can't even count the amount of times we would call each other a c**t. Our relationship was very volatile, and I do believe he thought a lot of me. Otherwise he would have stopped looking after me a long time ago. But the fact that he kept coming back to see me during that awful time, and just being there, I knew he cared. That was his way.

The problem was, I couldn't really face anyone. I didn't know what to do. I told them to leave me and I lay on the bed of my hotel room staring at the ceiling. What the fuck had I done?

My friends were texting me relentlessly asking if I was OK.

I couldn't talk to my mum either – I didn't want to be a burden on her. When she called I had to pretend I was all right. She was scared too and getting abuse from people who'd seen her behaviour in the *Big Brother* house. All I wanted was for her to come and give me a massive cuddle and tell me it was all going to be all right. But I knew she couldn't. She loves me, but she's not that kind of mum. I have always been the one to care for her.

Losing the use of her arm in the accident meant I had to do all the chores around the house because she couldn't pick anything up. I was five years old and I did it all – the cooking, cleaning, ironing (I don't even do this now, but I did then!). She had dreadlocks for a time, so I had to do her hair. I remember having to split it into sections so I could wash it. It took hours. I'd stay up until some stupid o'clock in the morning and then fall asleep at my desk at school the next day. Of course, I didn't always get it right, and sometimes I burnt the dinner or one of the shirts I was ironing. Then when I was older I would often come home and find a note from her saying she'd buggered off to party with friends for the weekend. That was what I should have been saying to her, not the other way round! My mum and I have a very unusual relationship. It's always been like I have to play the mother role. I'm the one she comes to when she's in trouble. But right now I needed someone to turn to. I was in big trouble and I needed some reassurance myself.

I spoke to Jeff. He was with the boys, but I knew I couldn't speak to them yet. I could never have them hearing their mum in the state I was in. They're so sensitive, they'd have picked up on everything. I was crying too much. For now I just needed to know they were OK.

Jeff's words were: 'So, Jade, you've put your foot in it this time, haven't you, eh? I'm sure you'll get out of it. It'll be fine.'

We weren't getting on very well at the time, so I knew he wasn't going to suddenly turn into this steady rock, but he really sounded odd and distant. And that made me realise things were certainly not good.

I had an overwhelming urge to let the people I'd worked with over the years know I didn't mean it and that I was sorry. I needed to speak to someone who knew – someone who could tell me what was really going on.

I rang Lucie from *Heat*. I was sobbing so much down the line that she couldn't work out who it was to start with. She said afterwards she thought it was one of her friends and that something awful had happened. I didn't know who else to call, and I desperately needed to know that the whole world didn't believe I was a racist. Lucie couldn't tell me everything was going to be all right, but she said she knew I wasn't a racist. But she also said there were going to be things that needed reporting and that it had to be told like it was. I knew that, and I wasn't after sympathy or pleading to be treated nicely, I just wanted to tell her that I wasn't a racist.

I also called Celina from *Now* magazine – I'd spoken to her loads because I used to have a column in *Now*. She's black too, so I needed her to know I would never cause her any deliberate hurt. But this was a magazine that had put a picture of me on the cover with the words: 'We hate you, Jade – the nation turns on thick racist bully!'

'Celina, I hope I haven't offended you in any way. I'm not trying to get into your good books, but I want to apologise to you.'

'Jade, it's fine. It's just all got out of control.'

It wasn't fine, though. Not at all.

The headline in the *News of the World* the next day read: 'Yes I am a bully. Yes I am a racist.'

I couldn't even see the words any more. I didn't want to. I hadn't said that – all I'd said was that I could see how people would think from watching some of the footage that I was a bully and a racist. But it's about selling papers, isn't it?

Later that day I had to go on *Big Brother's Little Brother*.

To say I didn't want to would be putting it mildly. I've known Dermot O'Leary for years. We shared the same agent, and when we met we would always stop for funny little chats. But when I saw him that day it was different. And again, because Davina had got such a hard time for not seeming to grill me enough, there was pressure on Dermot to do a better job. He had to be tougher on me.

I didn't see anyone beforehand, no producers, no other

guests, no audience members – I was just taken straight into the studio. I remember glancing over to the audience and seeing Andi Peters sitting there. You probably hate me right now, I was thinking. In the past you've liked me, but I know it's all changed.

I sat on the sofa and all I could feel were eyes boring into me, like I was getting dirty looks from all around.

I kept telling myself, 'Don't cry, don't cry.' After my *News of the World* interview people had started saying that I was putting on crocodile tears, and this just made me more paranoid. Everything was making me weep every time I opened my mouth, it seemed. There was no way I was putting it on, or would ever be capable of doing something like that. I'm not that bloody clever, but now I was obsessed that people thought I was.

'Don't cry, don't cry.' I didn't want anyone to think I was pleading for help or sympathy. But it was so difficult to sit there and face what I was going through and not shed a tear. You'd have to be made of stone for it not to affect you.

And of course I broke down.

Dermot asked me everything, showed me clips from the show, questioned and challenged my actions – and I tried to answer as best I could. Afterwards it was like I had never known him. I could understand in a way, but there was a big part of me that felt disappointed and upset. It was the same as with Davina. I had known these people and valued them as friends, but right now they didn't know what to say to me. And maybe they didn't want to associate themselves with someone the nation hated.

After that I was taken back to my hotel room, where I lay in the same spot on my bed for what seemed like hours. I stayed dressed in the same clothes – black leggings, a black top and a black Puffa jacket – and I don't think I took them off for the next week. By now I hadn't eaten since I came out of the house and everyone was starting to worry about me. 'You must have something,' said my bodyguard Mick. 'Please just try a sandwich,' said Katherine. But I couldn't. I couldn't do anything – except watch *Big Brother* and the news. Following that interview on *Big Brother's Little Brother* I became obsessed with what was going on in the house. Dermot had shown clips of what was happening in there and all I could see was how Jack was acting like nothing was wrong. It was as if my eviction had barely affected him – he actually seemed happier not having me around!

As I sat in my hotel room, glued to the TV, I felt jealousy and hatred. And I think from that moment the fate of our relationship was sealed because I could never get over the fact that he stayed in the house after I'd gone. I couldn't understand how he could be so disloyal to me. What was the purpose of him remaining in there? His girlfriend had been booted out and he knew full well that something was wrong on the outside (later he'd tell Danielle when she got evicted, 'Don't worry, you'll be OK – at least there's a crowd there, which there wasn't for Jade'). So, if he knew I was suffering, why did he stay? Where was his loyalty?

I sat there thinking, I'm sitting on my bed, red-faced from crying so much, and you're in the Jacuzzi laughing and splashing about with Danielle Lloyd. Something's not right here.

I wanted so much to see him upset; I wanted to see him mourning for me – or at the very least talking about me. But there was nothing. Whether he said stuff in the diary room and they just didn't show it I'll never know, but all I could see at the time was that he appeared to be enjoying himself much more than when I was by his side. It was like he suddenly had a personality, whereas he'd been so much quieter when I was there. Now he was chatting to people and joking away. I even started to question my influence on him. Was it my fault that he was a mute in there before? Did I stop him having fun? Every negative emotion I could possibly have thought I did – I was infuriated, I resented him, I was envious of him, I felt betrayed – yet still I couldn't turn the TV off. I was fixated with whether or not he was going to kiss Danielle. I hadn't worried about her in that way when I was in the house, but now I was out she was a threat to me. There was this pretty, leggy girl who was hanging around with my boyfriend and I was convinced something was going to happen between them. My head was fucked up.

Two of my mates, Jennifer and Kelly, came round and immediately tried to lighten the mood. 'Fucking hell, Jade, you've lost weight! Put us on that diet, will you, eh? We need a bit of that!' Then Jen said, 'You had me up all night last night watching that bastard boyfriend of yours on the telly – trying to make sure he was behaving himself.' They thought the same as me.

The next morning I was wheeled on to *GMTV* – I was told they wanted to interview me, and I didn't once stop to think that maybe it wasn't such a good idea. I just wanted to explain myself to as many people as possible, to try to convince people that I wasn't a racist. And despite the criticism I got afterwards for seeming to appear on every TV show as if I was on a sympathy trail (which was never ever the intention), I don't regret it. All I wish I hadn't done was say 'sorry' as many times as I did. I should have said it once only and disappeared. But I genuinely was remorseful. I needed people to know that. And who's to say what was the right thing to do? If I hadn't done anything I'm sure that would have seemed like I didn't care. I would have been criticised whatever.

I can't really remember much about the *GMTV* interview except that I got through it. Fiona Phillips got to the point, she wasn't horrible to me, she let me explain myself and that was that. Afterwards I walked past Lorraine Kelly, who said, 'You'll be all right, Jade, it'll be fine,' and then apparently (I didn't see this, but my friends told me) went on to write in her column that she hoped I would 'disappear into obscurity'.

The lady from the Perfume Shop was next to call me with bad news.

'I'm sorry, Jade, but we have to take "Ssh" off the shelves.'

I knew she had no choice and I understood why, but I was absolutely gutted. I know it sounds stupid because it's only a perfume. But it meant so much to me. I'd been the only non-celebrity to have a perfume out – all the others were big stars like Victoria Beckham, Paris Hilton and Beyonce. I was so disheartened because for once I'd been the first to do something. I was the first reality-TV star to launch a scent (and, without blowing my own trumpet, I think I was the one who raised the bar for other reality stars to have perfumes). It was personal to me and meant so much.

But now I was being told that there'd been letters and threats demanding my perfume was taken off the shelves – 'Goody's a racist, it's disgusting, she's a bully – get it off.'

111

Everything was crumbling beneath me. I felt like my life was a house of cards, and that once a couple of them were taken away the whole thing had come crashing down. My head couldn't deal with it. And despite what everyone might think it wasn't about the money. These things represented me and my life. The paperback of my first book had been stopped – the publisher pulled it from the shelves, even though thousands had already been printed. My DVD was taken off the shelves. Bit by bit I was crumbling away.

I was told that I'd have to move to a different hotel every night for the foreseeable future, because there were fears for my life. People were sending death threats against me to the police. I also had to have 24-hour security because one of the windows in my house in Essex had been smashed and no one knew what – or who – was going to be attacked next. I began to drive myself mad reading every newspaper I could lay my hands on. I felt like I was in a bubble that I couldn't get out of. I was either sobbing uncontrollably or numb and unable to speak.

But the thing that finally broke me was my interview on *This Morning*.

I'd been on the show numerous times before and always got on well with Phillip Schofield and Fern Britton. But this was one of the worst experiences I've ever had. I arrived with my bodyguard and Sally, my agent from John Noel Management. I wasn't taken to the green room with the other guests, but put in a room on my own. I wasn't thinking about the interview because I felt I knew the sort of questions they were going to ask. And surely nothing could be worse than the interview I'd done with the *News of the World*.

I was taken on set and sat on the sofa opposite Phil and Fern. Then the ad break ended and there I was, live on TV.

Then came the thing that finished me off. Fern started questioning my mothering skills and that nearly killed me. It's making me cry just thinking about it now, because my boys mean the world to me and for anyone to say I'm a bad mother is like ripping my heart out.

She said, 'Doing a deal with a newspaper, crying in the diary room, not having been able to see your children – it all looks like an attempt to save your career. Why do all these interviews? Why not just go somewhere quietly with your children and step back?'

'But I was just doing what I'd been told to do,' I said. 'I am in no fit state to see my kids like this – I think I'd be a bad mum if I saw them like I am now. I can't let them see me like this. I'm not allowed to see my children, as there are police outside my house. They can't come to where I am staying because there are people around there. I don't want my children to be rejected because of what I've done. That's why I'm doing these interviews. I am sincerely scared for my children.'

Tears were streaming down my face.

I was in bits. It must have been bad because there were people walking off the set after they'd started crying too. I think it was horrible to watch. On the studio floor there are usually loads of people milling about – from sound assistants to runners, producers and floor managers – but they were all leaving, like they couldn't face watching someone in such a mess.

People could clearly see I needed help because after the interview the counsellor from *This Morning* came over to me and said, 'You need to come and talk to me, Jade.'

After my interview the show had gone to a break, but when they came back on air Phil and Fern had a huge pile of emails in front of them. They'd been printed on pink pieces of paper and there were over 100 of them. Phil looked at the camera and said, 'Since our interview with Jade Goody a few minutes ago we've received all these emails from you at home, and I want to tell you that out of this many we've only received two negative ones against Jade. The rest of them are all supportive. And we just wanted to say that.'

But I was too far gone by this point to even register or care that I still had some supporters out there. The counsellor took me aside and was talking to me about how I felt, reassuring me that I'd be fine. 'You don't feel like you're really here, do you, Jade?' It was all hazy by now. I felt like an empty shell, like I was just a numb body sitting there in front of her. My brain felt empty.

I was in floods of tears and it seemed like it was never going to stop. Sally called John on the way to the hotel and told him what was going on. She said the counsellor would give him a call. But first it was decided I had to eat something. Back in my room I had to promise, before Sally would leave, that I was going to order room service. My bodyguard sat outside the whole time and assured her he'd make sure I did. But, of course, I'm thick as shit, aren't I? I got the menu and rang the kitchen downstairs. 'Can I have a chicken curry, please?' I wasn't even thinking. It arrived, I took the plate and closed the door. Then it clicked: oh my God, I've just ordered chicken curry! What if someone in the kitchen thinks I'm taking the piss? What if they hate me for what I've done? What if they've deliberately decided to undercook the chicken? What if they're trying to give me food poisoning?

It was like I was going mad. The hotel room didn't have much light so I couldn't really see the chicken properly. I stood on a stool so I could be close to the light bulb and I took each individual piece of chicken in my hand and started tearing it apart in strips, like it was those cheese-string things that are meant for kids, studying each piece to see if there were any red bits, any blood. Any sign of someone trying to poison me. I must've done it for over an hour. Of course there were no hints that it had been undercooked and, by the time I was done, my plate was covered in peeled-off bits of bird. I looked at it and started crying. I couldn't eat a thing.

I went to put it all outside my door – then I stopped in my tracks. I couldn't put it there uneaten! If I did that someone might see and think I'd done it on purpose and that proved I was a racist for not eating my food! The thought of eating it was making me feel sick, but the thought of leaving it there untouched terrified me. So I took each piece of chicken and wrapped it in bits of tissue, then I set about trying to dispose of it in every way possible. I flushed bits down the toilet, put others in the bin, even poked some down the plug hole of the sink – all the while racked with tears. I must've looked like an absolute fucking nutter. I didn't stop until every single bit of chicken had gone. And only then did I put the plate outside.

John told me I had to go and see a doctor and I was sent to Harley Street. She was quite a big lady and as soon as I walked into her room I felt safe. She was the first person to give me a cuddle like a mum should. A proper engulfing hug. And I cried and cried in her arms for what seemed like eternity.

She said, 'My God, you've gone through so much.' She asked me about how I was feeling, about whether I'd eaten, trying to determine my state of mind. Then she asked if I'd had any thoughts about wanting to end it all, to kill myself.

I shook my head. 'I've been feeling so low, but I would never do anything like that – I have my kids and I live for them.' But I told her how I was going out of my head watching the television and reading the newspapers. I must've seen more news programmes and read more news stories over the previous few days than I ever have in my whole life. I was sitting in the chair talking to her, and I was actually rocking. I looked like Arthur Fowler when he was in *EastEnders*.

She looked at me. 'I'm going to put you on anxiety tablets and antidepressants.'

And that was it. I started sobbing uncontrollably. 'I don't want to be on those! I've never been on antidepressants in my life. Please no!'

But there was no option. Especially if I wanted to see my children.

It was decided I could see my sons at my neighbour Lindsay's house. I couldn't see them at my mum's – she'd been sent to Champneys by John Noel to get away from the paparazzi – and, let's face it, I haven't really got any other family, so there was nowhere else to go. My windows had been smashed and the thought of going back to my house scared and upset me. I remember Bobby and Freddy pleading, 'Can we go home, Mummy? Can we stay at our own house?' and I tried to tell them that it would be too cold in there because the window cleaner had broken the window by mistake. Lindsay was brilliant. She has kids herself, so the boys were able to play with them. I slept the night in bed with my boys, cuddled up together. I must've squeezed them so tightly they were hurting, but they didn't say anything. Much as I tried to put on a brave face, they're sensitive soldiers and they instinctively knew to cuddle me and say nothing else. At one point Bobby wanted to put his football kit on for me but I looked outside and there was a street full of paparazzi. 'Bobby, you can't put your England shirt on.'

'Why? I want England!'

'You can't wear that one, Bobby. Put a different one on.'

I was so paranoid by now – imagine what a field day the papers would have if they got a shot of one of my boys in an England top. That would've been seen as racist too.

Somehow I talked him into putting something else on and they went to play in the street for a bit. I was trying to have fun with them, to be the happy mummy they knew. But outside, in front of all these reporters, I didn't know what to do or how to behave. I didn't put make-up on because I didn't want people to think I was trying to look nice. And I felt bad about smiling in case people thought I didn't care about what had happened. My mind was whirring.

Afterwards I sat in Lindsay's house and she must've been talking to me for about an hour. But I just wasn't there, I was blank. I'd reply to her questions but there was no feeling any more, as if all the life had been sucked out of me. All my emotions were drained. It was like I wasn't in me. Even when the kids were coming up to me and showing me things they'd done I was praising them but there was no real compassion there, everything had gone.

Then the bodyguards Mick and Tony came to pick me up. The boys were trying to stop me leaving. 'Mummy, don't go!' It was heartbreaking. 'I'll be back soon,' I promised. And I honestly thought I would be.

Then I had an interview with *Heat*. Again I wasn't paid any money; the magazine donated my fee to charity. If there was ever a symbol of how things had now come crashing down around me, this was it. My first ever interview – when I'd come out of the *Big Brother* house in 2002 – was also with *Heat*. They'd got me all dressed up like a princess with a bag of chips in my hand, and I'd been so excited and had so much fun. Now here I was again, and the circumstances couldn't have been more different.

Katherine was with me and I'd pleaded with her beforehand to tell them I didn't want to have any make-up or to dress up or pose for the shoot. It all felt wrong. I walked into the studio and saw all these familiar faces – Russ the picture editor, Dan the art director, Tom the photographer and Lucie the interviewer – but even though I knew them and had worked so closely with them in the past they all felt so distant. I felt so weird. They tried to give me something to eat but I couldn't touch anything. All I could do was drink Diet Coke and smoke cigarettes – and I don't even smoke! (I found out afterwards that I was unintentionally doing what's known as the Kate Moss diet – fags and Diet Coke.) Don't ask me why I thought smoking was going to help matters, but somehow when I had a cigarette I felt a little bit calmer for 20 seconds or so.

I was asked to talk about everything that had happened since I left the house and what I had to say to *Heat*'s readers about my actions. When I started speaking about my interview on *This Morning* I broke down again. The thought of anything upsetting my kids or people thinking I'm a bad mum is too much. I told Lucie how worried I was about my mum and my grandparents. Granddad had been getting phone calls, although he'd been refusing to tell me the details in case they upset me too much. But I knew they were bad and it killed me that I'd brought it all on them. My mum's fence had been kicked in and one night people started banging on her bedroom window and shouting abuse. She'd been scared shitless. I remembered how the police had said they were in fear for my life. I honestly didn't know if I'd be able to go home again.

When I was asked whether I thought Jack was flirting with Danielle in the house, it put my mind in even more of a whirl. Why was I being asked about them? Surely that meant something was going on that I didn't know about? At the end of the interview I had another one to face. A crew from CNN India had come to ask me questions about Shilpa. It was all just becoming so mechanical by now, though, that I felt like an empty vessel. But the reporter was really nice and fair – she just asked about what had happened and what I wanted to say to the Indian nation. It was 'sorry' – obviously.

11
New Beginnings

Then I was driven straight to see John Noel.

'Jade, you're not well.'

'I'm OK, I'm fine.'

'Stop kidding yourself, you're not well. I've spoken to the doctor – you need to go to The Priory.'

I turned to Katherine. 'I can't go in there! I used to laugh at celebrities who booked themselves into The Priory! Remember? Whenever we'd open a newspaper and see that someone had checked in we'd say, "Oh, there goes someone who needs to get their profile up again."'

I was petrified people would think I was going in there for publicity. And right now I needed more publicity like a hole in the head.

John said, 'It's not like you've booked yourself in there, Jade! You've been referred by a doctor who thinks you need help. You're ill, you're losing weight and you're on antidepressants.'

'But I don't want to go. I really don't want to go.' The *Big Brother* final was that night. 'I have to be at the final – it's in my contract.'

'The doctor says there's absolutely no way you can be there, Jade. You're in no fit state to be put in that situation, you're too fragile.'

So I was taken to The Priory in Roehampton. There was just me and the driver, my bodyguard Mick. I sat in the back with tears rolling down my cheeks.

'Are you OK, Jade?' he asked, looking at me in the rear-view mirror.

'I feel like I'm going into that film – *One Flew Over the Cuckoo's Nest*,' I told him. I didn't have a clue what to expect or what I was heading into.

As we pulled up the drive, I thought, This looks quite posh, a nice-looking building. It was night-time and I was taken straight to my room. There was a single bed, a cabinet and a television with no plug on it. I wasn't sure whether they'd taken the plug off for me especially or whether they were all like that. I didn't ask. By that stage I didn't even want to watch it anyway.

I hadn't been in there long before my mum arrived with Kate Jackson, the lady who's produced all my shows for Living TV. Kate could hardly speak, she was so shocked when she saw me. She'd never seen me looking so lost and weak. I don't even remember the conversation apart from hugging my mum and saying, 'I don't want to take my coat off' – I was still wearing the same Puffa jacket I'd had on all week. The same whole outfit in fact. My hair was greasy. I don't even know if I'd cleaned my teeth. I certainly hadn't had a wash. I just felt that if I took my coat off it meant I would have to stay in there. I was crying my eyes out.

'Come on, darling,' Mum said, stroking my head. 'You'll be OK. You have to take your coat off. You'll get too hot.'

Then they had to go. I was so scared. When I spoke to John, I asked, 'Is Jack going to come and see me?' I knew he would be out of the *Big Brother* house by now.

'We'll sort it, Jade. Don't worry,' he said warmly.

Later that night a doctor came in and talked me through where everything was, then he said he was going to come back in the morning for a check-up. Then the lights were turned out and I lay there trying to go to sleep. I still had my Puffa jacket on; it was like my security blanket and I didn't want to remove it. So I tried to sleep as I was. But the jacket was a really expensive one that I'd bought for skiing, so it was designed for thermal conditions, and it was making me sweat.

I couldn't sleep and I desperately wanted to smoke, so I got out of bed and started wandering down the corridor. I didn't know where I was going, but I knew there must be somewhere for people to have a cigarette. Then I found a room that was like a tiny dark space, crammed full of patients all puffing away madly, as if their lives depended on it.

'Hello,' I said meekly to the first guy I saw, and lit my fag.

He glanced up. 'Are you all right, girl?'

'Yeah,' I mumbled unconvincingly.

'What are you in here for?'

That was to be the question I'd get asked about 50 times

during my stay. It's the first thing that everyone says to each other, like you're in prison.

'I've got anxiety and depression,' I answered nervously. It felt like the oddest thing to say, but it was the truth. I told them a bit about *Big Brother*, but whether they knew or cared who I was they didn't show it. To them I was just another patient going through a tough time.

Then I had to ask, 'So, er, what are you in here for?'

I have to confess that, when I heard myself say the same words, inside my head I was smiling a little bit, although my mouth was incapable of showing even a smirk. It was such a bizarre thing to say.

He replied, 'I've got to get off the smack.'

Then a girl next to him piped up. 'Same here – mine's crack, though.'

Before I knew it, one by one, everyone in that room was telling me about their drug addictions. My heart sank. I was in a rehab place like my dad used to go to. Had I ended up the same as him? I had battled my whole life to be better than that, but now here I was in rehab – just like he was before he died.

He died during the time he was in rehab somewhere in Bournemouth. He'd just got out and went and jacked up in a fast-food place. That was where they found him.

My dad's death was a strange experience for me. I really didn't feel equipped to deal with it. When the police first told me – 'We're really sorry to tell you but your dad's died of an overdose. He was found in a toilet in Kentucky Fried Chicken in Bournemouth' – the first thing I felt was actually a wave of relief that it wasn't Jeff, it wasn't my boys and it wasn't Mum, but afterwards I felt incredibly nauseous and just flat. Then, when it did hit me, I was in pieces, mainly because I didn't know how to feel or act. I was numb. I'd never talked about my feelings towards my dad. I'd never shown him any kind of forgiveness for how he'd behaved when I was growing up – the lies, the drugs, being in and out of prison. I'd barely acknowledged his existence.

I couldn't face the funeral either. Although I desperately needed to say goodbye, I wasn't ready. And now, being here in this place for junkies, just like he was before he overdosed, I felt sick and ashamed that I had ended up like him: my dad, who had done so many drugs that he died without a single vein left in his body. In the end he'd injected every single part of it and all his veins had collapsed – even the ones in his penis. He was on heroin for so long that he'd run out of veins – they'd simply disappeared.

And now I was surrounded by people like him, shaking, chattering nervously, with hands like balloons from the swelling. What a waste of a life.

As I stood in the dark listening to these people who were in The Priory for drug problems, I was thinking, I don't belong here. I wanted to smoke my cigarette as fast as I could. But for some stupid reason, instead of putting it out, I just lit another one. What was I doing? I was acting like Dot Cotton. But I realised that, much as I wanted to escape these people, I didn't want to go back to my room either.

When I eventually left I made my way back down the corridor and as I was walking along I could hear a piercing scream getting louder and louder. 'Don't leave me! Don't leave me! No! Please!'

It was coming from the reception area, and I had to

pass there to get to my room. Part of me just wanted to run past so I didn't see what was going on, but another part was curious. All I could think about was films about those nuthouses where patients get injected and taken back to their room in a straitjacket. And I had to take a look. I stopped still to see what looked like a mother and daughter. The daughter was the one screaming, but she looked really well-off – she was in her thirties, she had nice clothes, a designer bag, good hair – but she was hysterical.

'Don't leave me in here! I've been off the drugs! I don't need to be here.'

I froze with fear and suddenly this weird shriek came out of my mouth. Everyone looked round at me. I had this big Puffa on and my hair was sticking up everywhere.

'Aaaaaghhhh!' I shouted, then legged it off to my room faster than I've ever run in my life.

I never saw the woman again.

I went back to my bed and sobbed. This place is full of drug addicts, I kept thinking. I don't want to stay in here.

Every five minutes or so someone would come into my room silently and shine a torch in my face to see that I was OK. In the end I must've cried myself to sleep because the next thing I knew it was the morning. It took me about 20 seconds to register where I was and what was happening. My first thought was: it's the day after the final – what's happened?

Then I looked at my phone. I'd had a text in the night from Tony my bodyguard. 'You OK, Jade? Standing here at the final now. Shilpa's won. The crowd are booing. But at home everyone can only hear cheers.'

I didn't think much of what he'd said at the time, but

when I spoke to Tony a couple of weeks later he insisted that what was shown on TV wasn't representative of what happened that night. He told me that when Shilpa had walked out of that house she was booed like you wouldn't believe. He was convinced that Jermaine was the real winner.

But that didn't matter right now, because here I was in The Priory and there was still no sign of Jack.

This is something that turns my stomach every time I think about it. The minute Jack came out of the house Katherine took him aside and said, 'Come with me. Jade's not well, she's in The Priory. You need to come and see her.'

And his reply? 'Oh, I have to go in here for a bit first.'

Then he went into the *Big Brother* party! Unbeknown to me, he spent the next few hours drinking away with the other so-called celebs in there and having his photo taken on people's mobile phones. (I found this out a few months later because I saw pictures of him on his mate's phone with drinks in his hand, laughing and larking about.) Katherine was so disappointed in him, but back then she didn't say anything about it to me. She knew I was too fragile. I've asked Jack since why he didn't come and see me that night, and he said, 'I didn't know you were in The Priory.' But I knew Katherine wouldn't lie – she never has done in all the time I've known her.

In the morning, the doctor came into my room and said they were upping the dose of my depression tablets. Then a lady came in with a Diet Coke for me and another one told me what I was going to have to do when I was in there. She said she'd booked me in with a therapist who would be doing some sort of regression treatment on me – taking me back to my past to begin confronting some of my issues.

It was like being hypnotised. The therapist's aim was to bring hidden memories into consciousness for me, and she said the first thing I had to do was to go back to my worst memory as a kid, which was watching my dad inject heroin in front of me.

'I first saw my dad doing drugs when I was three or four,' I told her. 'It was one of those times when he was out of prison for a bit. I woke up in bed to see him stood in the corner of the room putting a needle into his arm. I'll never forget the look on his face. His eyes were rolling into the back of his head and he was shaking. I was scared stiff in case he could see that I'd been watching him. I think I thought he'd tell me off, so I only dared to look a tiny bit. Then I closed my eyes so tightly I thought I'd never be able to blink again. All that was going through my head was: why is he sticking needles in his arms? What is he doing that for? It was his facial expression that scared me the most. I know that drug addicts can't help themselves, but surely there's a line you just don't cross? If your four-year-old daughter is lying in your bed, how can you jack up in front of her?'

When I'd finished telling her about it, she asked me questions about how it made me feel, what it was like looking back, and so on. It made me realise there were still so many things about my past that I hadn't confronted, let alone come to terms with. And this was just one tiny part of it. After we'd done, she told me how to close the memory, as if it was a chapter in a book, so that I had closure. But all the while she said it needed to stay at the front of my brain, not be pushed to the back. It wasn't something that should be forgotten and brushed aside.

Then I went back to my room and a lady sat with me to make sure I ate my food. I had zero appetite and I had to force it down. I think they were worried because of me making myself sick in the past. Also, because I was on so many tablets, it was important that I had food in my stomach, otherwise I'd get ill.

Another woman came and told me there was a garden outside that I could use and walk around in if I wanted to get fresh air. By now the Puffa had come off – I'd been told I needed to relax and that sitting in a stinking, hot, sweaty coat wasn't going to help me do that.

I was told about classes that I could do – there were different ones designed for different illnesses. I said I wanted to do one the next day. More than anything I wanted to do things so I could prove to the doctors that I was ready to go home as soon as possible. We decided I would do the class for people with anxiety.

That evening Jack finally appeared. I knew nothing of his previous night's partying. And I didn't think to question him at that stage about why he hadn't come sooner. I was so disappointed in him, but I couldn't confront the situation. I didn't have the strength. All I knew was that I needed him. In truth I just think I needed someone. It could've been Osama bin Laden – as long as he'd given me a cuddle and told me everything was going to be OK. The doctors let Jack stay the night, which they don't usually do, and it was so nice just to be held in his arms again.

He had to leave in the morning, and then I got up and walked into the garden to have a cigarette. As I walked past one of the benches I saw a newspaper. Shilpa Shetty was on the front cover with the headline saying something like 'The Queen Wants to Meet Me'. All I could think was: everyone in here is going to think I'm a racist now. For some reason it hadn't occurred to me that people would be allowed to read newspapers in here. I started to panic. I had an overwhelming urge to grab it and hide it in a drawer. As I went over and picked it up I noticed a man standing behind me. He was a huge fella and he looked a bit of a head case: his hair was all scruffy, his face looked a bit mean. I opened the paper, glanced over the article, saw my name staring back at me, closed it, put it back down and walked away.

As I left I could still see the man out of the corner of my eye. He picked up the paper and held it close to his face. Then he spat on it and put it straight in the bin.

I looked at him, confused.

He didn't even catch my eye, but just said, 'Fucking newspapers. They're worth nothing.' And off he went. I never saw or spoke to him again.

That was his way of saying to me, 'It will be all right.'

After this I went further into the garden and lit up a cigarette. I sat next to one of the other patients and started talking. Although at first I'd hated it in The Priory, by now I had begun to feel like it was the only place I was safe. Yes, I still wanted to leave and see my boys, but whenever I spoke to the other people in there I felt like my problems weren't as bad. It put everything into perspective a bit.

There were a few of us outside, sitting in a circle. One man looked at me and asked, 'So what are you in here for then?'

'Depression and anxiety. How about you?'

He sighed. 'I'm a fucking sex addict, aren't I? I haven't had sex for bloody ages. My balls are fucking filled with come, they are.'

'Oh, all right,' I replied, gobsmacked. Well, what else would you say to that?

Then he took a cigarette out of a packet. 'Got a light?'

I gave him one, he lit up and that was the end of the conversation.

At about 2.30 it was time to go to my class. I was feeling a bit stronger by now. The man spitting on the newspaper had given me a little bit of hope that people didn't hate me, and speaking to that sex addict had actually made me smile genuinely for the first time in days.

So as I walked to the class I felt like I could tackle anything. I got to the room where it was being held and opened the door. Inside there were about 10 or 12 people walking round in a circle with their hands clasped together in front of them like they were holding something. Except there was nothing there.

I saw the teacher, who was looking at them all and saying, 'Put it down, then pick it back up again.'

He looked at me in the doorway.

'Sorry I'm late.'

'That's OK, come in.'

Everyone stopped and turned to face me. All of a sudden I felt like I was rooted to the spot, unable to walk into the room. My hands started getting sweaty, my throat dried up, I started twiddling with my hair and my eyes welled up with tears (which is a problem I always have now whenever I feel nervous about something). I started crying.

The teacher took my hand. 'Come in and sit down.'

He told me to watch the others for a bit, then he persuaded me to stand up and do the same. To start with I didn't understand what I was supposed to do.

He said, 'I want you to think of a problem that you've got. Something that upsets and bothers you. I want you to hold that problem in your hand, and then I want you to try to put it down.'

I couldn't do it. This is fucking mental, I kept thinking. But after a few minutes I accepted that there was no point being here at all if I wasn't going to throw myself into it. Everyone in here was in the same boat, there were no egos here, no reason to be embarrassed about making a fool of yourself. I just had to do it and let go of my insecurities.

So I did. I thought of my problem. 'My problem is lies,' I told him slowly.

'And why can't you deal with lies?' he asked me.

'Because of my mum and her past,' I said. I didn't have to explain any more than that. He just accepted it.

'What happens when this problem of lying occurs, Jade?'

'I get into a rage, it makes me angry and upset. And no matter how small or big the lie is, it's all the same to me.'

'And if you try to put that problem down, how does it make you feel?'

I went to put it on the floor. 'It makes me feel ... lost. Like I don't know how to act without having it there. Because that's all I've ever known.'

'And if you pull it close – now how do you feel?'

'Ugly and horrible as a person.' Then I paused, starting to feel inexplicably angry inside. 'So what does that mean? What am I meant to do with the fucking problem then?'

'Stay with it, and walk around the room with it.'

As I was walking around, he was talking to other people

about their situations. Then he said to us all, 'Now I want you to try to love the problem.'

I thought, I can't love this problem! It's nasty.

He carried on. 'I want you to try to see past the problem and think about why you've got that problem and how you can overcome that problem ...'

Well, I thought to myself, I haven't got that problem now because my mum's not doing it any more. She's stopped.

I'd never admitted this to anyone before because it killed me to think about it. I deliberately didn't write about it in my last book because I couldn't face it and didn't want people to judge my mum. But now I have to face it if I'm ever going to get over my anger and my hang-ups. It goes back a lot deeper than 'it's just Jade's rage'. I've looked after my mum all my life and, as I told you earlier, I felt like she had stabbed me in the back.

I walked out of there feeling so much better. But then the next day I had to confront the problem again. And this time it was far from easy. I had another session with the therapist who had made me talk about my dad the day before. Now it was mum's turn.

Trust is a huge issue for me (which is why I can't actually understand why I stayed with Jack for so long – someone who clearly was lying to me about other girls, but we'll deal with that later). So at first I couldn't even speak to the therapist about it – I was so paranoid that whatever I said was going to get leaked to the press. I was going to have to talk about my mum and address stuff that I'd never vocalised in front of anyone. The therapist was so sweet. 'Jade, everything you tell me is between me and you. That is it. I might have to consult your doctor if I feel you need to change your dosage of tablets, but that's all. It goes no further.'

When I started talking about stuff, it was like it was never going to end. I told her about my relationship with my mum and how I'd looked after her after the accident. I told her about how I tried to protect Mum for the whole time – hiding her chequebooks, jumping out of a car for her. For as long as I can remember I was desperately trying to stop my mum becoming like my dad. But when I was 18 my whole world fell apart. Mum got in with the wrong crowd and started smoking crack. Everything was going wrong for me at that time and I needed my mum more than ever. But I had lost her. I had lost her to drugs, the very same thing that stole my dad from me. I had failed.

And the lies – the lies she told me every day. 'I'm not doing what you think, Jade, I wouldn't do that to you.' It was horrible. I thought I was going to come home one day and find her dead. Some of the addicts she was hanging out with had died. I was beside myself. I would come home and smell smoke and see remnants in the ashtray. I would feel sick at the thought of her doing drugs – it was like she was turning into my dad. And she continued to lie. I dreaded coming home. I was so frightened of seeing her sitting there all glassy-eyed. I told the therapist that after a period of time I couldn't take it any more, and I told her how I lashed out at Mum and punched her. How she hit me back and we had a proper fight. It was all so disgusting. I felt sick just speaking about it. After everything I had tried to protect her from when I was a kid, she'd thrown it all back in my face.

And she lied about it, over and over again. And that's why I can't stand liars. To this day, if anyone lies to me I have no capacity in my brain to differentiate between the lies – whatever it is I will just get really angry and shout, 'What did you lie for?' This was the exact same reason I shouted Shilpa down for lying to me about the stock cubes being the only thing she'd put on the shopping list. That's why I flipped.

Mum would continually ask me for money, and if I didn't give it to her she'd get all upset and erratic, and if I did give it to her I knew I was just feeding her habit. I used to cry myself to sleep at night because I felt so helpless. Neither option was the right one. I didn't know what to do. I couldn't face it any more.

The therapist had taken me right back to this horrible time all those years ago. I was feeling exactly the same way I felt when I used to walk into my mum's house. I could even smell the drugs. It brought everything hurtling back to me: the fact that I'd protected her since I was five years old, the fact that she'd thrown it all back in my face, and, ultimately, the fact that, when it came to it and I said it's the drugs or me, she chose the drugs. Knowing that devastated me. I gave up my childhood for her and this was how she had repaid me.

It makes me cry even now talking about it. I still haven't properly dealt with it all.

I had to talk through everything with the therapist, and I could see she was affected by it because she kept saying, 'I can't believe you've been through so much.' I was in floods of tears (as I seemed to be most of the time in those days) and eventually it got so much that I had to stop. The therapist told me that I was in too fragile a state to carry on.

After that I went outside for a cigarette because, well, I

bloody well needed one by then, and I got chatting to one of the male patients. He explained that The Priory is divided into sections according to what you're in there for. He told me that one block was for depression and anxiety, across the garden was the area for addicts (which was where I'd ended up on the first night) and then there was another bit called 'the Twiglet zone'.

'Twiglet?' I asked.

'Yep – Twiglets, anorexics, whatever you call them. The ones who don't eat. And if they stand behind one of the trees you can't even see them because they're so bloody thin.'

My mates Jen and Kelly came to see me that evening, and it was just the tonic for me. When they arrived Jen was eating a sandwich and Kel was eating a packet of crisps, but they'd gone into the wrong part of the clinic. They'd wandered into the Twiglet zone! Jen was busy tucking into her food when she suddenly noticed people looking at her and she said to Kelly, 'Are we in the right place?'

Kel shrugged.

'Can I help you?' a man asked them.

'We're here to see our mate Jade Goody. She's in here for depression.'

The man leant over and whispered, 'You're in the wrong part.'

When they eventually found me they were beside themselves laughing, and I couldn't help cracking up too. Jen said, 'I knew something was up when we were getting dirty looks! I thought someone was going to come and grab my sandwich!'

They were so worried about me. I still looked a mess –

I hadn't washed my hair or myself for days. They'd never seen anything like it. But they still turned it into a joke. Jen started pulling my hair and sniffing it. Kel tugged on my trousers. 'Please don't tell me you've had these on the whole time, Jade.'

'I think I have,' I smiled weakly.

'Oh, Goody! What's going on? Get in the bloody shower!'

Then I relayed all my stories, and explained to them how when everyone speaks to you they start with the words 'What are you in here for?' Jen and Kel were in stitches. Right on cue a fella walked past and said hello, followed immediately by: 'So, what are you in here for then?'

Well, that was it. Within seconds Jen and Kel were rolling about with laughter, and that started me off too. Then I thought, I can't do this to the poor man. He'll get paranoid. So I composed myself enough to tell him why I was there and asked him what he was in there for (at which the girls started pissing themselves even more). He replied sadly, 'I just turned sick one day.'

'What do you mean?'

'I drove my kids to school as usual, then, once I'd dropped them off, I suddenly found myself driving round the block four times, having to open and close the front door six times, redoing things until I felt safe, washing my hands over and over ...'

'Shit,' I replied. It turned out he'd developed that OCD condition overnight. I didn't realise it could happen like that.

As he left, Jen looked at me and whispered, 'Fuck, I thought you were the only head case in here, Jade!'

Soon afterwards the doctors said I wasn't to attend any more classes because they felt I was pushing myself too much too soon. The regression therapist wanted to continue to help me try to come to terms with Mum's drug use, but I couldn't handle talking about it any more. To this day I know I need to go back and face up to it, but it's still so painful.

There was a famous model in The Priory when I was in there. Everyone there knew who she was – she was gorgeous-looking (well, I guess she had to be if she was a model) and had long, blonde hair. She has her own brand of beauty products in the shops. She was about to leave the day after I was checked in and she sent loads of stuff to my room as a gift – there was a soothing CD for me to listen to and more beauty products than I've ever seen: top-of-the-range creams and perfumes; bits and pieces from a top-class make-up range; and various lotions and potions. And among it all was this beautiful card saying, 'Hang in there, Jade. You're a tough girl, you don't deserve what you're going through at the moment, but you'll come out stronger. I promise you xx.'

I went to thank her, but she'd already gone.

I was beginning to slowly rebuild my confidence, helped in part by the letters that were sent to me during my stay. One of the ladies who would come and visit me in my room and talk to me about how I was feeling said the staff were taken aback by the amount of mail I'd had. 'We've had top A-list celebrities in here,' she said, and went on to reel off their names, 'and not once have we been bombarded with this much fan mail.'

I was so touched. The things people had written to me

really helped – I was scared at first in case they were letters of abuse. But they weren't. And I read every one – all of them were offering support and telling me they didn't think I was a racist. People from all nationalities wrote saying they had nothing against me and knew I had nothing against them. One wrote, 'I'm a black woman and I think you're great, you don't need to say sorry any more ...'

I replied to as many as I could, but there were so many I couldn't possibly answer every single one.

I had started to feel safe again in The Priory, but despite this I wanted nothing more than to go home to my boys.

12
Making Amends

After five days I was allowed to leave – but only on the condition that I returned once a week to see the therapist, who had told the doctors I still had major problems to work through.

I asked Jack if we could stay at his uncle's place in Norfolk. We'd been there once or twice before and Bobby and Freddy had loved it because there were fields to play in, chickens clucking about and quad bikes to ride. Plus it's so remote that the paps would find it hard to get to. We arranged a break and my bodyguard Mick came with us, which gave me peace of mind.

Being out there was such an escape from everything that was going on around and being written about me. And gradually, as each night passed, I managed to wean myself off the tablets. I was determined not to stay on antidepressants any longer than I needed. In fact, I was very frightened of getting dependent on any drug whatsoever.

Then one day we ran out of food. The nearest shop was

Tesco but this was the countryside, so even that was ten minutes' drive away. Mick had gone out and Jack couldn't drive a car, so that only left me. And the thought of going out in public for the first time absolutely terrified me. But the boys needed feeding, so I had no option.

I decided to disguise myself by putting on a Barbour jacket that I found hanging up in the hallway, some wellies and a flat cap. I drove to the shop, my heart pounding so hard I could feel it in my mouth. I pulled into the car park, climbed out of the car, walked into the supermarket and headed towards the bread section. As soon as I got there my hands starting sweating, my throat felt tight and my eyes were filling up with tears. I froze. An elderly woman was coming towards me. No, no, I was thinking. Please don't say anything horrible to me.

But as soon as she reached me, she put her hands on both my arms and started to cry.

'I am so sorry for all the stuff you've been through. You didn't deserve that.'

Which set me off. And we both stood there sobbing. But, although I felt so comforted by her, I was still petrified and anxious, and all I wanted to do was to get out. So I left, climbed back into the car and drove home as fast as I could, having bought bugger all food.

Back indoors I was almost gulping for air. Jack was really worried that I was having a panic attack.

'Jade, what's wrong? Did something bad happen out there?'

'No, no. It was nice, but I still felt so scared.'

I sat in the kitchen for about an hour before I'd calmed down enough to brave it and go back there again. I had to, otherwise we'd starve.

So off I drove once more. And this time I did it. Having got past the initial dread of seeing people for the first time, I was OK. And I actually did what I was supposed to and bought some food. My disguise was completely rubbish of course, and everyone I walked past said something kind like, 'Hello, Jade, hope you're OK.' Not one person said anything nasty. I felt so relieved.

As I was driving back to the house I felt warmth spreading over me and as soon as I got inside I ran to Jack. 'Can we move to Norfolk, please? I love it here. Everyone's so friendly and sweet here. I never want to go back to my old house.'

Because I had to go back to The Priory as an outpatient, I had been given homework to do during my stay in Norfolk. I was told to write down all my thoughts and feelings throughout the week, to talk about whether I felt angry and, if I did, what I was angry about.

I continued to do this each week and the therapist and doctor would ask me about it in detail every time I went back. But I still couldn't return to the issue of my mum. And before long it started getting harder to return there at all. Each time I pulled up outside the famous rehab centre I'd get papped, which would give the newspapers an excuse to run a story saying something about 'Jade the racist'. So, ultimately, I had to stop. I know it disappointed the therapist because she felt like she had so much more to work on with me.

But I'm ashamed to say I haven't been back since.

There was one more thing I needed to do. I wanted to go to India and say sorry to the Indian people for any upset or hurt I'd caused their country. The papers at home had got wind of my idea and were making out I was doing it all for effect. One even said I was going to milk the trip and turn it into a documentary. But nothing could have been further from the truth. I wanted to go out there unnoticed, do my bit and come back. It wasn't a PR trip.

As it turned out it was a PR disaster.

I'd spoken to John Noel about it beforehand and told him I wanted to donate some money to an Indian charity. I had £100,000 that I wanted to give. It was a lot of money, but I felt that, if I could do good with it, it would go some way towards making up for my behaviour. Sally, my agent there, helped me research organisations to find the most suitable one. We landed on a charity called the Railway Children, and its story really affected me. These kids had either run away from their families or been abandoned. They ranged from babies up to the age of 18. And they had nothing.

I could've sat at home, written a cheque out and sent it to the charity without ever setting foot in their country. But I wanted to see where my money was going.

Sally came with me, as did a guy called Gurmej Singh Pawar, who was also represented by John Noel. John had thought it would be a good idea for him to come along as he was Asian himself and spoke the language. Gurmej wanted to film it on his video camera, so that we had something to remember it by. It was never ever intended for TV. Katherine, my PR, didn't come, but I bloody wish she had because it got completely out of control.

I stayed in a posh hotel and someone who worked there was clearly in cahoots with the press because by day two there was a media circus outside like you wouldn't believe. I had never seen so many freaking cameras in my life. It was as if I was the president or something. It was madness. And it was scary. There were a lot of British journalists but amazingly most of the photographers and reporters were Indian. People were firing questions at me left, right and centre.

'Are you going to meet Shilpa Shetty while you're over here?'

'You're going to the slums. You're our hero. Shilpa hardly ever goes to the slums.'

But, surprisingly, not one reporter said anything horrible to me.

There were so many people asking for me at the hotel that Sally called Katherine and asked for help. She wasn't a PR person herself, but just booked my TV work for me. Why wasn't Katherine there with me?

'Do a press call,' Katherine advised.

I didn't have a clue what I was doing but that's what we did in the end.

I felt like Tony fucking Blair. It was ridiculous.

I walked into this room that had been set up for me in the hotel and there was a sea of faces. Microphones had been set up and there were film cameras at the back, while at the front reporters were scribbling notes on their pads.

I had to sit there and take questions as if I knew what I was doing. And it was so bloody daunting. All I wanted was someone to put their arms around me and give me a cuddle. I was lost.

A British journalist asked me, 'So how's it been, Jade? How are you enjoying it?'

I said that I couldn't talk too much about why I was here, but that I was doing something for charity. I wasn't allowed to say the charity's name at the time, because they hadn't even decided if they wanted to be associated with me, so I had to respect their wishes. I didn't want it to appear as if I was just using their name to get me good publicity.

'So, Jade, how are you finding the food here?'

And that was the killer question. Because once again I put my foot in it.

'Well, you know, everyone knows I love an Indian.'

It just didn't occur to me at the time what I'd said. Whenever I refer to a curry I always say, 'I'm having an Indian tonight,' so it seemed perfectly normal to me to talk about the food in that way. It was only when I saw the headline 'Jade: "Everyone knows I love an Indian"' that I realised how bad it sounded and how easily it could be misconstrued. So, once again, my intentions had backfired good and proper.

In fact, as far as the UK press were concerned, everything on that trip had gone tits up. I was criticised for staying in a five-star hotel, even though I'd paid for the whole thing myself and was giving £100,000 of my own money to a charity. If I'd stayed in a shack that wouldn't have been right either, so I couldn't win.

But ultimately I didn't care because press attention wasn't the reason for this trip. It was about the charity. And there was no way I couldn't be affected by what I saw.

The kids being helped by the Railway Children charity were incredible. They were so young, but so streetwise and tough. One ten-year-old boy had this tattoo running up his arm. 'How did you get that?' I asked him. 'My friend did it with a needle,' came his proud reply.

Their stories were tragic. Most of the girls had turned to prostitution to get money to survive. The young boys were being abused by older men who took advantage of them (and who had probably had the same done to them in the past, so knew no different). Yet incredibly all the kids still wanted to learn and better themselves. None of them had given up hope that their lives could improve and they could grow up to be something. One young boy told me that he'd sniffed glue until a year ago. Tears were welling up in my eyes as he talked to me, but I tried to hide them as I didn't want to make him feel bad or like he'd done anything wrong. 'How old are you?' I asked him. 'Nine,' he replied.

They were all huddling around me, sitting on my lap and soaking up everything I said to them. I told them all about my dad and how he'd been a heroin addict and they sat there listening intently. They related to me because I'd been there myself and I really felt I connected with them. One of them said, 'You're famous because you said something to Shilpa Shetty, aren't you?'

'Yes, something like that,' I said.

I taught them all how to play Stone, Paper, Scissors, which they loved. Just the simplest things – stuff we take for granted – were enough to give them pleasure and put a smile on their faces. They were all amazing, but there were three in particular that I so wanted to pick up and take home with me. The place they were living in was so dirty and disgusting it made me feel very sad. Even the roughest parts of London are nothing in comparison with what I saw that day. But still the kids were upbeat, and at one point they did a little dance for me and I joined in.

Outside there were paps taking photos, and I knew the risk I was running by getting up and messing around with the kids. I would probably be accused of doing it all for effect, but I didn't give a shit. The fact that these kids had been at rock bottom yet could still see light at the end of the tunnel made me think to myself, How dare you feel bad? How dare you sit there in your hotel room thinking your life has come to an end?

How dare I?

They took me to the refuge they can go to if they need a bed to sleep in – if they're lucky and get there early enough, that is. There's not enough room for everyone. All it consisted of was a few filthy old mats on the floor, but to them it was heaven. I lay on one of the mats with a couple of them and they looked surprised. 'She doesn't mind lying on a dirty floor,' one of them said to the others.

'Of course I don't!' I laughed.

I wanted so much to be able to take them to the park to see the ducks. They weren't allowed in any public areas like that near where they stayed because the police would think they were stealing and causing trouble. I wanted to give them the things that my kids take for granted. None of them had even had a birthday party, and I so wished I could just go over and throw a huge celebration for them. One of the boys said he didn't even know how old he was because he'd never had a birthday. How fucking sad is that?

I asked them, 'If there was anything you could have, anything in the world that I could give to you, what would it be?' And the answer was cricket equipment and computers. So that's what I decided my money was going towards.

I really want to go back to see the Railway Children, but I can't. The press will write something negative about it and I could be back to square one. And I can't handle any more bad press – it affects my family too much, and at the end of the day they're the reason I'm here and I have to do whatever I can to support them.

13
Back to Reality

When I got back from India I was reminded of just how meaningless all this *Celebrity Big Brother* stuff had been. Whenever I picked up a magazine I seemed to see Danielle bloody Lloyd's face staring back at me talking about her heartache over splitting up with Teddy or some other rubbish. Her reputation didn't seem to have been affected at all – yet I was told by my mates that the things she'd said in that house were really bad, and seemed to have as severe implications as anything I'd said. Danielle had said she thought Shilpa should 'fuck off home', for God's sake! And there was one piece of footage in which Shilpa asks someone to get her a towel. As Jo leaves to get one, Danielle passes her one from the floor instead. And I'm the one who was branded a racist?

It was a joke. I couldn't bear it.

After a few weeks I moved back into my house. I couldn't keep carting the boys about from place to place, it was too unsettling. We'd had cameras put up in the house and alarms fitted. I found it really hard to sleep the first few nights because every tiny noise I heard I thought was someone trying to break in. But after a while I calmed down, and Freddy and Bobby were so happy to be back where they belonged, which made the decision worthwhile. Yet ultimately I didn't want to stay there, as it didn't feel like home any more. I wanted a fresh start, somewhere with no reminders of that year. So I put in an offer for another house that was a bit further away and would be much more secure.

One evening I went to Ikea with Jack's mum to get a few bits for the kids' rooms. As I was walking down one of the aisles I saw the profile of a familiar face looking at a shelving unit. It was Danielle Lloyd. She turned in my direction and immediately turned away, perhaps trying to pretend she hadn't seen me. Well, I thought, I'm not going to go out of my way to say hello to you. You're the one who's been bad-mouthing me since you've come out of the house. Be like that then. And I walked in the opposite direction.

When I was queuing up to pay at the cash tills I heard some girls talking loudly behind me. I turned to see where the chatter was coming from and noticed three girls standing there, two black girls and one white, and they were pointing behind them at – you've guessed it – Danielle Lloyd. She was standing with her mum, looking at the ground sheepishly. The girls looked at me and one of them said, 'Oh, it's Jade Goody, innit?'

I smiled, unsure of what they were about to say next. They were being so loud, everyone could hear.

'You all right, gal?' another of them asked.

'Yeah, I'm fine, thanks,' I replied.

'We don't mind you, Jade. We don't think you're a racist at all, you're all right, you are. But as for her over there ...' And they nodded over at Danielle. 'Look at her, who does she think she is? Standing there with her little Gucci bag. What's she famous for? Shagging footballers!'

They started laying into her, being really rude and calling her all sorts of names. I didn't know what to say or where to look. I was glad it wasn't me on the receiving end, and I felt a bit sorry for Danielle. But I have to admit there was a part of me that was smiling about it inside, because finally she knew what it was like to have people dislike you. It made me realise that, although the magazines and papers might put her picture in their pages, some of the general public actually thought she was a piece of toot. For me it was the other way round. And I'd much rather be able to walk down the street and have people say, 'You all right, Jade? I love you, when are you going to be back on telly again?' than have a magazine or newspaper be nice to me. I'm more bothered what normal people think of me than what the media think. That means so much more to me.

Saying that, there are some areas I'm still scared about walking through. One day I was in Camden with Jack, and a lady shouted, 'Jade, can I have a photo with you?', so of course I stopped. Just as we slowed down another woman was walking towards us with her friend. She looked quite posh and well-to-do, and as she passed us she mumbled, 'You racist bitch.'

I was shocked. She didn't look like the kind of person to say that. So I walked after her without thinking and said calmly, 'Excuse me, did you just say something?

I was busy talking so I couldn't hear properly. Is everything OK?'

'Yes,' she answered, 'I called you a racist bitch because that's what you are, aren't you?'

'I'm not actually but you're entitled to your opinion. To be honest, you look a bit too mature and above making comments like that to young girls you don't know. I thought you came from an upper-class background but obviously you're just as common as I am. Have a nice day.'

And I walked off.

It wasn't just my life that had been affected by the *Celebrity Big Brother* experience, though. My mum was getting grief too. She was attacked one day on the street by two Asian guys as she stood at a cashpoint.

I was also shit scared about anything hurting my grandparents and I kept thinking it was now my fault that they couldn't go on public transport again or do the things they used to without getting hassle. But thankfully they've been all right.

Not long after we came out of the house, Jack went on a skiing holiday with some mates. While he was away I got a tip-off that there were journalists there acting as beehives for male celebrities, so I texted him to warn him. Of course at first he wondered what the fuck I was going on about because as usual I had the word wrong – I meant honey trap, not beehive. That meant there were female journos trying to set men up so they could write about it for the papers. On cue a story appeared saying Jack had tried to come on to one of them. But for once I knew this wasn't true because even Jack wouldn't be so stupid as to fall for it when I'd warned him it could happen.

One night after Jack was back I locked myself out of the house, so I had to call him to come round with his keys. For normal couples this would have been fine, but we're not normal. Jack had been drinking a tiny bit with some of the lads round the corner, he was the one driving and he also only had a provisional licence. Doh.

The police caught him and then he was banned for six months.

Meanwhile, I was panicking about how I was going to bring up the boys. The offers of work had, unsurprisingly, dried up. I had £100,000 in the bank, which might seem like a lot but it was potentially going to have to last me for God knows how long without work necessarily coming in. Rightly or wrongly, by then I'd somehow managed to land myself with monthly outgoings of about £11,000 (too many posh cars, Jade) and most of that was needed for food and the kids. People seem to think I've got loads of money, and yes I have earned a fair bit in the past, but it's been six years since I was first in the public eye and that cash soon goes. I have nice cars, nice holidays and send my kids to nice schools – and that pretty much uses it up. And now it was all over and I was sick with worry about how I was going to survive.

Jeff wasn't helping the situation at home much. We weren't getting on brilliantly and there were constant battles about money and maintenance. Like me he wasn't working, so he said he couldn't afford to pay me more than £11 a month. But I couldn't understand how he had three houses if he was so skint. We'd bicker about duties too, like babysitting or picking the kids up from school. Our relationship was up and down at the best of times.

And right now, it was down. We were just constantly niggling at each other. We'd send texts about whose turn it was to look after the boys and there would always be something to fall out over – whether it was time changes, money for maintenance or what food they were eating. Every time we rowed Jeff would try to hit me where it hurt by throwing the *Celebrity Big Brother* stuff back in my face.

'Well, everyone in the whole entire world knows you're just a fucking bully, Jade.'

'Jeff, grow up, will you. This is just about me, you and our children.'

But there were pressures from all directions and I was having sleepless nights. I was the breadwinner, but now there was no bread to be won.

And then, after over six years, I split from John Noel Management.

A few months after coming out of the *Celebrity Big Brother* house I was summoned to a meeting with John at his office. He wanted to talk to me about what we were going to do moving forward. I was a bit late because my driver got lost, so that put him in a bad mood from the off. And, believe me, as I've said before, John's not one to mince his words. He was seriously pissed off; he thought I was up my own arse – and he had no qualms in telling me so.

I was so unhappy at this time. The idea of moving into a new house was all that was getting me through it, but John was having none of it. He kept telling me that the press would crucify me and that I should be saving money, not splashing the cash. He even said I should try taking a leaf out of Angelina Jolie's book!

Me? Behave like Angie?! Come on, everyone knows I'm not like that!

I couldn't believe it. I told him, 'I do my bit for charity and I like doing that. Whenever I go to an auction I'm the only bloody celeb who ever buys anything – the others just sit there quaffing the free booze. And I've already given £100,000. But I can't agree to go round pretending to be someone I'm not.'

He was having none of it. He said I needed a reality check and that maybe I should think about selling my car.

But all I wanted to do was be true to myself.

I didn't want to sell all my nice things. I'd grown up with nothing, and now I'd been lucky enough to be able to afford all these luxuries. I couldn't understand why I needed to give it all away. I knew I had a huge hurdle to climb, and I wanted to do whatever it took to get back on track. But I begged him to not make me sell the things I'd worked so hard for or try to turn me into somebody I'm not.

I think he had some idea about me travelling the world and building houses in poor countries or something. But I've got two kids, they're my priority and I want to build a future for them here. I can't suddenly uproot them and start pretending to be Angelina fucking Jolie.

John didn't like it when people disagreed with him. He always believed he was right, and he'd had enough. So he told me that was it. And, just like that, he ended it.

I couldn't quite believe what I was hearing. I looked over at Katherine and Sally, who were also in the room. He didn't mean it, did he? We'd rowed before loads of times and it'd always blown over. Surely this was just him being all hot-headed again?

But he didn't budge.

After a few minutes' silence I realised he was deadly serious.

All I could say was: 'How can you sit there being like that to me when you put me in that situation in the first place? If you hadn't made me go back into the *Big Brother* house, none of this would have happened! You are the only person I've ever looked up to as a father figure, you've been my rock and now you're flicking me away like I'm a piece of shit on your shoe? Well, that makes me feel just great, John. Thanks a lot.'

I stood up, tears rolling down my face. 'I feel sick. You have let me down in a bigger way than I'd ever have imagined.'

I looked at Katherine, but she couldn't say anything. I think she thought it was one of those arguments that John and I had always had in our pretty volatile relationship and that it would sort itself out. But I knew this was it. I felt shattered. I was in bits. And I felt so empty. As I left John's office all I could think was: Who am I? What the hell has happened to me? What have I done wrong? My life is over.

I sat in my car and sobbed.

After about five minutes Sally rang me.

Then Katherine called. 'Are you OK?' she asked.

'Not really, Katherine. I can't believe I've been dismissed just like that. How can he do that after six years?'

'I know, Jade, I know. But whatever happens I'll help you find someone to look after you.'

'Don't worry, I don't want anyone's help.'

'John might come round ...'

'I don't care. I don't want him to now, I just feel so let

down. The fact that he can end it like that. I can't ever forget that.'

So that was it. My surrogate dad had kicked me out. And it hurt like hell.

I drove home in tears. The next day I woke up thinking, What do I do now? I had no agent. I felt lost and didn't know where to begin.

I rang Kate Jackson, the lady who'd worked with me on the Living TV stuff. 'Why don't you try Sean O'Brien?' she said. He was a journalist at the *People*, but now had branched out into being an agent and a PR guy. He was also friends with two paparazzi I'd known for years, and they liked him. Besides, I had nowhere else to go.

14
Hot and Bothered

I needed a break. I just had to get away from everything for a bit, so I decided to take Jack, the kids and Jack's brother Louis and his girlfriend Gemma somewhere hot. I picked Tobago, not really for any reason except that it looked nice in the pictures. I paid for it all and didn't think twice about the cost – mainly because I didn't want to believe everything was coming to an end. I was burying my head in the sand.

Normally when I go on holiday we'd stay in a hotel, but because I wanted to be away from everyone who might recognise me we decided to get a villa.

But, as usual with my life, it wasn't that simple. We arrived – the villa was lovely, near the beach with its own pool – and unpacked. It wasn't until it came to dinnertime that it dawned on me that staying in a villa actually meant cooking your own food. Not that I'm incapable of making food, but this meant it wasn't going to feel like a holiday for me at all because I was the only adult in the entire group. Jack was 19 going on 12, Jack's brother and his girlfriend were 16 and Bobby and Freddy were toddlers. So I was going to have to do lunch for everyone, evening meals for everyone and clean up after everyone. But that was nothing compared with what happened next.

One evening we were sitting out on the terrace watching the sun go down. The boys were in the pool and Jack was swigging on a beer in the hammock. Suddenly, to one side of the villa, I saw a flicker of light in the distance.

'Jack, there's a fire over there, look.'

'Oh, don't worry about it, Jade.'

'Don't worry about it? I think it's one of those bushfire things! This is what you see on *Holidays from Hell*. It's going to get bigger and come towards us!'

'No, it won't.'

'It will!'

What can only have been about six minutes later – *whoosh*. The flames were crackling near the house. It had spread quicker than Jodie Marsh's legs! I jumped up screaming, 'The kids!'

I pulled them out of the swimming pool and shouted for Louis and Gemma to take them somewhere down the road.

'Call the fire engine!' I shrieked at Jack.

'How do we ring them? It's not going to be 999, is it?'

'I don't know!'

Then I remembered that there was this boatyard nearby where they kept petrol and all the boat supplies and I started panicking even more that everything was going to blow up. By now some of the neighbours had come out of their houses after hearing the commotion, but they're used to having fires like this, so it wasn't so scary for them. I think what was more terrifying was the sight of me running about like a loon with no bra on (I was wearing a vest but that doesn't help much when I'm jumping about), hair sticking up on end from the shock with a gob on me like they've never heard before.

Then one of the neighbours called the fire brigade, but because they were putting out so many fires in the area they didn't get there for over an hour. So we had to take it into our own hands – the locals filled pots of water and we splashed one after another on the fire.

And, because a couple of days earlier a nearby hotel had tipped off some paps about me, the whole extravaganza was being caught on camera.

After about the eighteenth bucket of water I clocked that something – or rather someone – was missing. Jack. I looked over in disbelief. He was half-heartedly spraying water on the fire – still holding his beer in his hand! There am I thinking I'm going to die and he's just casually boozing like it's a normal holiday occurrence!

The fire was spreading and spreading. I ended up screaming at the paps, 'Put your fucking cameras down and help us please!' – which eventually they did.

Finally the fire engine arrived and put out the flames. The boys returned thinking I'd just been playing a big game of Fireman Sam and that I was a hero and Jack went back to his beloved beer.

The next day I nearly drove us all into the sea.

We had hired a minibus-type van so we could take day trips and get provisions for meals. We decided to get out of the villa for the day and drive to the beach. Bobby loves the beach but for some reason Freddy has an aversion to the sand and the sea and anything connected to it, which means that whenever we go there I have to bring a tent for him to play in, along with loads of distracting toys. So the van was much needed, and it would have been OK but for the fact that I nearly killed us. I spotted a few cars driving on the beach itself, so I made a move to do the same, but as I started to drive forward Jack yelled, 'Shit, Jade, we're on the edge of a cliff!'

I quickly put on the brakes, but the nose of the van was hanging over the edge. Then I saw some builders waving their arms and shouting, 'No!'

The boys were in the back acting like it was all a game, and I just froze in a panic. Jack was quick-thinking for once and grabbed the steering wheel and put his foot on the brake so I could move mine off while I tiptoed round the side of the van and carefully got Freddy and Bobby out. All the while I knew that if Jack let the brake go he would be over the cliff and a goner. I sat the boys on the verge out of the way while a growing group of locals surrounded us – once again having to come to my rescue. They must've been thinking, Who's this girl causing danger in our town?

One guy tied a rope to the van's bumper, then the others pulled on it to try to get the van, with Jack still inside, away from the edge of the cliff. But they pulled so hard that the bumper came away! Suddenly the van lurched even further forward and there was a point when I seriously thought it was going to drop. Jack was amazingly calm throughout the whole thing – he probably had a beer in his hand somewhere under the dashboard. I was shouting, 'Just jump out of the van! Quick! You're going to die!' Which I'm sure really helped the situation.

Then for some unknown reason I decided to take

pictures of the event, so I took out my camera and started snapping away from all angles.

Suddenly I heard a voice bellow from the van, 'Stop fucking taking pictures! Are you mental?'

Somehow or other the locals pulled the van back and Jack got out alive. One man looked at me afterwards and put his hands on my shoulders. 'You are one crazy lady! You should never be allowed to drive again!'

You'd think that would have been enough drama for one holiday. But no.

Next day comes and we hear a loud crash, bang, wallop outside the villa. A drunk driver had crashed into an electric pylon and it had fallen on to the road. That was our power gone, and with it the air conditioning. And it was God knows how many degrees outside.

The electricity repair guys turned up and Freddy and Bobby sat on the side of their van half-naked, happily sucking on lollies, while they were in the villa trying to sort things out. I was sitting in a towel because everything had cut out while I was in the shower and Jack was swigging on another beer in the hammock. We were told our electricity would be on again within an hour.

It didn't come back on again for 24 hours.

Jack had to set up beds for the boys to sleep in outside because they were too hot indoors and he sat watch all night (again drinking beer, but it was sweet of him to stay awake with them). Meanwhile, I went to sleep in the van with the air con up to the max. I get really itchy if I'm hot and I start getting all paranoid that there will be flies on me biting me alive. Not that I'm dramatic in any way of course. After that we had about two days left before we had to come home.

As if the holiday hadn't been enough of a disaster, not long after we got back my dear mum put her foot in it again. For some ridiculous reason she told a newspaper that when I was younger she used to clean my face with piss! I opened the *Daily Star* to see the headline 'Jade's Sick Wee Secret – *Big Brother* Star's Face Wiped Clean With Dirty Nappies'.

What the fuck? I love my mum, but sometimes I just want to chin her.

I phoned her up. 'Mum, what the hell have you been saying about me?'

'The reporter just started saying what good skin you had and asked what your secret was ...'

'So you said you'd washed my face with pissy nappies?' She laughed.

'Mum – if you had ever really washed my face with nappies I would report you to the social services because that is sick and wrong. And you said you did it too!'

I read the article out to her. 'You said, and I quote, "I've been putting my own urine on my face since the age of 11. I get it really hot then put it on my face so it opens up the pores and sinks in."'

She chuckled again. 'Oh, Jade, I was just having a laugh!'

'Why would somebody say that? What were you thinking?'

I can't even explain what goes on in her mind, I really can't. She amazes me sometimes. I honestly don't know whether she washes her own face in urine. All I can say is that having grown up with her through all these years I've never smelt piss when I hugged her! She was actually ridiculously hygienic when I was growing up. She was super-strict about my teeth. At school all my friends would be allowed bags of sweets at break-time and I'd have to make do with an apple and some crisps. Whenever I asked her for chocolate she'd just shake her head and say no. And even when I was a teenager she watched me like a hawk to make sure my teeth were brushed before I went to bed. She used to get up in the night and feel my toothbrush, and if it wasn't wet she'd wake me up and march me to the bathroom. I even remember coming in drunk from a nightclub when I was 16, staggering into bed, then hearing this banging on my bedroom wall. Mum was half-asleep in the next room but awake enough to shout, 'Oi! Brush your teeth!'

So how that explains her washing my face with wee-soaked nappies I'll never know. And what Jackiey does in her own time, I couldn't honestly tell you. All I can say is that she manages to single-handedly dig more of a hole for me than anybody else! If there's ever something embarrassing to say or do, Jackiey will stick her right arm up and do it.

15
Hopes and Fears

Then I realised I'd missed my period. I knew there was no way I could go out and buy a pregnancy-testing kit as there were still paps following my every move. For some reason the photographers weren't as bothered about trailing Jack, so I asked him to go when he was sure he wasn't being followed, and he managed to get one. I think most women just know when they're having a baby; it's like an instinct. And deep down I knew that weeing on a stick wasn't going to tell me anything new. I was up the duff.

It was a complete accident and neither I nor Jack really had time to take the whole thing in before it was out in the open and it was too late. A day after I'd done the test I got a phone call from a journalist at the *Sun*.

'Jade, congratulations, we're really pleased for you.'

Now, most clever people in my situation, having got used to the ways of the media after six years, would have replied, 'What about?'

But I blurted out, 'How do you know?'

'Oh, so you are pregnant!'

'I, er, yes, but I'm only early. Please don't print it, I don't want anyone to know yet.'

I spoke to Sean and he said, 'They're going to run with it, Jade.' Which I already knew really. Since when have papers done someone a favour and not run a story unless they're going to get another, juicier story in its place?

This meant Jack and I had to tell our friends and family. It all felt a bit sick and wrong to me, though, because I knew you had to be at the three-month stage to be properly sure everything was OK. Jack and I hadn't even really discussed what we wanted to do, as there hadn't been time. But there was no way I could have an abortion now. Even if we'd decided we weren't ready for a baby together, if I chose not to have it the papers would accuse me of being a murderer as well as a racist and a bully. And I certainly wasn't mentally strong enough to deal with any more blows to my character.

Don't get me wrong – I'm not saying I think I could've seriously gone ahead with a termination. Bobby and Freddy mean the world to me and I can't imagine not being a mother. And the thought of getting rid of something that could be their brother or sister would kill me. But I was in a dark place at the time and part of me really didn't know if Jack and I were ready to be parents. In the past – before I had the boys – I've been in a situation where I've had to have an abortion. So I don't disagree with it in certain circumstances, for instance when people are too young or really don't feel ready. But as a mum already I know I would've struggled to make that decision. It's just that half of me wished I just hadn't got pregnant in the first place because it wasn't the right time. Then there was the other half of me that thought this new little child might be able to bring us all happiness – and it was the first piece of good news I'd had in ages.

But we had to tell our families. They were going to find out in a matter of hours anyway, because there were paps surrounding my house, journalists doorstepping me, sending me bunches of flowers to congratulate me, chocolates, toys, the lot. I knew they weren't doing it to be nice – they were doing it to butter me up because they know I am the sort of person who finds it hard to be rude to them if they've come all the way to my house. I can accept that they were only doing their job and if it hadn't been for them I would never be doing what I'm doing now. But this time I hid inside the house.

Jack's family have always been very welcoming and lovely to me, but when he told his mum Mary I think she was a bit shocked to start with and just wanted to make sure her son was doing the right thing. She asked him if he was sure and if he loved me, and he replied that of course he did, even though I already had two kids by a different guy. He felt close to them and wanted to become part of their family even more. So his mum understood and accepted it. I would have asked the same questions if it had been my 19-year-old son who had got a girl pregnant. And once the news had sunk in, his family welcomed the idea with open arms. In fact, they got so excited about the prospect of having a grandchild they talked about virtually nothing else.

My mum's so easy-going she just said she was happy for me whatever. If I'd told her I was expecting a herd of elephants she probably would have shrugged and said,

'Well done.' She loves kids and couldn't wait to be a grandma again. It seemed to take her only about two seconds before she was out shopping for babies' clothes. She started buying pink babygros, convinced I was going to have a little girl.

Jack couldn't hide how chuffed he was either. He kept putting his hands on my belly and saying, 'I can't believe that's my baby in there.' It was really sweet.

As predicted, it was in the newspapers the next day and so officially out there. Sean phoned me and told me I should do a set-up interview and talk about it, but at first I didn't want to because it seemed weird when I didn't know the baby was safe. Besides, it was all such a rush and Jack and I had barely had time to talk about it all ourselves. And, on top of all that, I wasn't sure the public was ready to hear about me gushing about having a new child. I didn't think anyone wanted to read anything about me any more.

'I've had lots of offers for your first chat about it, Jade – people do want to know,' Sean reassured me. 'Anyway, it's been printed now, and if you don't say anything there'll be speculation about it and more stories that might not be true. Also, this is a bit of good news after all the bad surrounding you – so it might help focus people on something positive instead.'

So I did my first interview with *OK!* – Jack, Bobby and Freddy were with me – and it felt nice. Somehow, gradually, I was being accepted again. And having the pregnancy to talk about was such a relief after having answered questions about my time in the *Celebrity Big Brother* house. Jack doesn't usually say much in interviews but this time he was really vocal, as if he'd found something he just couldn't stop talking about. And it was lovely.

I remember reading something that Chantelle Houghton had said in an interview or a column she was doing, insinuating that it was a bit 'convenient' and a bit of a 'coincidence' that I was pregnant now. As if I'd done it on purpose to stop the negativity after *Celebrity Big Brother*!

Jack's sister kept going on the internet and finding things she wanted to buy for the baby. Everyone was buzzing around us wanting to talk about baby toys and presents. It was impossible not to get caught up in the excitement of it all.

Maybe this was the new beginning we all needed.

Before my pregnancy went public I was approached by a guy called Mark, one of the organisers of the Soccer Six celebrity football tournament, about playing in one of the female teams. I'd politely declined and said I couldn't tell them why, but now it was out in the open I was able to get back on the phone and explain my reasons. Mark was really sweet about it and said that they'd still like me to come down on the day and do some publicity for them, and invited Jack to play in one of the boys' teams instead. I was terrified, though. This was going to be my first big public appearance, in front of huge crowds, and I felt there was every chance I would get booed right back out of the stadium. Later I found out that an argument had gone on behind the scenes among the other Soccer Six organisers about whether I should be allowed there at all. Mark was fighting my case, but some of the people higher up said they were worried in case it got them bad press or caused a riot.

In the end they took the chance, and I was so pleased

because it did my confidence the world of good. The matches were taking place somewhere in West Ham, which meant we were near enough for me to take the boys along. If I'd gone on my own I think I'd have felt so much more self-conscious, but with my kids with me I had to focus on them and make sure they were enjoying themselves. And they had a great day – all the other celebs kept fussing around them and giving them loads of attention. The funniest thing was that Jeff was also playing in the tournament, so Bobby would run from Jack's team to Jeff's and back again, reporting back on who was the better footballer. Jack and Jeff get on really well, thank God, but there could've been some bruised egos after Bobby's stirring.

Kate Moss was there with Pete Doherty, who was playing on Jack's team. She didn't come down to the pitch but she had a box with loads of people in it and was watching from above. Someone came down and invited me up there. I was secretly pleased because it meant that Kate hadn't turned against me after all that had happened – in fact, she knows more than most what it's like to have the press calling you names – but I said I couldn't come up because I had the boys with me. Then at one point I was crouched at the side of the pitch watching one of the matches and Pete came and sat beside me. He was so much more gentlemanly than I'd ever imagined from seeing pictures of him and reading about him in the papers. And he looked quite clean too!

'How are you, Jade? Are you all right?'

'Yeah I'm all right, thanks, Pete.'

'Kate's up there. We're having a party later – you should come.'

I was explaining that someone had already asked me and I'd have loved to but I couldn't because of the boys, when Freddy suddenly ran over to Pete and started thumping him on the head! I was screaming (and half laughing), 'Freddy! What are you doing? Stop hitting the man!'

But Pete just swung round, grabbed Freddy and rolled him to the ground in a play fight, tickling him and saying, ''Ere! You little rascal!' I felt like I saw a completely different side to him that day. He told me that he has a son of his own, which I had never realised. But you could tell, because he's great with them – unless he's just like me and has the mental age of a toddler, which is why we connect with them so well!

It was all a bit surreal. Pete was asking how old Freddy was and seemed really interested in what I had to say. He told me that he used to want to be a footballer before he got into music, and I replied, 'What, you? You fancied yourself as a bit of a Gazza, did you?' and he laughed. Then he high-fived Freddy and walked off.

Then it dawned on me and I quickly grabbed Freddy's hands and checked them for cuts and grazes. I know that sounds bad, but if Pete Doherty was the drug addict people say he is I wasn't taking any chances.

The papers afterwards made out that Pete was doing drugs all throughout the matches, but I've seen people when they're high and I can vouch that he was clean that day. He was a really good guy. I could see why Kate was attracted to him (and I never thought I'd say that!).

It was such a good day. And the crowds were all so supportive, shouting things like, 'We love you, Jade! We know you're a good sort!', which put a smile on my face that I still couldn't wipe off by the time I went to bed.

Because that event had gone so well, Jack and I got

invited to another Soccer Six tournament, this time up north. Obviously I couldn't kick a ball about because of my condition, but Jack was on one of the teams and I was going to do a bit of radio and TV publicity for them.

We left the boys with my mum and drove up together. The games went on throughout the day, then there was a charity auction in the evening and I bought a Maradona football shirt for £5,000 which I was going to give to Bobby. All the celebs were staying in the same hotel and getting pretty pissed (apart from me of course) and for the first time I met Michelle Scott-Lee, who was really sweet. We ended up chatting for hours about nonsense, and I thought she was a great girl.

Jack was with one of our mates, Michael, who'd joined us for the day, and they were getting bladdered in a corner. By about 11, I was feeling really shattered, so I told Jack I was going to bed and asked if he'd come and help me bring the football shirt upstairs because it was in a big glass case. He took me upstairs, gave me a kiss and said, 'I'll be up in a bit.'

I woke up at about 3am and thought, Where the fuck is he? I called his mobile, but there was no answer. So I rang the bar downstairs and they said the party was still going on. I asked if they could see where Jack was, but the reply came: 'We can't find him.'

So I rang Michael's phone. 'Have you seen Jack?'

'I don't know where he is – I've lost him.'

I rang Jack's phone again. No answer.

I was starting to get really stressed by this point. I left him a message: 'Where the hell are you? What's going on?'

About ten minutes later Jack appeared in the doorway. He could barely stand.

'Where the fuck have you been, Jack?'

I couldn't get much sense out of him, he was so hammered. But eventually I worked out what he was ranting on about and I couldn't believe it. He was calling me a slag and accusing me of having it off with some other guy. As if I'd been with another guy while he was downstairs!

'You fucking think you're *it*,' he was shouting.

I was gobsmacked. 'Jack – you know what? You can leave this room right now.' He was talking like someone who had a guilty conscience and was accusing me of doing what he'd probably been up to himself. 'Just get a life, Jack,' I said. 'I'm pregnant with your child! What would I be doing with another fella?'

He refused to leave the room and was heaving himself about the place, falling into the table, the bed, the chair. When he came towards me I chucked an ashtray at him. I just wanted him to leave me alone. By now I was in tears.

Then he lost it completely.

'You want to smash things up do you Jade? Well, I'll show you!'

And with that he started throwing things around the room, hitting the walls, picking up the TV, breaking vases and lampshades. Really frightened, I lay on the bed sobbing and shouting for him to stop. I got up and tried to leave – 'I'm going home, I can't stay here with you' – but he blocked the door and refused to let me out of his sight.

Then all of a sudden he pushed me on to the bed and stood over me shouting. My instant reaction would usually be to shout and swear back at him – but I couldn't move. I was terrified. He'd never behaved like this before. He pushed his head against mine and started mumbling words I couldn't understand. I feebly scratched his neck, but it was as if he couldn't see me – his eyes were glazed over like he was a zombie.

I was screaming at him to stop, but he didn't listen.

'I'm pregnant!' I cried out.

Then he stepped back, screaming at me. He didn't seem to know what he was saying. He even shouted things about the baby not being his.

I rang Michael to beg him to come and help, but Jack snatched my phone out of my hand and threw it to the ground. I couldn't believe what was happening. There was blood all over the sheets and up the walls where he'd cut his hands on the vases. It looked like there'd been a massacre in that room.

In the end I knew I was going to have to pretend to sleep, otherwise Jack wouldn't calm down. Tears were streaming down my cheeks and I lay there on the bed with my eyes closed, praying he would stop.

After a few minutes he did stop. But only to be sick all over the bathroom.

I can't face this tomorrow, I lay there thinking. After all I've been through, the thought of having to walk downstairs and see all these people who've heard our row – it's too much. Besides, they'll probably all think it's my fault and that I was hitting Jack. After all, I'm the 'bully'.

Finally, after puking all over the place, Jack passed out. I picked up my mobile phone and dialled Lewis Day Cars, the cab firm I always use to take me about when I'm in London. Thing is, we were in north Wales, so a cab home was probably going to cost me as much as a small house, but I trusted them, and at the moment I needed someone I could trust.

It must've been about 5.30am by the time the car got there, which the driver said was really good going and he only made it in that time because the roads were so clear. Jack was still out for the count, so I carefully picked up the football shirt in its frame and crept out as quietly as I could. As I left the room I burst into tears. I was a total wreck.

As I got into the lift I was so frightened that someone would shout out and ask me why I was going home. I walked past reception with the framed shirt covering my face, which must've looked even more bizarre, like some dodgy robber in skinny jeans who'd stolen the thing.

I climbed into the taxi and sobbed for the entire journey. I kept thinking, Is it my fault? Why do all my boyfriends turn psychopath on me?

It was about 7.30am when Jack called me on my mobile.

'Where are you?'

'I'm at home, Jack.'

'Why? What did you leave for?'

'Have you seen what you've done, Jack?'

He was silent.

'Jack, what about the state of the room? Do you actually remember last night? I don't want to talk to you any more. You've made me feel ashamed.'

I put the phone down. I couldn't bear to talk to him.

Then it rang again. It was Mark, the organiser from Soccer Six, the same guy who'd put his neck on the line for me when the others were worried I'd cause trouble.

'Jade, is everything OK? You've got an interview to do in a minute. I've been calling your hotel room but there's been no answer.'

He didn't know I'd left. And now I was going to have

to explain that I was leaving him in the lurch and he had to cancel all the publicity I was booked to do for him. I was going to look like a prima donna who'd had a hissy fit because she couldn't handle having a fight with her boyfriend.

'I'm so sorry, Mark, I've had to come home because there's been a bit of a crisis with my children.'

I couldn't bear that I was using Bobby and Freddy as an excuse but I didn't know what else to say.

Mark was really sweet. 'I can't believe you've been let down by your babysitter, that's awful,' he said. 'Don't worry. I understand.'

The worst thing was that I wanted to do the interviews that had been set up for me. I needed to do them in order to try to get my life back on track again. And because of Jack I was having to turn down things that could lead to potential work. I felt so low.

Half an hour later Mark rang again.

'Jade, your hotel room's been trashed.'

'Yeah, I know.'

I was so sheepish. I had to come clean and apologise in the end. I felt so guilty for putting Mark in that position.

I tried to explain that Jack had started to go a bit mad, but even as I was saying it I was questioning whether he believed me. I wouldn't have blamed him if he didn't. I'm portrayed as this psycho woman who hits her boyfriends and gets angry all the time, so would Mark think it was my fault? I asked him to give me the details of the hotel manager and I called him and used my card to pay for all the damage, which came to about two and a half grand. He was incredibly nice considering, and assured me that it would go no further. I found out afterwards that the press had gone down there asking to take pictures of the room and the staff didn't let them, so I sent a huge bunch of flowers to say thank you for their discrepancy (although I've since found out I meant discretion).

So as usual I was left footing the bill for Jack. And I was starting to get really bloody fed up with it. But what could I do? I was carrying his baby and we had to make a go of it. When Jack got back to Essex he was full of apologies, but as far as I was concerned they were starting to go in one ear and out the other. I was just tired of everything. The press were once again outside the house after getting wind of our row.

When I told Jack's mum about what had happened at the hotel, she couldn't believe how he had behaved. Mary immediately came over to my house and when she saw me her face seemed to crumble. She seemed mortified and in absolute shock at what Jack had done. I sat down at the kitchen table with her and said, 'I am disgusted with your son. And I want you to know exactly what happened so he gets embarrassed about what he's done.' Jack was sobbing by now. He claimed he couldn't remember. All he kept saying was: 'I'm so sorry.' But words were meaningless.

Mary insisted on taking me to their house, she was so worried about me. I didn't want to see anyone, so I agreed and, I have to say, for the whole of the next week Jack's mum and dad were amazingly attentive. I don't think they spoke to Jack once, they were so disgusted. They couldn't stop apologising and spent that week fussing around me and cooing about their grandchild-to-be.

Jack seemed really upset about what he'd done and I wasn't going to make things worse by letting the papers sniff out what had gone on. After that, I don't really know how it happened, but Jack somehow managed to win me back round. And since then, thank goodness, he's never scared me in that way again.

That doesn't mean he hasn't behaved like an absolute dick, though.

But that came later.

During this time I had been calling the lady who ran the Perfume Shop, begging to know what was going on with my perfume. It was my pride and joy and I was desperate to know whether it would ever be in the shops again.

'When's it going back on the shelves?'

'I don't know, Jade.'

In June 2007 I got the call I'd been dreading. 'Shilpa's releasing a perfume, and we're going to stock it. I'm sorry, Jade.'

But what I didn't realise was that Shilpa's perfume did me a favour. In a way I have her to thank for getting my perfume back on sale. A few days after I'd had the call about Shilpa's perfume being sold, the Perfume Shop lady was back on the phone. 'Now that we've sold Shilpa's, we think we can put yours on the shelf again, Jade. It seems right again now.'

A week later my perfume was back in the shop, and by September I was outselling her by three to one. My fans are bloody loyal, that's all I can say.

Jack's behaviour at Soccer Six wasn't the only thing that was starting to grate on me. It was the fact that he seemed to have no desire to go out and earn any money. When I first met Jack he claimed to be a 'football agent' and ever since then the newspapers have referred to that as his 'job'.

But the truth is, when it came to having ambition and drive, Jack was severely lacking. He seemed happy just to bum about and seemed like he was always waiting for some thunderbolt to strike and say, 'Here's the job you're meant to be doing!' He always said he still didn't know what he wanted to do. One time he was approached in the street by a scout from Select Model Management, but nothing ever came of it – he seemed too embarrassed by the whole thing – but I'd have loved him to be a Calvin Klein model, it would've made me so proud. But the truth is, I'd have loved him to do anything. And his laziness was starting to piss me off.

One day I got so frustrated I even asked Sir Alan Sugar if he'd give Jack a job. We were at my house and I was on the toilet – most of my brainstorms come when I'm on the loo – when I suddenly had a light-bulb moment. '*The Apprentice*! It's clear Alan Sugar needs people to work for him! So I might try to get Jack a job!' I rang up my agent and said, 'I need Alan Sugar's number. I'm trying to get Jack a job.'

'What? Jade, are you bonkers?' he laughed. 'You need to get it yourself. Why don't you try directory enquiries?'

So I found out the number and, still sitting on the bog, rang it.

'Hello, it's Jade Goody here. Can I speak to Sir Alan Sugar, please?'

'Er, let me put you through to his PA. Hold on a minute.'

'Jade? How can I help you?' said his PA.

'Well, I'm just ringing up because I know Sir Alan needs people to work for him and I'm trying to get my boyfriend a job. He's an entrepreneur or something, isn't he? So I just want to know how he became an entrepreneur and also does he want to take Jack on for a job?'

She wet herself laughing.

'Sir Alan Sugar's away at the moment, Jade. He's a bit busy.'

'Oh, really? Or is he in the office and you just don't want me to talk to him?'

She laughed again. 'No, he is actually away at the moment. But I can give you the number of a gentleman who works closely with Sir Alan and he can explain how he made his money and he also might be able to help with guiding your boyfriend and getting him a job.'

'Thank you very much, that's really kind.'

And then I eventually got off the loo.

I called the number she gave me – I think the guy was called Dave – but it went to his answerphone. I left what must've been the longest and most waffly message in the universe about me wanting to get Jack a job, and then hung up. It wasn't until I told my mates afterwards that I realised this kind of thing isn't exactly normal. Jen cracked up. 'Jade! I can't believe what you've just done! You rang Sir Alan Sugar and begged him for a job!'

But I just wanted Jack to have a bit of ambition.

As if Jack's lack of drive wasn't enough to contend with, I got banned from getting behind the wheel for six months. Admittedly, it was my own fault. I'd managed to clock up three motoring offences, including driving my BMW X5 the previous November with only a provisional licence. I'd passed my test a while before but I didn't realise you had to send off the forms to the DVLA. I just thought that once you'd passed your test you automatically had a licence and that was it. Because of this I had to retake my test, which was slightly embarrassing. Thankfully I passed. I was also forced to plead guilty to driving while uninsured in Brentwood in March. I was ordered to pay more than £1,500 in fines and I had 14 penalty points added to my licence – resulting in a ban. Just what I needed. At least it wasn't for a whole year though as I later won my appeal at Basildon Crown Court. I don't know how I'd have coped with that, as I'm totally dependent on my car.

16
Lost Treasure

Then in July 2007 I lost the baby. I'd been getting period-like pains for a few days but it'd been a stressful week and I didn't think they were bad enough to go to hospital. I had a scan booked for the week after, so I wasn't too worried. But then the evening before the appointment I had a strange feeling, like I was empty. It sounds odd but I almost felt like I knew it was going to happen. When I woke the next morning at about 4am in a lot of pain I knew something was very wrong. I went to the toilet and lost a lot of blood. I'd seen my mum have a miscarriage in the past and I just knew it – I knew I'd lost it. I was in shock. I didn't scream and I didn't cry. I tapped Jack on the shoulder to wake him up and said really calmly, 'I think I've lost the baby.'

Jack seemed a bit stunned and he called the NHS helpline. Bobby and Freddy were asleep and we didn't want to disturb them by having an ambulance turn up.

The doctor I talked to confirmed that I'd probably had a miscarriage. I put the phone down and broke down in tears. Jack was sobbing as well and we fell asleep holding each other. When we woke up again we felt numb, and neither of us knew what to say to each other. It hit me a lot harder than I thought it would and I really felt like I couldn't deal with it. I made an emergency appointment at the doctor's and he confirmed our worst fears. That morning I walked out of the surgery like a zombie and spent the next few days in a haze. I tortured myself asking why it had happened. What else could go wrong? Hadn't I put up with enough? It was a really dark time but I had to put on a brave face for my sons.

Jack's parents were really upset too, although they tried not to show it because they knew they needed to be as supportive to us as possible. A few weeks later Jack was clearing some things from his house and came across a card that his dad had sent to his mum saying what a great grandmother she was going to make. And that really choked me.

Jack was really supportive in his own way. He'd make sure the boys were OK while I sat upstairs staring at the walls like a mute. But I don't think a man can really understand the grief a woman goes through when she loses a baby.

As odd as it sounds, once I managed to leave the house after about four days, one of the first things I did was go on a sunbed for 20 minutes, as I hadn't been able to use one while I was pregnant. I don't think that's in the 'Coping with a Miscarriage' handbook, but there you go. I think I felt that having been in rehab for depression in February I didn't want to go back, and I knew I had to do something to pick myself back up.

The launch of my first perfume, Shh… I put everything into getting the right smell for this, and I can honestly say getting my own perfume on the shelves is one of my proudest achievements.

Inset: Always the life and soul of the party, it wasn't long before I made a move for the decks!

© *Matrixphotos.com*

A romantic holiday with Jack …

Below: … and me and Carly, my business partner for Ugly's, soaking up the sun and enjoying the atmosphere at the 59th Cannes Film Festival. © *Matrixphotos.com*

The London Marathon, April 2006.

I got slated by the press for giving up before the end, but I'm proud of what I achieved that day. I raised loads of money for the NSPCC and completed 21 miles, which I don't think is too bad!

Above left: Getting a bit carried away as I sink my ball during a round of golf with the Tweed family (believe it or not I was actually damn good at putting!).

Above right and below: On stage in my West End debut. For one night only I appeared as a guardian angel in *The Vegemite Tales*. I had a bit of an unusual costume – yes, my angel wings are made from condoms – but it was real laugh.

Freddy's second birthday party. I organised a 'Pirates of the Caribbean' themed party and we had balloons, clowns, an amazing cake and lots and lots of party games.

Captain 'Freddy' Hook.

Above: Freddy, me and a group of the other little pirates having a good old giggle at the clown.

Below: Bobby and Freddy, either side of their dad Jeff, playing a game of pass the parcel.

I was persuaded by Sean to speak to *Closer* magazine about my loss. He reasoned that once it was out there in the public domain the press would be knocking at my door again, pestering me for an interview, so it was easier just to get it over with in one go. It was a surreal experience talking about losing a baby to the same journalist I'd met on numerous occasions before, when I usually rabbited on about some sort of new diet I'd been on or my relationship problems with Jack. This time we didn't do a set-up shoot, thankfully. A photographer just took my picture as I spoke to the journalist in real time. And inevitably I was down in tears for most of it.

Again I started to get worried that readers would judge me for crying. Since coming out of the *Celebrity Big Brother* house I'd had such a lot of criticism over this. Whenever people saw me crying they would accuse me of crocodile tears, but anyone who knows me knows I'm incapable of doing something like that. I get emotional (in a good and bad way) really easily, and what you see is genuinely what you get. But the interview was a much more difficult experience than I thought it would be. I told them that part of the reason I wanted to do the interview was that, while I'm not the only woman to have miscarried, I somehow hoped that speaking out might help others cope better.

But it was one thing to talk about losing a baby on the pages of a magazine, and something else again when it got picked up by the newspapers and suddenly everywhere were headlines like 'My Miscarriage Was God's Punishment for *Big Brother* Race Row'. I was furious. Never once did I say anything about God punishing me, and I never would. They had completely twisted things to give themselves the headline they wanted. I'm not religious, so I would never use a phrase like that. I remember saying, 'When you lose a baby there are loads of things that go round in your head like did I do something, did I eat something? Did I drink something? Maybe it's God's way of saying it's not your time to have a baby yet?'

But I didn't say, 'God's punished me,' and it made me angry, as it's not my way. I don't go to church or spout on about religion, so how dare I start saying God has punished me? I knew this would be just another reason for people to criticise me – and they did. There was even one newspaper article where a reporter had spoken about it to a vicar, who felt he had to say, 'Jade Goody can be sure that losing her baby wasn't a punishment from God. God doesn't punish people. He stands by them and shares in their suffering as we see in Jesus Christ.'

I was so sad, and talking about it now makes me feel a bit weird because it's an odd feeling to think that there was a child I never had.

I was at rock bottom. I felt so low. And on top of the miscarriage I was still ridiculously paranoid about what people thought of me. All I wanted to do was to change myself so that people couldn't recognise me any more, or so they would see that I was a new person. I hated my old self and I didn't have a clue who my new self was meant to be. I was thinking things like, maybe if I change the way I dress? Or my hair?

That's the reason I changed my hairdo about 50 million times – I was just trying to be someone I wasn't. I thought that having a different hair colour would allow me to dress differently and become a new person. It sounds weird to me now, but that was the reasoning going through my head. So I made the decision to dye my hair blonde again. I thought there was something in the fact that when I came out of the first *Big Brother* house in 2002 I was a blonde, and I so wanted to escape from the image of coming out of *Celebrity Big Brother* as a brunette. I honestly thought that by changing my hair colour back to how it once was I'd change myself back to the same dizzy blonde that everyone once liked. I also wanted to distance myself from the picture of that awful night when I argued with Shilpa and I had that nasty look on my face. I wanted to wash myself clean of it all. Clearly, though, I'd washed myself clean of all sanity because the resulting look was like something out of *The Muppet Show*.

The idea was to go platinum blonde, but it went yellow. And for some reason I decided that it wasn't enough just to have my hair blonde in the style it was. I wanted it long too, to make myself look totally different. So I asked my poor hairdresser, Terri, for hair extensions. I have a vague memory of her trying to persuade me against it but you know what I'm like once I've made up my mind about something.

'Your hair's so short, Jade, it might look odd.'

'No, I want it, I want it. It'll be fine.'

After hours of gluing and bleaching I sat and stared at myself in the mirror in the salon and thought, What the shit have you done?

It was vile. It was like I was trying to be some Page 3 model.

I could see that there were paps outside, and for

some unknown reason decided to put on my reading glasses – as if that was going to somehow make me look all sophisticated.

I saw myself in the paper the next day. You look revolting, I thought. Like Miss Piggy's librarian sister.

Jack said he liked my hair shorter and Bobby said no when I asked him if he liked my new look, but at that stage I really didn't care what anyone thought. It was different and that was all that mattered.

I kept the extensions for about a month until I finally reached the end of my tether. And I nearly made myself bald in the process. I was at Jen's house with Carly one night and we sat there until about 3am pulling out each strand. Problem was, it was all glued into my scalp, so I almost ended up with less hair than Bruce Willis. We tried everything to get the extensions out, but nothing was working. We put nail-varnish remover on the roots and that was no use. Jen even went downstairs and came back with some pliers. We went on pulling and yanking until I looked like I had alopecia. I was crying at one stage because it hurt so much, but then I realised there was no point and started laughing hysterically instead.

Eventually we got most of it out but now it was shorter than it had ever been. And without wanting to sound like a mad person, it was like getting rid of all that hair was the start of getting rid of the rest of the mess in my life – Jack.

After we lost the baby we never fully recovered and I was getting more and more fed up with his lack of oomph. We were at breaking point. I looked at my life and realised that I was mothering Jack and I thought, I don't want to be your mother. I want a man to look after me and put his

arm round me and tell me everything will be OK. I want
to be able to open my bills one day and think, Jack can
pay this month, not, shit, how can I afford this? I've
always taken charge of everything – from looking after my
mum, to the kids and now Jack – and for once in my life
I wanted someone to make everything all right for me.

I couldn't understand how Jack could be in the prime
of his life – he was 20 now – and have no motivation to
do anything. With all the magazine interviews and stuff
we were doing – plus his *CBB* appearance – he was
making more money than most blokes his age, but he just
pissed it up the wall. I'd say to him, 'Why aren't you
saving it or investing it in something? Why don't you buy
a property or something?' Once I suggested buying a car-
wash business, as I thought that would be a good way of
making money. But he just shrugged and said, 'No, I
don't know what I want to do.' My head could not take
it. How could a guy of his age just sit there on his arse
and the highlight of his day be watching fucking *Family
Fortunes*. I'd had enough. Then one day he looked at me
and he knew.

'Jade, what is it?'

He knew something was wrong. I didn't want to lie to
him but I find it so difficult to deal with any situation
when I know someone's going to get hurt. He asked me
again, 'Jade, what is it? Don't you want to be with me
any more?'

I simply looked back at him and said, 'No, Jack, I
don't.' The words were so difficult to say, but I couldn't
carry on like this.

Jack pleaded with me, tried to talk me round, but I
knew I'd made the right decision – for now anyway.

'No. I've fallen out of love with you because you're lazy, you've got no ambition and I feel more like your mum than your girlfriend. I'm sick and tired of nagging you. I've got two kids that I nag, I don't need another one.'

I needed to give him a wake-up call. I still loved him really, and I knew the kids adored him, but I knew I couldn't go on as we were. So I told myself that if Jack really wanted to be with me he'd do something about it, and this would be the shock to his system he needed.

We were both in tears. Neither of us really wanted it to end but we both knew it had to happen. I don't think for a second he'd seen it coming or had a clue what to say or do. I told him I needed him to learn to stand on his own two feet and to do something with his life. Even if it meant sweeping floors. I didn't care how much he earned. I just wanted him to earn something.

As soon as he'd gone I took down all the pictures of us and cleared the house of all memories. I was trying to prove to myself that I was doing the right thing.

Jack kept calling and begging me to reconsider, but I had to stay strong. In the end I knew the only way was to be nasty to him and try to feel hatred. I had this thought that, if I was worth it and he really cared about me as much as he said he did, it wouldn't matter what I threw at him.

Then I started hanging out with a guy called Dave Wickenden. I'd been friends with him for ages and I knew he'd always had a bit of a crush on me, so it was nice to get a bit of male attention. He was never my boyfriend, we weren't dating, but he wanted to take me out and he was a nice bloke, so I didn't see any harm in it. I also didn't see any harm in Jack knowing I was moving on. Of course we were papped – and the papers and magazines went all doolally over it – but there were never any shots of me holding Dave's hand or kissing him, because it didn't get that far. There was one snap of us in a toy shop and it looked like he was buying presents for the boys, but that was just because he'd given me a lift to town so I could buy one of them a birthday present. Dave knew he was never going to be my boyfriend, but he seemed to be happy just to be my mate.

By now Jack's reaction had gone from sad to bitter and I had a few abusive phone calls from him when he saw the reports about me and Dave in the paper. But I just had to grit my teeth and ignore it.

Then one night I went to Embassy with my mates and Jack was there. I'd just been reading that one of the magazines had said we had ended because he'd been calling me 'Cashpoint' and, although I knew deep down he would never say such a thing, I was still seething that someone could even suggest it. I felt a bit humiliated. Suddenly Jack started shouting at one of my friends and then turned towards me and called me a slag. I just shrugged and said, 'Whatever,' and immediately the bouncers came over and asked if I was OK. The owner, Mark, has always been good to me – he's become like a friend – so when he saw what was happening he stepped in and had a word with Jack.

'Jack, I'm sorry, mate, but when Jade's in here she gets priority. You're not going into the VIP area while she's in the club. She's my baby and I don't want you causing trouble.'

I can't tell you how good that felt.

One day I opened my door and the postman presented me with this large box. 'It's from a secret admirer, Jade,' he smiled.

I ran inside and tore it open. There was no message with it, so I didn't have a clue who it was from. But as soon as I saw what was inside I didn't care, to be honest. I'd been sent a gorgeous pair of Jimmy Choo shoes and a Louis Vuitton bag! Wow! I knew for a fact it couldn't have been from Jack; he'd never have been able to afford them.

But who could it be?

After I'd worn the shoes out a few times I bumped into my cousin, who clocked my feet and said, 'Dave got you them, you know.'

I was in shock. I rang Dave. 'Did you send me that present?'

'Yes.'

'How did you know my shoe size? That's scary!'

'I'm not saying,' he laughed.

I thanked him, and I was really chuffed. But it didn't change the way I felt about us.

Then it was time for my annual trip to Marbella. I thought it would be the perfect way to let my hair down after splitting up with Jack. If I had any hair, that is – it was still all burnt at the ends with remnants of glue in the scalp. I went with a few of the girls, oblivious at the time to all the pap pictures that were going to be printed of me afterwards. If I'd been aware of so many photographers hiding in the bushes I definitely would have worn a full-on swimsuit rather than letting all my bits hang out in a bikini. But, boy did I have a laugh!

We went to this champagne party at the Ocean Club,

and I got rat-arsed. There were a few other celebs there, including Danielle Lloyd, Nikki Grahame and Michelle Marsh. I remember looking over at them sipping their champagne in their diamante bikinis at the bar, looking all ladylike, then glancing down at my kebab belly as I took another swig out of the bottle that had just been sprayed all over me by one of my friends. But I knew who was having the better time. Danielle and I were completely blanking each other by now, there was no point in me even pretending to like her, or her me, so we didn't.

I remember this boy slipping over because he was so pissed and his head fell right in between my boobs. I nearly wet myself I was laughing so much. I must've looked like a drowned rat. I was running around all over the place, playing dares with this big group of people we were with, and crying with laughter.

At one point I was sitting in the pool smoking one of those funny bubble pipes that my mum used to be so into. We went to Egypt when I was young and she spent most of her days smoking them in the cafes. They're called *sheesha* pipes or something, and they come with different flavours of tobacco, like apple and orange and things. Mum used to put her puff in them, though, and just sit around with a big fat grin on her face, chatting up the locals. I stuck to the legal stuff of course.

While I was smoking away a man swam across the pool and handed me a magnum of champagne. I took it from him and swigged it back – it was all dripping down the side of my face but I didn't give a shit. I could see Danielle and the others looking at us and I could have sworn they seemed a bit jealous. They might have looked the part, but they weren't having half as much fun as I was. Calum Best was with them and when I got home I found out there was a story in one of the papers saying that I'd got off with him. I've never even kissed him, let alone had sex with him. Yes, he's a good-looking fella, but the main point is that he's been through the whole celebrity pack. Urgh!

I was missing my mum too. She's always been there to help me with the boys, but in the autumn of 2007 she had got all loved up with her new girlfriend Mel. I was pleased for her, and splashed out on an exotic holiday for the two of them. I thought it was the least I could do.

I'd also put a bit more of my money to good use – on my barnet. I saw pictures of me on holiday and realised I seemed as if I had a light bulb on my head, it was so stupidly blonde. So I put a few darker streaks in my hair, gradually moving back to my roots.

17
Jack's Back

I still loved Jack, though. And I knew I wouldn't be able to pretend for much longer. We'd been split up for a couple of months and I'd bumped into him a few times when I'd been out before, but this night was different. I was in Funky Buddha, absolutely plastered, and I spotted Jack in a corner. This time there was no abuse, and I could tell what was going to happen from the moment we clapped eyes on each other. We began flirting like mad. Admittedly, if anyone saw us they might think I was flirting just as much with the vodka bottle I was carrying around in my hand (classy!) but that night I just wanted Jack and no one else. We ended up leaving the club together and I slept with him that night.

After that I didn't want him to leave, as I realised how much I'd missed him. We lay in bed the following day and talked about our relationship. He told me how much he'd missed me and how he'd been working towards getting some club nights going so he could earn a bit of money as a promoter. And, at that point, hearing those words was enough for me. So we were a couple again.

And true to his word Jack got off his arse and started putting on events. I knew he wasn't going to be able to get a normal job, because it's hard when you've been on a TV show – people won't take you seriously in most other careers. Some might think that 'promoting' isn't a proper job, but Jack was earning good money in the end, sometimes raking in £2,000 a night. He and his mate Mark set up an evening called 'Last Request', which started in Essex but soon branched out into a couple of London clubs too. I was pretty proud of Jack and I couldn't knock him.

He acted like a bit of a good-luck charm to me for a while too. When we got back together we decided to go to a casino and Jack gave me £200 (who'd have thought it?). I had a bit of a flutter on the poker without much luck, so I tried roulette. I couldn't be bothered to try to be clever, so I put the whole lot on number 18 – that's how old Jack was when we first got together. He laughed at me for doing it, but 18 came up and I won £3,000. I couldn't believe it. I screamed the place down. We had an amazing night and, unsurprisingly, got very drunk.

When I'd split with Jack I'd been really careful not to make too much of a big deal of it to the kids because they were so fond of him. Whenever they asked where he was I replied, 'You know when you stay at Daddy's house and you miss your mum?' – and they nodded – 'Well, Jack's been missing his mum, so he's had to go back and stay there for a bit.' That was all they needed, but I knew they still pined for him.

After Jack and I got back together I took him with me in the car to pick Bobby up from school. And I've never seen Bobby smile so much in his life. He sat in the back of the car, grinning from ear to ear. It was so sweet. After a few minutes he leant over and whispered, 'Can we rock out now, Jack?' Jack simply nodded and then all of a sudden started shaking his head and jumping up and down in his seat. Bobby did the same and they didn't stop the whole way home.

What better way to celebrate getting back together than by embarrassing yourselves in front of the nation by dressing up as a poor man's Posh and Becks for a magazine? It was the funniest photo shoot I've ever done in my life. We were asked to recreate the raunchy images that Victoria and David Beckham had just done in their underwear for a fashion magazine called W. They'd been splashed all over the papers and billed as their sexiest shoot ever, and some of them were pretty steamy. So when we were asked I jumped at the chance – mainly because I like dressing up as other people. I would never have done something in my bra and knickers if I'd had to be me. But this was like playing a part.

Hmm. A car part.

Cut to me and Jack half-naked, sprawled across a car bonnet in the middle of Hackney on a pissy rainy day with locals walking past shouting, 'Put your clothes back on, dirty girl!'

I think they thought we were doing a porno shoot or something. I was in hysterics. I looked vile. But I thought it was brilliant.

Later we did another shoot dressed up as Amy

Winehouse and her husband Blake. I've always liked Amy and I found out not long ago that she's a fan of mine too. I used to live round the corner from her cousin, who told me that Amy used to watch me when I was in *Big Brother*. Her dad, Mitch, always talks to me whenever he sees me and he knows how I like singing so he was going to set it up so that me and her could have a singsong in her local pub, the Hawley Arms. But every time we'd arrange it some drama would occur (with her – not me for once!), so it never happened in the end. Mitch is wicked. He's what they call 'the salt of the earth'. I wish I had a dad like him. He'd say, 'My Amy loves you, gal, you'll be all right.' Not sure what she'd have thought of me dressing up as her, though – I looked like Bluto from Popeye with all those fake tattoos down my arms. But I don't care how stupid I look. I like it when I can take the piss out of myself and do something funny. It's been my dream to dress up as Miss Piggy while Jack plays Kermit the Frog – although for some odd reason no one bought that idea.

Bobby and Freddy have always loved the programme *Rosie and Jim* and had been going on about the boat they live on for ages. So one weekend I decided to treat them to a canal boat trip and my mate Jen came with us. Of course I didn't quite realise that once you're on the boat you're left to your own devices and that means steering the bloody thing yourself! I thought there was a man there to do it for you. We were so rubbish at going through the locks that Bobby would see one ahead and sigh, 'Oh no, not another lock, Mummy!' because he knew it was going to take us about an hour to fathom out how to get through it. We were so useless that we couldn't even manoeuvre the thing to a nice grassy verge for lunch.

Instead we ended up stopping under a dirty old railway bridge near a Chinese restaurant and went in and bought a greasy takeaway for lunch.

Talking of travelling, my life on the road hasn't got much better since I've got older either. Aside from being caught out for texting while driving and, another time, driving without a licence, I got pulled over for driving the wrong way down Oxford Street. But that was the direction my satnav had told me to go! The police even had to breathalyse me because they couldn't understand why someone would drive down a road that was clearly marked for buses and taxis. When I tried to protest that it was my satnav I think I saw one of the coppers suppress a smile. I'd made a mammoth mistake, as usual.

In spite of my string of driving offences I was still asked to do a show for ITV called *Call Me A Cabbie* where celebs have to learn how to be cabbies and drive the general public around while being filmed. I was over the moon at being asked to do it because it was the first proper bit of work I'd been offered since everything that had happened in *Celebrity Big Brother*. I did all the training – I got on really well with the cab driver who was teaching me and we had a real laugh – but then, just as we were about to start filming the show, the TV watchdog Ofcom brought out a report criticising Channel 4 over *Celebrity Big Brother*. This sent all the newspapers mad again and my name was brought up along with more negative coverage. Even before I got Sean's phone call I knew what all this meant for me. He told me, 'ITV have called and apologised but they feel it's not appropriate to use you on the show any more because of all the bad press surrounding you again at the moment.' I understood, but

I was devastated. I couldn't stop crying for days. I thought I was never going to get another chance again.

Even though I was struggling a bit for money, I've always wanted my family to have what I never could – no matter what it might cost. And this applied to Bobby and Freddy when it came to choosing what school they went to. As with most things in my life, though, it didn't come without a smattering of confrontation. I wanted to get Bobby into a private school called Oaklands, near where we live in Essex. It costs over two grand a term, but I was willing to put all my savings into giving my kids a good education.

Typically, there were a few people who didn't like the idea of me sharing the premises with their kids and a couple of mothers lodged complaints, which were then picked up by the newspapers. Someone said that they thought I would 'lower the tone and spell trouble', while one mum threatened to pull her kid out and there was even talk of a petition. Luckily it never got that far, though, and in an odd turn of events the *Sun* actually started to stick up for me and encouraged readers to support me against 'snobby mums'. It was a bit upsetting, and the paps started circling the school, which was probably one of the reasons some of the parents were against me being there in the first place. But it calmed down in the end and Bobby was accepted and started in September 2007.

I will never forget his first day. It makes me well up just thinking about it, he was so cute. I videoed him as he was getting dressed. 'How are you feeling, Bobby?' I asked.

'A little bit nervous ...'

Then there was a pause as I tried to stop the lump in my throat.

'Mummy?'

'Yes, darling?'

'I need to tell you something.'

'What is it?'

'I don't want you taking any pictures of me at the school gates.'

'Bobby! You can't say that to Mummy! You only have one first day at school. I need to get a photo so we can remember it!'

'Mum, I just don't want it.'

'Why not?'

'I just don't think it's cool.'

In the end I was virtually begging him to agree to a photo opportunity. But we had to just agree that I'd take photos of him outside the house in his uniform instead. I must've been snapping away for ages because he had to shout, 'That's enough now!'

It was so sweet seeing him in that uniform, he looked like a little man. Before we left he called to Freddy, who was standing at the bottom of the stairs completely naked as usual, 'Bobby's going to big school now,' and he leant over and kissed his little brother's head. 'Have a nice day!' said Freddy, waving, and we left him in the house with my mum.

I took Bobby into the classroom and could hardly hold back the tears. He sat down in his little chair and looked at me and said softly, 'You can go now, Mum. Don't cry. I'm going to be all right here.'

I walked away sobbing my eyes out.

I love the joys of being a mum because the stuff kids come out with is amazing. Bobby behaves like he's a miniature grown-up. It's genius. After he'd been at school a few weeks he came back, threw his bag on the floor and sighed really dramatically, 'Ooooh, I've had the worst day ever!'

I looked at him trying not to smile because this was obviously serious business and not to be laughed at. 'Why? What happened?'

He stared at me stony-faced. 'Yoga.'

'What?'

'What the hell is yoga, Mum?'

Yoga is one of the classes the kids get taught in the year above Bobby's, so I fathomed that he must've been told about it that day or had an introductory lesson. I tried to keep a straight face. 'Yoga relaxes you, Bobby. It's good for you.'

'I don't need relaxing.'

'It helps you stretch.'

'Stretching? Surely that's a girls' thing?'

'It helps you de-stress.'

'Mum!'

'What?'

'I'm only four years old. I'm more stressed that I'm doing yoga in the first place!'

I didn't know what to say – he had a fair point. And with that he ran upstairs and left me rolling about laughing. I don't know where he gets it from.

Bobby's big into his football – he goes to the David Beckham Academy in Greenwich every Saturday. He loves it there.

When we first moved to the house we're in now we were left with a couple of sheep on our plot of land. They're harmless enough, and I quite like having them there because it makes me feel all countrified. But Bobby had other ideas. One day he turned to me and said, 'Mum?'

'Yes, Bobby.'

'Just so you know, I don't want to be a farmer when I'm older.'

I started laughing. 'What?'

'I don't want to be a farmer – so let's get rid of the sheep, yeah?'

Then the other day he ran into the lounge and groaned, 'Aaargh! Keep Freddy downstairs, will you, Mum? I'm going upstairs to relax and don't want to be disturbed!'

Recently I had to go to a parents' evening at the school to check Bobby's progress. He's doing brilliantly and I'm so proud. He's definitely the most common little kid in that place, though. His mates are all so posh and well spoken, but he's a right little geezer. One of the mums told me that he's a heartthrob too. Apparently her daughter came home the other night and swooned, 'I love Bobby. I want to marry him. He's so cool.'

He is a bit of a dude actually – he's taken to wearing rock T-shirts and aftershave now. It's my fault really because I began spraying him with a little bit of Creed one day. But that's really expensive, so I tried weaning him off it and on to Versace Blue Jeans instead. He immediately told me it smelt 'odd' and insisted on a different one. He now has either Chanel Sport or Polo Black. He told me the girls love sniffing his neck!

18
Family Values

My children mean everything to me, but because of my stupid addiction to slimming pills a couple of years ago I've just about ruined every chance I had of becoming a mother again. I've fucked up my body so much that it's now irreparable (ironic really that I was once offered £2.2 million to be the face of a brand of slimming pills – which, thankfully, I turned down flat). Towards the end of 2007 I was interviewed on *Tonight with Trevor McDonald* about my addiction because I wanted to warn other women of the dangers. In my case, it had gone too far before I had a clue what slimming pills could do to you. Obviously there were critics saying it was just my way of trying to get back on the telly, but it honestly wasn't. I wanted to try to help people.

The harsh fact is that, because of my own actions, doctors have now told me that if I give birth again I could die. Until now I've been too scared to tell anyone about this. It's been well documented that I've had a series of collapses and had to be rushed to hospital, but no one has known the real reasons behind it. I suppose I just haven't wanted to accept it and hiding the truth makes it feel like it's not a reality. But every time I collapse I lose scary amounts of blood and it's happened so many times now that the doctors have warned me it's deadly serious. When I gave birth to Freddy in 2004 I was told that my blood loss was so extreme that there was a point when the surgeon thought he might have to take my womb out. I have blood cells that don't clot well and it makes me black out. It's fucking scary. And it was nearly fatal. I had to sign papers to say I was OK with my womb being removed in a life-or-death emergency, but thank God it's never come to that.

Just before the end of 2007 I'd been losing loads of blood again, so I went to see the doctor. By now I was used to this happening, so it almost seemed routine for me. It wasn't until I got there and the doctor sat me down that I realised how serious it was. I was told I'd had another miscarriage.

I hadn't even realised I was pregnant.

The doctor was really concerned. 'Jade, I have to strongly advise you not to try to have kids again, because if you do you're putting your own life at risk.'

I didn't speak about it afterwards. Not with my mum, not with Jack. No one. I didn't want to face it. When I'm scared of something I don't talk about it. I hide things. I have two beautiful kids, but that doesn't mean I don't want any more! I was devastated.

I always knew I was a high risk when I was pregnant, because Bobby and Freddy came a month early and I had to have blood transfusions with both of them. But now, because of all the mess caused by the slimming pills and so on, it's even worse.

Not only that but I've had a history of problems with my cervix. Even before I was sexually active, when I was 15, I had to have pre-cancerous cells burnt off and removed. And that nearly traumatised me for life, it was so painful. Earlier this year I was having all sorts of tests, one of which involved having another smear. And the abnormal cells had come back again. This was the fourth time I'd had to have the same operation now, even though it shouldn't happen – once you have them burnt off they shouldn't come back.

I was so scared.

It still doesn't seem real that I can't have more kids. I don't want to believe it. I didn't even cry back then because I didn't want to think about it.

I found all this out in one of my worst weeks ever because that was also the time when my little Freddy was diagnosed with a hernia.

My mum was staying at my house. Freddy adores her, and she's always the first person he calls for when he wakes up in the morning. That particular morning he'd shouted for her, 'Nan, I want to go for a wee!'

But when she took him into the bathroom she noticed that his groin was really swollen. I was so panicked. I didn't have a clue what it was. I rang the doctor and they said to see if it went down, and if it didn't to bring him in the following day. Whenever he lay down it seemed to disappear, but when he stood up it was there again. I immediately booked him in for the next day.

The day of Freddy's appointment I dropped Bobby off

at school and quickly nipped into Morrisons to get some shopping as we weren't due there until the afternoon. As I stood at the checkout my mum rang.

'Jade, you have to come home. Batman has ripped his whole paw off.'

'What? He's only a puppy! Shit.'

Mum had been cleaning out his cage and hadn't yet put his bedding back in, so as he'd climbed back in he'd cut the pad of his little paw on the metal of the cage. We had to rush him to the vet, who informed me that because he was only eight weeks old there was a chance he could die during the operation. I was beside myself.

Then I had to take Freddy to the doctor!

'It's a hernia,' the doctor said.

I started sobbing uncontrollably. He kept saying it was fine, and nothing to worry about, but no matter what he said he was talking about my baby.

There were paparazzi following me that day too. And when I got in the car to take Freddy home I was trying my hardest not to break down again, but I was sure my face looked swollen and red. I felt so upset and confused. I always related hernias with old people. I didn't know what was going on. In the end I could hardly see the road because I was sobbing so much. Freddy was oblivious to it all and sat humming happily in the back.

When I got into the house I ran straight past my mum to the toilet and threw up.

Although I've been told a zillion times now that Freddy's hernia isn't dangerous at the moment (it is only if it becomes painful or if it's still sticking out when he lies down), we still booked him into the hospital to get it removed.

Batman was all right too, thankfully. But how much can happen in one week, eh?

I've been in and out of the doctor's surgery most of my kids' lives. Every time I think there's something wrong with them I worry. But then I tell myself it's better to be safe than sorry. I remember taking Bobby to the hospital when he was a couple of months old because he had all these little spots on his cheeks and I was convinced he had acne! I took him to A & E in a right two and eight. 'Oh my God, I think he's got acne! What am I going to do?'

The doctor came over, took one look at Bobby and said, 'Miss Goody, your son has milk spots from having the bottle,' then laughed and sent me home.

19
Fat Chance

Although I lost a silly amount of weight from stress after *Celebrity Big Brother*, towards the end of the year it had crept right back up again. And then some. So I decided I needed to do something about it.

I've released three fitness DVDs in the past, the last one hitting the shops on the Boxing Day of 2005, a few days before I went into the *Celebrity Big Brother* house. And the release of this one, like everything else around that time of my life, had turned into another big hoo-ha. When I came out of the house I found I was facing another scandal aside from the racial allegations. Newspaper reports were saying that I'd cheated on the DVD and that my weight loss had been down to liposuction, not exercise. I was fuming at this. But as usual I only had myself to blame. You see, I have actually had liposuction before – I've just never come clean about it. I got it done at the same time as I had my boob job in 2005. After

Bobby was born I was desperate to get something done to my chest because I felt my tits had gone like saggy chicken fillets. I didn't want to look like Jordan with great big balloons. I just wanted my droopy bits to be filled out.

In the end I went from a 36C to a 36DD/E. And while I was at the clinic I had some lipo on my tum too. At the time, though, I didn't see the point in telling anyone about the lipo (even my agent, who wasn't best pleased when she found out later), but the real reason for that was because the bloody thing didn't work! I had it done on my waist to try to sort out my flabby belly but apparently I've got the kind of stretchy skin that it won't work on (there is a medical term for it but of course I can't remember it and wouldn't be able to spell it even if I could). So my body will never take to liposuction. The doctor who did it for me has now become a bit of a mate of mine, and he gives me cheap botox in my forehead, so I see him a few times a year. I'd known him for a while through a friend of mine and he gave me a really good deal.

Paps have seen me go to this clinic, so, when the story came out suggesting I'd had lipo before my DVD, one newspaper reporter found my doctor, who had just done my botox. The problem was, the same doctor does something called 'Smart Lipo' and when the paper clocked this they realised it was just what they were trying to prove I'd had done.

As soon as the article came out, the doctor rang me up in a panic, and he was so apologetic. 'Jade, I was asked if I did Smart Lipo on you and all I said was, "No comment."'

'Why didn't you just say no?'

'Because I wanted to get it out there that we did it in the surgery. I just thought it wouldn't hurt for PR. But, Jade, I'm so sorry.'

Part of the reason the paper had targeted him was also because he was Indian and they wanted to get his comments on the racism allegations.

'They were asking me all sorts of questions, Jade, and I told them you were a great girl and not racist in the slightest and that we'd been out together for a curry before. I also told them that you could not have achieved your figure by having Smart Lipo.'

Of course, because reporters choose to ignore the things they don't want to hear, none of this information ever made the paper. I was more upset because I'd sweated my flaming arse off for that fitness DVD – it was fucking hard work. And I was proud of the figure I'd got because of it. I felt fitter than I had in ages before I went into the *Celebrity Big Brother* house.

My boobs were starting to weigh me down now, though – in more ways than one. Because I'd lost weight they were starting to look silly and, no matter how small I got, there was this massive great pair of bazookas sticking out in front of me that made me look bigger than I was. I asked the doctor about getting them reduced, but he warned me I'd get really bad scarring. Apparently it's a much more complex operation than an enlargement, because they have to move your nipple and stuff.

I read somewhere that Jordan was going to sell her old implants on eBay. Who'd buy them? I don't think I'd even rustle up 50p for mine.

Every part of my body was getting floppy or droopy and I really needed to sort it pronto. Yet, although for years I've been saying I wanted to have a tummy tuck, I finally decided against quick fixes like that. I realised that my stretch marks were there because of my kids – it's like a constant reminder of them and I don't want that taken away from me. Also, having a tummy tuck would be like me sticking two fingers up to all my fans, as if to say, 'Do you know what? You've followed me with my weight problems through all the years but now I'm just going to do something you can't afford and pay to have all my lumps and bumps cut off.' And that wouldn't be fair.

So instead I enrolled myself into a two-week 'boot camp' to fight the flab. I'd never actually been told about it by anyone. I'd seen people going on about places like 'Brat Camp' on *The Jeremy Kyle Show*, so I just assumed there'd be something similar for fatties and searched 'fat camp' on the internet. I was surprised how many came up, but a lot of them were abroad. Finally I found one in Wales.

'You'll last two days,' laughed Jen. But I proved her wrong. I went with my mate Charlotte and it was bloody hardcore. On our first day we had a chat with a nutritionist called Marissa. The first thing she did was set a crisp alight. I watched in horror as it turned to oil and melted. 'Most crisps are practically pure fat,' she said. 'If you want to get a bonfire going, throw a load on.' That was scary. Then she poured my beloved fizzy drink into a glass bowl and threw in a penny, a tooth and a chicken bone. After just a day the penny was clean, the tooth had turned brown and the bone dissolved. 'Now think about what fizzy drink does to your insides,' said Marissa.

The rest of the week was a haze of 5.30am starts, jogging, lessons in nutrition and PE-type games led by army-style instructors. We had 12 hours of training a day. We climbed mountains, went on 15-mile hikes, boxed, played rugby and football, did squats, lunges and sit-ups. All we got to eat for breakfast was porridge and water with a single raspberry and a cup of yukky green tea. All fatty food was banned, along with alcohol and too much caffeine. Instead we had to eat chicken salads, omelettes, grilled fish and fruit. There were no weights used in the exercises – instead we had to lift bricks!

On my third day, when we tried abseiling, I burst into tears and said I couldn't continue, but everyone cheered me on and I ended up loving it. I even won a 'Best Rugby Tackle' certificate after dumping one of the male instructors in the mud. We had to do a night-time orienteering trek crossing a river using a makeshift bloody bridge. At one point I thought I was being sent to my death, it was so fucking intense. By the end of the week I'd also jumped off a 40-foot cliff into a waterfall. Apparently the fear you feel doing this makes you lose calories, but to me the theory sounded like a load of crap.

Admittedly, I lost just under two stone in two weeks through training solidly, going on those long hikes and eating ant-like portions. I was even seeing double at times because I was so dizzy from exhaustion. By the second week I was close to breaking point. It got so bad one day that me and Charlotte made out to one of the organisers that we had to go out for colonic irrigation because we were in such pain, but we got a cab to the nearest sushi restaurant instead. I've never eaten so quickly in my life. Then we started fretting that the organisers would smell fish on our fingers when we got back, so we grabbed the mints you're given on your way out and started crushing them up and rubbing them all over our hands to disguise the stench. We must've looked like we were losing the plot.

I have to say I felt great when I got home. I don't think

I've looked so feisty-fit in my life. I was a size 16 before and I now I was a 10. I'd dropped six and a half inches from my waist, five and a half inches from my hips, three inches from my boobs and three inches from each thigh. Jack couldn't believe it and the boys ran around shouting: 'Look at skinny Mummy!' I felt so proud of myself and immediately ran to the wardrobe to put on this titchy pair of size-ten trousers that I'd bought from Zara on a whim and had been hiding in the back of the wardrobe for yonks. When I first got them I was living in cloud cuckoo land, thinking they would fit one day, but now they did. What a feeling!

As soon as I was home I decided to enrol the help of my old personal trainer Kevin Adams. Kevin was the first person charged to get me fit when I came out of the original *Big Brother* house back in 2002. I remember when I first met him he scared the hell out of me. You're a big black man with the biggest eyes I've ever seen in my life, was my first thought. And he was so strict. I'd be on the treadmill shouting, 'I feel sick,' and he'd shout, '*Keep running!*' and I'd be wheezing, 'I can't! I'm going to faint.' '*Keep running!*' I had to do it every day and it was awful.

To be honest, I didn't pay much attention to all this exercise lark with Kevin and the call of the shops was often too much for me to resist. This meant that, instead of turning up at the crack of dawn like I was supposed to, I'd often spend the morning shopping and getting my nails done, which meant I'd be really late for training. I'd arrive laden with shopping bags and Kevin would shout at me, 'You're not taking this seriously!' He got so pissed off once that he phoned John Noel and said he'd pull out if I didn't make more of an effort.

This time round he nearly fainted at my discipline. He's

no less of a task master nowadays but I accept I need someone who'll shout at me (mainly so I don't feel guilty when I shout and scream back). We were doing all sorts – speed walking, jogging, sprinting – and I even did ridiculous chin-ups on trees! We still argued loads, just like we did the first time. But Kevin seems to thrive on me answering back and it makes him more determined to break me. I need someone who wants to boss me about otherwise I'll walk all over them.

We do most of our training outside because it's nicer than being in a sweaty, stuffy gym, but this means there are plenty of opportunities for paps to hide in bushes and capture me wheezing and straining. *Heat* has printed several pictures of me looking mighty ugly on a training session. I didn't realise I was capable of pulling such contorted faces!

After a while I found I wasn't even tempted to raid Bobby and Freddy's sweet cupboard. And that, believe me, was a miracle.

Scarily, Jack and I sat down and worked out that in one year alone we'd spent thousands of pounds on takeaways – we were having them at least three times a week. My mates would call me 'the Bear' because I'd been so big. Mind you, one of them had the nickname 'the Tank', and I don't think I'd have been quite so happy with that one!

So I was trim at last. I felt better than I had in months. And I was ready to face anything. Including Danielle Lloyd.

I'd like to be able to say that now the dust had settled on *Celebrity Big Brother*, Danielle and I were back on speaking terms. But that would be a lie. In fact tensions couldn't have got worse between us. It seems like fame has really changed her.

In December 2007 Embassy opened a sister club in Abu Dhabi and Jack and I were lucky enough to get an invite. Loads of celebs were there, including Danny Dyer and Simon Webbe, who used to be in Blue (I love that man – he's one of the nicest fellas in showbiz, although that's not exactly hard considering most of the others are knobs). Unfortunately, Danielle was also on the guest list. But Mark Fuller, the owner, is my mate and I wasn't going to let anything spoil his night. He'd paid for everyone to be there – flown us all out on a private jet and put us all up in a seven-star hotel (I didn't even know there was a seven-star rating!).

When Jack and I arrived we spent the day by the pool drinking cocktails and feeling like royalty. Then evening came and we were all treated to a banquet of a meal (which must've cost Mark a fortune). Danielle certainly seemed to be enjoying the luxury!

Then it was the opening of the nightclub. And I was so happy for Mark. Before everyone starting arriving he took me for my own private guided tour and I could see he was so proud of what he'd achieved. He pointed to one of the VIP areas and said, 'That's where I want most of you guys to sit if possible, so we can get some photos for the press.' Then he paused and looked at me. 'Will that be OK? I know there's been a bit of tension between you and Danielle ...'

'Of course, I'm here for you, Mark. I'll do whatever you want me to.'

Slowly everyone started spilling in. Danielle was typically late. I stood with the others getting our pictures taken and everything was going according to plan. I started chatting to this girl called Rachel who was Miss Great Britain at the time, and I thought she was a nice girl. Then Danielle swanned in with Danny and Tamer. They headed straight to the VIP area, so after a nod from Mark I followed with Jack and Rachel so we could all get some photos done with them. But as soon as we arrived Danielle's whole group stood up and sat in a different area.

When they changed places I felt like a right idiot. But I knew Mark wanted publicity photos, so I walked over to where they were again. To my disbelief Danielle started to get up one more time, so I leant over and said, 'Have you got a problem, Danielle?'

Suddenly she was all sweetness and light. 'No Jade, I don't have a problem with you, why would I?'

'Danielle, Mark has paid for you and everyone else to be here so we can promote his new club. The least you can do is have a picture taken with the rest of us.'

'I'm not going to do that, Jade.'

At that I gave up and walked off. Maybe she wasn't happy because I'd brought along my own paparazzi photographers. But the truth was Mark had asked us all to bring our own snappers so that he could maximise coverage in the UK press with our different contacts.

I was so upset. I rushed right out of the club and went back up to my room in the hotel. As I sat on the bed I couldn't hold back the tears.

Jack had followed me upstairs and he said, 'Jade, don't let anyone ruin your night. Just remember what Mark is to you. He's your friend and this is his event. Come back downstairs with me and we'll show them all that they're not going to win over you.'

It took some persuasion but finally I thought, you know what – you're right. So I went back down to the club, determined to have a good time. In the end I had great fun – I was laughing and joking with people all night, and Danielle ended up leaving early.

But that little episode didn't spoil my whole holiday. I loved Abu Dhabi. One day Jack and I went for a camel ride down the beach, which was really romantic. The camels didn't smell like I thought they would. These ones were posh, more like racehorses (they obviously had seven-star camels out there too).

When I got back to the hotel that night I was really red-faced. I remembered I'd left my dirty knickers lying around the room and the butler was in there folding them up into a neat pile. The shame!

20
Friends and Fun

Towards the end of 2007 I found myself with a surprising new friend. A nice one this time. I was on holiday in Dubai when I got a call from Sean.

'Jade, the Prince of Brunei wants to meet up with you.'

'The Prince of Brunei? Are you having a laugh? What does he want with me?'

'The Prince of Brunei – Prince Azim's his name – he's one of the richest men in the world and he wants to meet you.'

I was convinced someone was playing a joke on me at first, but apparently he'd read about me and liked me. So a few days later I headed to his mansion in Kensington, along with Jack and Sean (he wanted to come along for a nose around, I think). A butler opened the door and we stood in the hallway staring open-mouthed at this massive chandelier and jewelled furniture dripping and glittering around us. We were ushered into another room where I saw a few other people just hanging about chatting. It was like a nightclub in there.

A few minutes later I heard this high-pitched voice calling, 'Jade! Hi! Lovely to meet you!'

I looked behind me to see this short, young-looking boy with spiky black hair, that had glitter spray in it, wearing trousers with tassels hanging off them. One leather-gloved hand was waving madly at me and the other hand flashing the biggest diamond ring I've ever seen in my life.

'You're amazing!' he cried. 'I've read about you, I love you. Come on, let's go and party!'

I warmed to Azim instantly. This is going to be a wicked night, I was thinking. He was such a character – everything he did and said made me laugh.

'I thought you were going to be a posh snob or something,' I said.

'Oh, only when I have to be like that! I'm just normal really!' he answered with a wink.

With that he took me on a tour of the house, which was the most surreal experience in the world. Normal was not the word. One room was full of photos of Azim and virtually every celebrity under the sun. There was Johnny Depp, Michael Jackson ... everyone. My mouth was on the floor.

'I can introduce you to all these people, Jade,' he said excitedly. 'They're cool! They're my friends!'

We went out for a Chinese meal, along with everyone who was in the house when I arrived. There must have been about 20 of us sitting at the dinner table.

'Do you know all these people?' I whispered to Azim.

He shrugged. 'Not all of them, no.'

'I'm going to say this to you, but please don't be

offended,' I said, leaning towards him. 'I think most of them are cling-ons. They're using you because of who you are. You want to be careful.'

He looked at me and sighed, 'Oh, Jade, why do you have to point out the nasty truth?'

Azim's sister and his best friend Naz were there, and they looked at me and smiled in agreement. I don't think there are many people who actually tell it to Azim like it is, and it made me a bit sad for a second to think that someone so lovely has to put up with leeches sucking up to him just because of his fame or fortune. He didn't seem the person to let anything bother him, though. He's a good-time party boy and that's just what he wanted to do that night.

We headed to a club in the West End called Aura, which for some bizarre reason is one of his favourite places. It's quite glitzy in there but certainly not what I'd say was fit for a prince! He was ordering drink after drink while we sat there surrounded by the club's security men and his own bodyguards. Then the bill arrived and he wasn't looking, so I paid. He didn't know I was doing it, but I just really wanted to show my appreciation and let him know that I liked him for who he was rather than for what he could get for me. It came to about £1,500 (not the cheapest night I've ever had, but there you go). When Azim found out I'd footed the bill he went a little bit mad. 'You shouldn't be paying for things, Jade! That's not right!'

But I explained that I wanted to because now he was a friend of mine. He seemed so taken aback that he took his ring off – the whopping great diamante number I'd spotted earlier (although, to be quite frank, you'd have to be blind not to notice it) – and handed it to me! 'I want you to have this, Jade,' he said seriously.

'I can't take that! I honestly don't want your ring, Azim.'

I was embarrassed, but he wasn't having any of it, and was actually starting to look offended. In the end Naz and Azim's sister begged me to take it from him to keep the peace. 'All right, I'll take it,' I said. 'But tomorrow I'm going to give it back to you.'

Immediately, in a grand gesture, he turned his back and shouted, 'I don't want it back!'

I looked down at my new bling possession. It was a joke! It had baguette diamonds that spread virtually the length of my whole hand. I couldn't take my eyes off it. And true to his word I've still got it. I don't know what it's worth to this day because I haven't had it valued – it seems rude somehow. But I've got it locked away somewhere very safe, believe me (and it's not in my house, in case any scallies are reading this and get any bright ideas).

After the club we all went back to Azim's pad, where he began jumping around like a big kid, getting all excited. 'You can all stay the night!' he said, pointing to the 20 or so rooms upstairs. 'In the morning we can stay in our pyjamas and watch movies all day!'

'Azim, that sounds lovely but I have to get home. I've got a babysitter looking after my children.'

'Don't worry, we'll get a cab sent to them and the babysitter can come with them in the car and they can all come here and watch Disney films!'

'I can't, honestly. I have to take them to a park tomorrow.'

He was so upset, bless him. Life is just one big entertainment show for him and he wants everyone to be a part of it.

That night I was wearing a wig. It looked like my real hair only glossier and fuller, even though I'd got it from Brick Lane for just 20 quid. I'd started to wear it in tribute to a little girl with alopecia who'd been writing to me. When she first told me she was going for a wig fitting it had coincided with me being on some TV show, so I'd worn it then so that she could see it. I'd even attempted to start a charity for kids with alopecia called 'Wiggy Wednesday', but it hadn't taken off. It's much harder than you'd think trying to set up a charity.

Anyway, I told Azim it wasn't my real hair and took it off, which really amused him. He took it from me and wore it round the house while doing impressions of various celebrities. I was crying with laughter, he was so funny. After giving the wig back he disappeared upstairs and returned with wet hair. When I asked him why, he told me that whenever he gets drunk he has to wash his hair straight away before going to bed. He said that one night he didn't do it and woke up with a rash on his face because of all the glitter from his hair that was left on the pillow.

By now I was stupidly pissed, and it was only a matter of time before Calamity Jade struck in full force. We were all dancing around, when I fell backwards and bashed into a table. As I recovered myself I shouted, 'It's all right, don't worry,' and I looked at my hand, which was clutching this jewel-encrusted flower. In slow motion I realised, to my horror, that the flower was meant to be attached to the table, not to me. It was covered in rubies, diamonds ... and God knows what. My heart leapt to my mouth. 'Azim – have I broken your table?'

He glanced across casually. 'Oh, it doesn't matter, Jade.'

'Shit, it must be worth about 50 grand!'

'Oh no,' he said. 'Probably a couple of hundred grand, but it's nothing.'

I was in a right state. 'Oh my God, I feel sick! Oh God, what do I do? Please – are you going to make me pay?'

'Don't be stupid. We'll get it fixed,' he shrugged as if I'd just spilt water on his shoe.

He was so cool about it. But you won't be surprised to learn that Jack, Sean and I scarpered back home not long after that.

Luckily, my near destruction of a prized possession doesn't seem to have put Prince Azim off being my mate. He texts me asking what I'm up to and we've been out a few times since. At the moment he's studying in London (supposed to be, anyway) and when the papers reported we'd been hanging out together I think his father went a bit mad because he thought I wasn't the sort of person his son should be mixing with. There was one picture in particular that upset his dad, where I was walking in front of Azim, holding his hand. And apparently when you're royalty you're not supposed to behave like that, and the person you're with should always hang back and walk behind you out of respect. Azim stuck up for me, though, and said it wasn't going to make any difference to our friendship.

He's so happy all the time – it's infectious and great to be around. He'll send me little messages saying things like, 'Hi, girl, how are you? What are you up to? Come out to play soon!' and he's always got stories about one celebrity or another. Mariah Carey once invited him to her birthday party but he couldn't make it, so he flew her a diamond-and-platinum necklace worth £2.4 million in one of his private jets! And you know how I love Mariah. I nearly choked when I found out he was friends with her. That's one woman I want to meet.

I looked in his phone and the amount of famous people he has in there is like a who's who in Hollywood. Michael Jackson actually called him up while I was at his house one day! Azim was so 'whatever' about it too. 'Hi, Michael, what've you been up to? When are you coming over?' They were chatting away for ages. Azim said that he thinks Michael would love me and that when he gets drunk he's the best character ever because he's really funny. Now that I have to see!

Azim's studies will be finished soon and he's managed to bag himself a part in one of the episodes of *Ugly Betty* and says he wants to take me with him over there. I might seriously consider it (maybe I could give Ugly Betty a run for her ugly money).

Every time I go out with the prince – and that sentence is still one I never thought I'd write – I always offer to pay my way, but it's always refused. One night we were out with Naz and Azim's sister, and Naz was dancing around throwing her Louis Vuitton bag about the place. She kept leaving it on the side while she went to the loo, putting it on a seat while she danced, really not looking after it at all – just like most girls when they're pissed on a night out. But when the bill arrived at the end of the evening (it came to £5,550!) Naz insisted on paying. I thought Azim's sister would have a credit card or get cash from one of her security guys, but instead she reached into her Louis Vuitton bag and I was nearly sick. She pulled out wad after wad of cash – all in £50 notes – and I even had to hold a candle so she could see to count the money. You were just chucking that bag about all over the place, I kept thinking. Anyone could have nicked it!

Fucking hell. These people lived in another world.

Unfortunately I did pick up one habit from them, though – a taste for Cristal champagne. Not really ideal when it costs around £3,000 a pop.

Christmas time was coming and, considering what had happened over the last year, I was so looking forward to putting a line under the whole lot and trying to start again. There was loads of press speculation that Jack and I were going to get married but we both knew we weren't anywhere near it at this stage. I didn't want to find a big sparkler under my Christmas tree. In fact, I'd have been very unhappy if I'd seen a little ring box. I'd told Jack I wanted to be proposed to on my own special day, not someone else's. This year I was just happy we were back together, and that we'd be waking up treating the kids. A sloppy kiss would do me fine. Jack offered to buy me a microwave for Christmas, which I thought was particularly romantic (that was a joke). In fact, I was bloody furious when he suggested it. I think it was his way of saying that he wanted me to start cooking. Hmm.

Then I was asked by a magazine if they could come round to mine and take pictures of me cooking Christmas dinner. Luckily they gave me cookery lessons beforehand, and when they saw the results the crew nearly fainted (not from food poisoning either, before you say anything). I was quite good! Move over, Nigella Wilson! (At least that's what I told them until they informed me her surname was actually Lawson.)

The boys wrote their letters to Santa. They'd seen a

really cool computer gadget that they could draw with – it even plugs into the TV and displays their artwork. I told them with a wink that Santa might well be bringing them one of those but that they knew they were only allowed five presents each as he has so many children around the world to make presents for. I'd be lying if I said I didn't spoil them, though. As far as I'm concerned, Christmas is the one time I get to go really overboard. And they truly are good boys. Every year they have to give away a sack of toys to a charity shop to make room for the new ones and I've never heard them moan about it once.

We always have two Christmas trees. The boys get their own to decorate with the stuff they make. I get a real one too, which I put classy decorations on, and that's the only one anyone sees when they first enter the house!

You might remember in my last book I spoke about my grand ideas about breaking into Hollywood. Well, it might still seem like a silly dream to some people but it's still what I'd like to do more than anything. In fact, if I could uproot and escape to America now without disturbing the kids' lives, I would, because I feel like I could start a new life there without anyone knowing who I was or judging me for the mistakes I've made in the past. Drama was one of the only subjects I was good at when I was at school, and I got an A plus for it. The problem is, no one will take me seriously enough to find out that I'm actually any good. People may laugh when I say I want to be an actress but everyone has a talent and I truly believe that mine is being a great performer. As you may recall, I won *Celebrity Stars in Their Eyes* back in 2006! I can do accents too. If I rang you up and put on a different voice there's no way in hell you'd know it was me. I can do posh (upper class, that is, not Victoria Beckham), Jamaican, African, Irish and cockney. I know I'm not bright but I'm actually very good at remembering lines too, especially when under pressure, and that's when I perform best.

Are you hearing me, Kenneth Branagh?

Since meeting Samuel L. Jackson on a flight to LA a few years ago – he shocked the life out of me because he knew my name and said, 'Well, hello there, Miss Goody!' (what a flight that was! I sat near to Kate Moss and Orlando Bloom on that trip) – I've had the pleasure of bumping into him again. What's even nicer is that it's been since *Celebrity Big Brother* and he doesn't seem to have changed his opinion of me. I can't remember where I was – it must've been the set of a TV show or something – but he said hello, asked how I was and started enquiring about what I wanted to do next.

'I want to act!' I declared.

'Well then, you should, girl,' he smiled. 'When you're in LA make sure to look me up!' and with that he walked off.

I love America. I went to New York with the girls recently. Jack stayed at home with the kids and we had a real girly one – I took Jen, Kel and Caroline as a treat. One night we went out to the Buddha Bar and I decided to buy a bottle of Cristal for £3,000 (yes, I am officially mental, but I blame Prince Azim for my expensive tastes) and when it arrived I couldn't believe it because I had my own bodyguard! It was brought to me in this amazing ornate case, and I was immediately given a table in the club, because they clearly thought, This girl must be famous as she's spending some serious dollars. The bodyguard actually followed me when I went to the toilet. I felt like Britney Spears.

Considering what had happened to my barnet that day, I was looking pretty like Britney Spears too – when she had her head shaved, that is.

Rewind to a few hours earlier to when I'd discovered what I thought would be my new favourite beauty salon. I'd found it up some stairs in a shop and thought it was so quirky – the women working there were mad and loud – and I immediately told the girls we had to try it. So we all booked appointments to get our hair done ready for our big night out. Except when we got there we found out they'd slightly overbooked, so there weren't enough hairdressers for all of us. I was unfazed, though. 'I'll wash your hair,' I announced to Caroline, and then Jen agreed to wash mine while we waited for someone to dry it.

Meanwhile, we looked over to where Kelly was having hers blow-dried straight. Or so she thought. Her hair is naturally curly so it takes a lot to get it looking sleek, but the woman who was doing her hair just seemed to be making it bigger and bigger and bigger. Jen and I couldn't help ourselves – we were crying with laughter. It turned out the lady who was drying Kel's hair didn't even work there! She was a friend of the salon and had popped in and seen that they were understaffed so offered her (not very good) services!

While Kel was getting a balloon hairdo, I sat in the chair for my turn, and luckily my hairdresser seemed to know what she was doing. Before she began I told her that I had extensions in (this time I was back to a brunette, having moved on from the Miss Piggy look at last). 'Be careful with it,' I warned. 'When you blow-dry it make sure you don't put it on the hottest setting.'

She was a Thai lady and didn't speak any English but she seemed to understand what I meant, and nodded. As she started drying my hair I was pretty pleased with how it was turning out. Then suddenly she said, 'All done, all done!'

I reached to feel the back of my head and nearly fell off my chair in shock. Some of my hair had been burnt off and I had other bits sprouting out all over the place!

Now it was the girls' turn to fall about laughing.

'You've burnt my hair!' I shouted.

She shrugged. 'It's fake!'

'But I told you it was fake! And I told you to be careful!'

She just looked at me blankly. I still paid her, though, I was too polite not to. But when I gave her the cash she looked at me in disbelief. 'No tip?'

'You think I'm going to give you a tip for burning my hair?'

We all left that place looking a right mess. Kel had hair like a thatched cottage. Jen had ended up with a third of a manicure because the girl had started filing all her nails away so much Jen had begged her to stop. And Caroline still had wet hair because, after all she'd seen in that salon from hell, she'd been too petrified to get it blow-dried. We got back to the hotel, trying to get dolled up for our night out, and all I could see were burnt patches on the back of my head. But I had to laugh. What was the point of getting upset? Instead I tried to focus on my outfit, and I pulled out the silk dress I was planning to wear. I had spent a ridiculous amount of money on this dress and had only worn it once before. But when I put

Above: Me and Jack being whisked away in a helicopter to a secret hotel in the country. We were both very excited!

Below: Entering the *Celebrity Big Brother* house. Jack and I entered first. Mum followed a few minutes after.

One of my lowest points. I hardly got to see my kids after my eviction from the *Celebrity Big Brother* house – I wasn't in a fit state and it was considered unsafe – and when I did there were always police around.

The couple of hours I did get to play with my boys meant the world to me.

My trip to India. It wasn't intended as a PR stunt, but somehow the press got wind of where I was going and I was hounded by journalists and photographers everywhere I went. It was totally mental – there were people everywhere!

Above: A press call my agent arranged because we were approached by so many people wanting to ask me questions.

Below: One of the beautiful temples I saw on my trip. © *Matrixphotos.com*

Above left: My best mates Kelly and Jen. They've both really stuck by me over the past couple of years.

Above right and below: In Norfolk with Jack and the boys. After leaving The Priory I was desperate to escape from everything that was going on and Jack's uncle's house in the country was the perfect place for us to have some quiet time together as a family.

Getting into the Easter spirit at an Easter party I organised at Bobby and Freddy's old school.

© *Matrixphotos.com*

Above left: Out and about with one of my wigs on. I love wearing wigs. I just think it's great to be able to change your hairstyle anytime you like.

Above right: With Perez Hilton, the queen of celebrity blogging.

Below: Trying my hand at being a London cabbie.

© *Matrixphotos.com*

it on it was like I was trying on a child's party costume. My mum had taken it upon herself to wash it for me and it had shrunk – completely.

So not only did I have burnt hair, I now had a dress that would barely fit a chimpanzee. But I was still determined to go out. This was New York and no amount of burnage or shrinkage was going to stop me.

I marched into the bathroom.

When I hadn't emerged after five minutes the girls poked their heads around the door.

'Jade. What are you doing?'

I was hacking at my hair with nail scissors, trying to tidy up the burnt bits – which to them looked as if I'd lost my marbles and was doing a Britney Spears to my head!

Afterwards, of course, my hair was worse than when it began. I put it up, it looked awful. I tried to put a hat on and looked like a mental patient. Oh, fuck it, I thought, and left it as it was.

So there we were, about an hour later, sitting in the Buddha Bar looking like a group of misfits, with me deciding to forget my worries by blowing three grand on some Cristal! We had such a great time. And having a bodyguard for the night made up for whatever state my hair was in.

It was an expensive night, and I woke up the next day with a seven-grand hangover.

On that trip I'd also paid for us all to go to a Knicks game at which I bought the T-shirt, the hat and the 80-foot hot dog to go worth it. If I was going to a basketball match I was going to do it properly. I'm sure I cheered for both teams because I kept getting confused about who was scoring, but I didn't care. I loved it.

As well as my newfound love for expensive alcohol, I've started to become a bit of a tattoo addict (but don't worry, I'm not quite in the same league as David Beckham yet). Back home, I was bored one day and found myself in a local tattoo parlour getting three red hearts inked on to my inner arm. I decided they were to represent Bobby, Freddy and me (although I told Jack at the time that he was the third one). I've also long been a bit of a fan of semi-permanent make-up – back when I had Ugly's I used to get my eyebrows tattooed on (which gave a few people a bit of a shock when I first saw them) – and now I've had my eyeliner tattooed on and also some lip liner. It doesn't look as drastic as it sounds, though, and to me it makes perfect sense because that way you wake up in the morning looking as fresh as you did the night before (and I can do with all the help I can get when it comes to my appearance at that time of day).

I've even done a course in tattooing myself, although for some reason none of my mates are jumping at the chance to let me get to work on their face. I'm in partnership with a mate of mine named Julie who's got a salon in Loughton in Essex called Femme Fatale. It's more of a silent partnership this time (if it's possible for Jade Goody to ever be silent) but now I've done the course it means I can go there and have my own clients if I want to. We're also thinking of branching out with another salon purely for men called Homme Fatal.

Whenever I want to try out a new product it's usually my mum who's nominated as the guinea pig, whether she likes it or not. She's like a little doll that I can play around with sometimes. One of the funniest moments was when I tested out on her a new fake tan I'd been sent. She was going out that evening (good timing, Jade) and she saw me open the post and take out this spray tan. 'What's that, Jade?' she asked.

'Come here, Mum, let's see if it works. Let me give you a nice glow because you're going out.'

'What?'

I dragged her to the bathroom and made her stand on the wooden slats on the floor. 'Stay still and I'll spray you.'

I was in fits of laughter because every time I asked her to move to the left she moved right and then when I had to spray her sides she couldn't hold her left arm up because of the accident, so I had to hold that in the air while trying to get the tan even. She was laughing too. But we were in a right pickle. And because I didn't put a towel on the floor the colour was going everywhere it shouldn't, including all over the bottom of her feet. Which, as fake-tanners are well aware, is a complete no-no. Her hands were bright orange too. It was a disaster.

She was looking down at herself in horror. 'What am I going to do? Look at me!'

I was rolling around on the floor in fits of giggles. But as much as she scrubbed her feet, the stains wouldn't come off.

'Jade! What am I going to do?'

'I've got some exfoliator,' I said, wiping away the tears. 'Let's try that.'

It didn't work.

I went to look for something else to remove it, but by the time I'd come back Mum had taken it upon herself to stand in the bath and spray Domestos (yes, you heard right – that's hardcore toilet bleach we're talking about here) – on to the soles of her feet.

'Mum, you can't do that. It's bleach!'

'It'll get it off, though!'

Well, it got it off all right. Along with most of her skin. By the time she was done her feet were red raw and covered in blisters.

It was one of those priceless moments that can only happen with my mum. She still managed to go out that night, but God knows how she walked anywhere. I did try to suggest that she soak her feet in vodka (well, I thought it would numb the pain!) but she didn't listen to me for some reason.

I like to make Mum do things. I dare her because it makes me chuckle. I'll often stand in the kitchen with an array of different food and say stuff like, 'If you eat this I'll give you a fiver.'

It's always things I know she won't like too. Like me, she hates ketchup – for some reason we both have a phobia of it, and it makes us cringe – so I'd do things like mix up a bowl with ketchup and mustard or something. 'I'll pay you five quid to eat this, Mum!' She'll shake her head. So I'll up the dollar. 'I'll give you a tenner.' Still no. Eventually she'll have a price, though, and to see her nearly puke when she's trying to put some rank concoction in her mouth is hilarious. I gave her a drink once that she thought was orange juice, but it was orange, sugar and pepper. I love her reactions – she pulls faces like a little kid and it makes me laugh so much.

Talking of laughs, Jeremy Beadle, the famous prankster, died at the beginning of 2008. Now you might wonder why the heck I'm mentioning it here, but there's a very good reason. I was chosen by the *Sun* to be the victim of the last-ever 'Beadle prank' in their two-page tribute to him. And, although at the time I fell for it hook, line and sinker and it gave me the fright of my life, in the end I was so chuffed that I'd been the person they'd chosen to play the trick on. It seemed to symbolise that they'd forgiven me somehow.

It was about 9.30am when I heard a buzz at my security gates. It was two policeman (who were really actors, but I didn't know that), then there was a guy (who was actually a *Sun* journalist) who they said was their driver, and another guy (also from the *Sun*) dressed in a fluorescent jacket. I let them in through the gates and opened the door in my pyjamas – no bra again – holding my boobs to stop them wobbling.

'What's all this about?' I asked. 'Is there a problem?'

'You might want to go and put a coat on,' said one of the officers, so I went inside and grabbed a Puffa jacket and put on a pair of Ugg boots.

'Do you want to come in?' I asked. I didn't have a clue what they wanted from me.

'No, it's best we talk out here because it's regarding your car.'

'What?'

They asked me if I owned the Bentley in my driveway and said they had to do a few 'routine checks'. How long had I had it? How much did it cost me? Where did I get it from? I began to get worried.

'Don't tell me I've bought a stolen car. It's not one of them cars that's been stuck together with another one, is it?'

One of the policemen, who said his name was DI Dickens, looked at me sternly and asked, 'Are you familiar with the term "cut and shut"?'

The colour drained from my face, and I squealed, 'Oh no!'

They then proceeded to tell me that my car was evidence in an international investigation involving a ruthless gang in Bulgaria, and I had to hand over my keys.

Another policeman then radioed for a lorry to reverse up my drive and I had to quickly clear the car boot, which was full of fancy-dress outfits belonging to the boys.

I was shitting myself. What had I got into? I didn't know I had a dodgy car. Did that mean I was in trouble? I was panicking. I didn't have any paperwork and I didn't know where the car was being taken.

As the mechanics jumped from the lorry and prepared to load the car on and take it away, I held my head in my hands in despair.

Then, all of a sudden, the guy who'd said he was the driver jumped out with a massive mocked-up cover of the *Sun* with the headline 'Jade Goody, You've Been Beadled!'

I shrieked, 'For God's sake, I'm nearly having a heart attack.'

But my distress soon turned to relief and I burst out laughing. 'Oh my God. I just spent all that money on the car, £135,000. I've only had it three days. I'm still shaking!'

I'd totally fallen for it.

'Where did you get the police uniforms?' I asked. 'I can't believe I gave you the keys. I was in my pyjamas. I had to clear all the kids' stuff out of the boot. I was shaking, I felt sick. I thought I was a suspect in a crime. I didn't know what to do. I was about to phone the car dealer and go mad!'

I read in the paper afterwards that they'd spoken to Jeremy Beadle's co-host from *Game For a Laugh*, Henry Kelly, who said, 'He'd have found it very funny. It's a wonderful tribute to him.'

What's more, they'd videoed the whole thing and put it up on the *Sun* website. It's very funny. And all in all I found it a huge compliment.

Mind you, some may say I'm usually asking for trouble. One day when I dropped Bobby off at school I was in a rush because we were late (typically). I was in such a flap that I'd left the car unlocked, with my handbag in the passenger seat. Clever, huh? Lo and behold, when I returned it had gone, so I had to go to the police, who virtually rolled their eyes at me in a 'Not again, Miss Goody' kind of way. I had about £700 quid in it, plus it was a designer handbag – one of those Thomas Wylde skull bags – worth about a grand and I had untold amounts of expensive make-up in there (which was what I was most bothered about out of the lot). What an idiot.

When you lose money you have to go back out there and try to make it again. And my latest venture is G. I. Jade, a fit camp that was inspired by my intense workout fortnight at the end of 2007. But this one was going to be different. The boot camp I'd been on was hardcore but it didn't always maintain results. We'd been virtually starving ourselves when we were there and when we came out we were advised to buy the meals they'd been giving us in order to maintain our weight loss. This consisted of a box full of packet food which cost £250 a month. That seemed expensive to me. So I was determined to offer something to people that was a bit more realistic. With that in mind I've set up a new company with my business partner, Nelam – she's tried loads of diets like me in the past, most of which haven't worked – and we've really researched the market properly. She worked in Ugly's for a bit, which is how I met her, and now she has three salons of her own. She's a really successful lady and she's really well known in the beauty industry.

We've hired a mansion with baths, a swimming pool, Jacuzzis – all the pampering essentials I didn't get in Wales – so that people can feel like they get a bit of a treat at the end of a hard day's slog. The point I want to get across is that crash diets don't work – only about one person in 100 sheds weight permanently from that sort of thing. So G. I. Jade is about retraining people's minds and eating according to the three Rs – if it roams, if it's raw or if you can recognise it (if you can't tell what it is you don't know what's in it). Also, you should never talk about 'losing' weight, because that's a bad thing. People lose keys, they lose husbands and they lose their marbles. Instead it's about 'shedding' weight. We've hired personal trainers from the army, top-notch nutritionists, the lot. I've had to put a lot of money into it but it will all come back round in the end. Each person who enrols pays £950 for a week (which is cheaper than most, believe me) and we promise they'll shed up to a dress size, get cookery lessons, hypnotherapy and a whole change of lifestyle. I think it's going to be a success and I'm really excited about it.

I've now been lucky enough to have a second perfume in the shops. This one's called Controversial (see what I did there?) and I'm just as proud of it as Ssh. Just a year ago I would never ever have believed I would be lucky enough to get another attempt. But when I found out that Ssh had shot back to number two after being off the shelves longer than it had been on them, I knew I must have done something right. And it's not necessarily about me – it's the smell, and people like it. I get so much joy when I smell someone wearing something I've created.

I control everything, from the shape and design of the bottle to the scents that go in it. I loosely based Ssh on a perfume called Viktor & Rolf's Flowerbomb, but obviously there are plenty of differences otherwise I'd get sued! The people who make my perfume take some of the ingredients but suggest others to mix with it, and then I choose the one I like from five or six different options. The new one, Controversial, is based on Creed (which costs a £160 a bottle). It's got a similar freshness and is lovely, if I say so myself.

I had a big launch party for it at the beginning of the summer of 2008. It hit all the headlines because I dropped the bottle as I arrived. What a muppet, I know … but I'll get to that in a bit.

The night before the perfume launch I was sat in the lounge on my own and for some reason decided it would be a good idea to sing a song at the party. Well, I didn't want to just arrive and look at all these people sitting down, then say 'all right?' like a stupid nugget. So I thought that if I made up a little tune then it would give people something to talk about and also remind them all that I'm not someone who takes themselves too seriously.

I stood up, faced the window, and started humming that Jackson 5 ABC song. Then it suddenly came to me. And like that it all started flowing like a thing that, er, flows …

(When you sing this to yourself, make sure you do it to the tune of 'ABC'. It fits … sort of.)

People think –
That I am controversial
But I am just a young girl
Trying to get through the little
Life on my own
I've taken tumbles
But got back up again
And that's why you're here to celebrate
The launch of Jade Goody's Controversial

OK, so not exactly Mozart, but I was quite chuffed that I'd come up with it all on my own.

The following night, just before the launch, I was so nervous. It was the first time I'd invited the press to come to something of mine – something that I was actually promoting – since *Celebrity Big Brother*. And I knew, although there had been a lot of water under the bridge, that I could still fall flat on my face. As it was, the only thing that fell that night was my blinkin' perfume bottle – right out of my hand! The paps all got pictures, but luckily all seemed to think it was really funny (and typical of me). Talk about making an entrance!

When I arrived at the venue – Embassy, of course – I made sure the music for the song was playing so I could start singing as I walked in. Because people couldn't see me at first I think they thought it was a CD playing and some of them seemed really shocked when they saw it was actually me – and that I could actually sing! As I finished I had a little giggle and said 'well, am I gonna get a clap then?!' and at that everyone laughed and started applauding. It was such a nice feeling.

I knew calling the perfume 'Controversial' was asking

for a bit of trouble in the interviews at the launch, but it was only really Radio 1 who quizzed me on it, asking whether it was a bit wrong of me to try and make money out of bad situation. I managed to turn it around though when I said 'well, you tell me which *Big Brother* housemate hasn't tried to make the best of a bad situation!' In the end they couldn't help laughing.

It was a great night, and the smell of the perfume seemed to go down well, which was a bonus. So we'll just have to wait and see if the public like it now ...

Ricky Gervais sent me tickets to see his stand-up show *Fame* a while back because he speaks about my perfume as part of the show. I went with one of my mates and was crying with laughter by the time I left. It's pretty close to the bone, but that's what all comedy is really. He mentioned *Celebrity Big Brother* and said things like, 'Oh, I'd better not say that otherwise my perfume might get taken off the shelves like Jade Goody's!'

Everyone in the audience kept looking round at me after that, and it was really funny. I didn't get to meet Ricky afterwards but I just felt chuffed he'd invited me. Anyway, he must think I'm a numpty because I wrote to him once when I was doing one of my reality shows for Living TV. It was the most nonsense letter I've ever sent. 'Dear Ricky, I really want to meet you. Will you come on my show?' I'd stuck a 20-pence piece on the paper and added, 'Here's 20p, so now you can't make an excuse saying you didn't have enough money to call me.' I sent it to his home address, so he must've thought, Psycho!

His agent called me a couple of days later trying not to

laugh and said that Ricky was very flattered but unfortunately too busy to come on my show at this time.

My business might be picking up, but my management has changed again. I'm no longer looked after by Sean O'Brien. He was a good guy, but deep down I needed more than an agent. I needed guidance and a father figure. So I called Max Clifford. And as soon as I said who I was he replied, 'I've been waiting for you to come to me, girl.'

'Really?'

'Yeah.'

'Max, I'll be honest. I need to have a father figure in my life. I need someone who I can turn to and who'll look out for me. I know that might not sound very professional but that's what I need.'

'But, Jade, I'm not an agent.'

'I know that, you're a PR guru, but I also know you look after Kerry Katona and she refers to you as her rock – and I want the same thing.'

'Don't worry, I'll look after you. I'll be your PR man and I'll sign you over to someone else who'll work as your agent.'

Work now seems to be picking up too. God knows if anything will come of this but MTV have spoken to me about doing a show with them. They're talking about me running a dating agency or maybe a hotel. When I told my mates this they laughed – which I couldn't understand.

'What's so funny about me running my own hotel?' I asked them.

'The very fact that you even feel the need to ask that question,' they replied.

There's been a request for me to appear in *The Vagina Monologues*, which as far as I can tell is some touring production where three women sit on stage and talk about sex stories. It's acting, though, which will be great for me. I've heard they say 'c**t' a lot too. Not something I'm very familiar with myself. I never use such foul language ...

You're not going to believe this, but *EastEnders* was another job that was on the cards once – going in as Ronnie and Roxy's cousin. But now Bianca's back the ratings have gone up again, so they don't need me. The producers have said they're still interested at a later date, though. How mad would that be? I wouldn't even have to act for that role – all I'd need to say would be 'Awwrright?'

And, finally, after months in exile, Living TV took me back on board as one of their faces, which really meant the world to me. In July 2008 I started filming a new reality series for them – this one is called *Living with Jade* (which, as many people know, ain't always easy!). Could this mean I have been forgiven after all?

I feel very grateful to be given a second chance and I know there are people out there who think I don't deserve it. I know I've done wrong, but I can honestly say that everything I've done or been through has been a learning curve for me – and I hope I've come out a better person because of it. I've said my 'sorrys' and I've learnt from my mistakes (even though, admittedly there have been an awful lot of them). But for all my critics there have been ten times more people who, throughout the past two years, have come up to me in the street, hugged me and said things like, 'You shouldn't have been taken to task in the way you were. Now let's get back to the important stuff – when are you going to be back on our TV screens?'

I've had such a wide range of people, from all walks of life, feeling the need to come up to speak to me and offer support. From the 'Jeremy Kyle' types of folk (the ones who don't give a shit and say whatever comes into their mouth), to really posh-looking types who I'd never expect would wash their hands with me, all saying, 'You've had such a tough time.' But it's the old people who affect me the most. They break my heart because they'll totter over and hug me, with tears in their eyes because they think I've been hard done by. And whenever I see an elderly person cry I just lose it.

The other day I was in the supermarket and these two little old ladies were staring at me near the fruit counter. I could hear one of them whispering, 'Where have I seen her before?' and I smiled to myself. Then the other came over and said, 'Excuse me, are you my dentist?'

'No,' I said, trying not to laugh.

'I know!' piped up the other one. 'I've got it! You're the optician!'

I didn't want to say, 'I'm off the telly,' because it sounds so awful, so I just said they must be mistaken. As I walked off they said, 'I'm sure I've seen you, though.'

'My name's Jade.'

'That's it! I knew it! Lovely gal. You went through it, didn't you, eh? Don't worry, it'll be all right ... Don't you look slim in real life?'

Mavis and Beryl were their names. I love old people; they just don't care what people think. I remember not long after I'd come out of the *Celebrity Big Brother* house I met an old war veteran, with all his medals still pinned to his chest, and he told me, 'Don't go hanging your head down any more, girl. It's done now, it'll be OK.'

21
End of the Road

As for me and Jack? We were to split again at the end of March 2008, for what I thought was it. Of course, there was a horror to come that brought him back into my life ... but I'll come to that later. I think back then it came to the stage when I simply realised I didn't care any more. There had been so many stories about his infidelities. I'd even stopped wasting my time arguing with him about it. And of course there was always a part of me that thought the stories were true. I wish he'd been a man and admitted it. But he never did and never will. I stuck with him for so long because, although the things I read in the papers made me feel upset and betrayed, when I was with him I'd think, We're really good together. He was amazing with my kids too. I remember when I lay on the bed with Jack, dressed in my ridiculous lingerie outfit that Valentine's Day, and I felt completely swept up by him and would have done anything for him.

But those feelings died when he hurt me. And I don't think I ever truly fell back in love with him again after he failed to follow me out of the *Celebrity Big Brother* house. That cut through me like a knife. On the night of the final I was at my lowest ebb in The Priory and he was larking around getting pissed and taking photos of himself and the other housemates on his mobile phone. How could I really get over that? If you haven't got trust what have you got? The crunch point came after there was yet another rumour floating about concerning him and some girl. I'd had enough. One evening I said to him sadly, 'You know you can trust me completely. I give you everything; the best bits of me and the worst bits too. You have all of me. But with you I've just come to the point that I don't know when you're telling the truth or when you're lying to me any more.'

And there was nothing he could say. If anyone had said to me, 'Do you see yourself with Jack in the future?' I would have said no. So there was no point in me wasting any more of his life. He took it better than he did the first time we split up, but he was still really sad. 'I can't believe you're putting me through this again,' he said.

But this time I knew it was the right decision. And the reason I knew that was because I wasn't remotely concerned to make him jealous or show him what he was missing. At first this meant we could just be friends. I'd phone him up and say things like, 'I want to go and watch this film at the cinema but none of my mates will come. Can you?' And I'd encourage him to visit the boys whenever he wanted, which was great for them and meant us splitting up wasn't such a sudden change. After all, Jack had been there throughout most of Freddy's life, and he feels a lot of affection towards him. I knew if I found out he had another girlfriend I'd be slightly miffed at first, like any woman would, but ultimately I'd deal with it because I'd know it was OK. I realised I wasn't bitter any more.

But peaceful times in my life don't have much of a tendency to last very long, do they? And in this instance it was Jack who decided to upset the balance. In fact, to put it bluntly, he turned into a bit of a psycho. All loonatickified, he went.

Despite me telling him I had no feelings for him in that way, I started to get texts in the middle of the day saying, 'Let's have sex' or 'I'm horny'.

I'd reply, 'What? I'm not a brass!'

I thought he'd lost the plot. But there was part of me that thought it was funny, so I'd bat it away good-naturedly and tell him to stop being a wally.

Then one night I went to Faces nightclub in Essex with one of my mates, Angela. Jack and his friends were there, but it didn't bother me in the slightest because I knew we were just friends. So I went over and said hi to all of them. We had a bit of a chat, then me and Angela went to the bar and got down to business (buying drinks, that is). Suddenly this guy called Anthony came over to talk to us – we both knew him from years ago because he used to go out with Angela's sister. He's not the most gorgeous man on the planet, but he's quite pleasant-looking. He bought us both a drink and we started having a bit of a joke. Then, out of the blue, I saw something fly past my face and hit Anthony on the head. I looked over to see Jack standing on a seat across the bar, chucking ice cubes at Anthony. He wasn't even as pissed as I've seen him in the past. But the ice cubes kept on coming. Anthony was gobsmacked. 'What the fuck is he doing?' he asked me.

'I honestly don't know, Anthony. Hang on.'

I marched over to the chair on which Jack was wobbling about like an idiot.

'Jack, what the hell's going on? Why are you chucking ice cubes at him? That's psycho behaviour!'

'He's all over you,' he slurred back.

'He's a mate – I've known him for years. I'm not the sort of person who would get it on with another guy in front of your face – unlike you have in the past.'

'He makes me sick,' was all he could manage before I walked off. Did he have no pride? If I was behaving like that my mates would've stopped me or dragged me away. But I guess that was a sign of Jack's age. He just didn't seem to care how he behaved or what I might think.

I thought it was best to leave Anthony at that point, so Angela and I hit the dance floor. But we could still see what was going on at a distance and I watched as Jack waltzed over to Anthony. I found out afterwards he was 'apologising' but you certainly couldn't tell that was what was going on from the body language. Jack fronted up to him, arms waving all over the shop and his face virtually nose to nose with the poor guy. Understandably, Anthony wasn't too enthusiastic about talking to the fella who'd just been pinging ice cubes at his head, so I could see he was telling Jack to leave it. Thinking they were having an argument, I ran over and told Jack to go. To which he mumbled, 'Oh, whatever,' before rejoining his mates.

'See you later, Anthony,' I said, and dragged Angela into another room, away from the pair of them.

By now it was nearing the end of the night and we were pretty tipsy. The DJ played Boyz II Men's 'The End of the Road' and we went nuts. I *love* that song. It was just me and Angela and we swayed around the dance floor like we were the only two in the whole place. We loved it.

Just as the song was coming to an end, this boy/man came over to me. He leant in close and said, 'You look really pretty. Your hair looks lovely.'

'Thank you,' I replied. It's always nice to have a compliment, even if it might be someone's beer goggles doing the talking.

'Can I ask you something, Jade?'

'Go on …'

'Have you had your lips done?'

At this, both me and Angela burst out laughing. You see, just that day I'd been to the beautician and had this injection in my lip called 'Cinderella kiss'. It's a temporary thing that lasts for about two weeks and plumps them up a bit. Not that I need it really – my lips are huge anyway.

'No …!' I grinned

'Yes you have!' shouted Angela. 'Don't lie! Look at the injection mark!'

'Shut up!' I laughed.

Meanwhile, behind me, Jack had reappeared and all he could see from where he was standing was me laughing with another guy. He stormed over and punched the bloke in the head, then turned and whacked his mate who was standing beside him, just for good measure.

I didn't know what to do. I looked at the guy on the floor and said, 'I'm so sorry,' as Angela tried to pull me outside.

'Jack, you fucking wanker!' I shrieked. 'Can you learn to behave yourself, please?'

By the time I'd finished having a go at Jack, the guys had dusted themselves off and left the club. Jack then walked off in a huff.

By the time Angela and I had followed, there was a full-blown brawl going on. Jack was chucking a load of punches, and getting a good pounding himself as well, and everyone was circling around them trying to get a glimpse of the action. There was a photographer out there too. I don't need this! I thought.

But even though I knew I should walk away and leave them to it. I couldn't. I was too worried about Jack getting hurt. The problem with him is that he won't stop – he might go down, but he will get right back up again. And no matter how small he is, he's got no fear. Some people might think he deserves what he gets, but at the end of the day I'd been with him for nearly three years and I didn't want to see my ex end up a battered lump on the floor.

I pleaded with Jack. 'Get in the cab with us.'

'No!' he stuttered and tried to throw another punch. 'Fuck off!'

The bouncers were still trying to break up the fight when the police arrived. That was all I needed. Eventually I managed to get Jack into a cab and Angela and I took him home. Not that he showed us much appreciation, mind you. All he could mumble while he was rolling around in the back of the cab was: 'You're a fucking slag! You make me sick!'

I told him, 'I've just saved your bacon, mate, so you need to learn to be grateful. You're on trial soon because someone's accused you of smacking them with a golf club, so I think you need all the help you can get if the court is going to believe you're a respectable character.'

'You make me sick. I've got no respect for you.'

'Yes, Jack, I gathered that last bit a long time ago. So for you to tell me that now just makes me feel better in the knowledge that I made the right decision to finish with you. I don't need this, Jack.'

As soon as we got to his mum's house we pushed him out of the cab and said, 'Good riddance.' In my head I'd written him off completely. No more trying to be friends.

Of course, he was back on the text the next day. 'Jade, I miss you. I was just jealous. We can't go to the same places any more.'

I replied, 'I'm a grown-up. We live near each other. I'm not going to do anything with other guys in front of you, but I'm not dodging places just because I think you might be there!'

After that I went on my first holiday as a fully fledged single mum – to Butlins in Bognor Regis. I did suggest Dubai or Spain but Bobby and Freddy were having none of it. They'd seen an advert for this holiday camp and that's where they wanted to go. I felt the blood drain from my face. It's going to be hell, I thought. I quickly rang my mate Danielle, who's got a two-year-old called Rosie. 'You coming to Butlins?' I blurted out.

'What?'

'Butlins. Come on – I'm paying.'

'Oh, all right.'

With that I put the phone down and booked the holiday quick as a flash so she didn't have the chance to change her mind.

I rang her back. 'It's all sorted.'

'What? Already?'

'Yep, we're going in three days' time.'

'Oh ... er ... OK.'

We drove there and the day we arrived we found we'd

255

been 'upgraded' to a cabin, which contained about 50 beds (OK, slight exaggeration, but you get my drift). I felt really awful but I had to go and ask if we could move rooms as there was no bath in there, just a shower, and the boys need a bath every night. This time we got properly upgraded, to the Butlins Shoreline Hotel, which was much nicer! When we woke up the next day we were given our itinerary and I've never had such a packed, eventful holiday in my life. We watched *The Barney Show*, *The Mr Men*, *Aladdin*, a Madonna tribute act – there was so much going on. The kids absolutely loved it, and I've never seen them so happy. When they were asleep me and Danielle would climb out of the window and sit up on the roof – like Robson and Jerome – with a glass of rose, putting the world to rights. That is, until we got told off by the hotel manager because it was against health and safety.

Much as I loved our trip to Butlins, my annual trip to Marbella is the thing I get most excited about. And this year I was going with the girls – on a proper singles holiday. As soon as Jack found out the dates, though, he booked an identical trip for him and his mates. That boy really has no shame at all! I warned him in no uncertain terms that he had to behave himself this time. If he so much as attempted to come near me or my hotel room door again I would call the police and have him arrested. I didn't want to feel like I was looking over my shoulder for the entire holiday.

In typical me fashion, I ended up in the newspapers again several times at the beginning of the summer of 2008. The first time, because I'd been burgled to the tune of £56,000. I'd been round at my mate Danielle's for the evening (the kids were at their dad's) and when I came home at about

11pm I instantly knew that something was wrong. Whenever I come back to the house my little dog Batman always scuttles down the stairs straight away to meet me, but this time he wasn't there. I went into the kitchen and my first thought was, I'm sure I didn't leave that window open ... So I called for Batman, who eventually came down the stairs, and started looking around the house. The doors in the front room were open too – I wouldn't have done that, I thought, anyone could get in from the garden!

My heart stopped. Someone was in the house. Without giving it a second thought I grabbed Batman in my arms, opened a drawer in the kitchen and pulled out the biggest knife I could find. Then I crept upstairs – trying not to breathe in case I was heard.

Yes, I know, what the heck was I thinking? How on earth was I going to fight a burglar? I know I'm not Wonder Woman, but that was my first reaction and I just went with it.

When I reached the top of the stairs I heard rustling and stopped dead in my tracks. Where was he? I looked into the bedroom and there were muddy footprints everywhere. I slowly walked inside – no one was there – but, oh my God, no! – my dressing table was glaringly bare. That's where I kept all my jewellery ... and it was all gone.

Gone.

All £56,000 worth.

Thankfully the ring that Prince Azim had given me was away being valued, and another yellow diamond ring of mine was away being mended. But I didn't know this at the time. All I thought was, Fuck me. What have I lost? Then, probably more to the point, Is he still in here?

I ran downstairs with Batman still in my arms, grabbed the car keys and, with my heart about to fly through the windscreen, started the engine and drove in the pitch black to the end of my road. I live out in the sticks, so there was no one about – and that frightened me rigid. I rang Danielle, who tried to calm me down, and she kept me on the phone while she rang the police, who said they'd be here as soon as possible and not to panic.

Panic? I could have died!

An HOUR later the police arrived.

Thanks for that.

We went back to the house and I had to give a statement, then they told me not to touch anything as they needed to get people in to check for fingerprints. Fenetics or forensics I think they called them. They asked me if I was OK in the house on my own and I nodded. My friends have since said that there's no way they'd have stayed there the night after a burglar had been in, but I was just exhausted from all the drama. Besides, I thought, it's my house – I'm not having some fucker kicking me out of it.

Once the police had done their business with the fingerprints I bleached and scrubbed the place from top to toe.

I wasn't covered by insurance. I was only covered for small amounts – I'd been meaning to change it, but naturally I hadn't got round to it. Yes, I felt sick at the thought of losing all that money, but ultimately I was more relieved that the kids weren't with me that night. What's money when you've got the safety of your family?

Epilogue

I know I need to go back to therapy. I have to come to terms with my past. I'm at the stage in my life now where I've taken some blows in the face and I like to think I've pulled myself out of it. But in doing so I've lost a lot of me. Yes, I'm doing all right now, but I'm not complete again. And I know that in order to get to that level of self-acceptance I need to face up to my issues. After *Celebrity Big Brother* people said I had a problem with anger – and yes, I have a temper on me – but, contrary to what the papers say, I don't go out picking fights wherever I go. About a year after *CBB* the newspapers accused me of having a go at a girl in a nightclub. Admittedly, the photo they printed wasn't me at my most demure, but, while it looked like I was fighting with a girl, I was actually being calmed down by my friend Danielle because a girl had chucked a drink in my face. I'm not the prettiest thing, but my boat race means a lot to me and because of what happened in the *Celebrity Big Brother* house people now think they've got the right to come and have a go at me or threaten to bottle me. And that thought petrifies me. When that picture was taken of me looking all shaken and angry I was simply in a state because of what the girl had done. Why should I put up with it? And far from what the papers said, the bouncers didn't kick me out of the club. They all know me and told me to stay where I was because they knew full well I hadn't done anything wrong.

There was a point in mid-2008 where I finally thought I'd picked myself up, dusted myself off and learnt a hell of a lot along the way. I was gradually starting to become Jade again. After *Big Brother* I lost all my confidence and felt like I had no identity. I know now that it's really important for me to feel liked. I never used to worry about what people thought about me. I'd been of the mind that you're either loved or hated, and that's life. But the reaction I got after *Celebrity Big Brother* was different because I was being hated for something that I wasn't – a racist – and I couldn't handle it. To know that people didn't like me was the worst feeling in the world.

I can understand people disliking me for the way I spoke to Shilpa, and the fact that I'd got so angry towards her, but that wasn't the cause of the national uproar. What I did was perceived as a racial attack and that's so not what it was. To be hated for something I wasn't made me lose all sense of who I was and all self-belief. Every time I walked past someone who I'd met before I would convince myself that they hated me. Each time I saw someone famous that I'd chatted to in the past and I knew had liked me once, I would think, Has *your* opinion changed of me too? Do *you* think I'm a racist? When you know that someone genuinely liked you before, it's hard to face the reality that they might have changed their opinion of you. I had a complete identity crisis – I didn't know how to act, what to wear or who to be.

I always used to put on the bravado that I didn't care, but deep down I did. I need to feel accepted. It's a huge thing for me.

I'm also starting to address the other issues that are wrong with me. I know now that I struggle with men – because of the way my dad was I have severe problems with trusting them. I've realised too that I have a kind of three-year barrier, by which point I end up pushing the men in my life away for fear it might get too serious and they might hurt me too much. It happened with Jeff and now it's happened with Jack too.

But do you know what my biggest worry is? I feel like the whole world sees me as this loud, pig-faced, fat, foul-mouthed girl. Sometimes it's made me cry myself to sleep just thinking about it. How am I ever meant to find Mr Right when everyone perceives me like that? How am I meant to get away from attracting the wrong type of blokes when that's the way people see me? No man with a decent job and grown-up lifestyle would ever look twice at me or say, 'I'll take you under my wing.' I've got a stigma attached to me and it's never going to go away. I can't ever imagine meeting a distinguished-looking man and saying, 'Hi, I'm Jade,' without him thinking, I've heard about you, and walking away. My dream has been to meet someone older, who's successful and has come from a nice family, but I've often wondered how that will ever happen. For a start, my mum's a raving lunatic. With her telling people she used to wash my face with wee, how the hell am I meant to keep a man?

At the time of finishing this book, after severely pissing me off a few months earlier with his childishness, Jack has started creeping back into my life. And this time – I'm not sure if it's just because he seems more mature (and has stopped pestering me for sex!) or because my outlook has changed – something feels different. I've been seeing a life coach recently, as well as doing all my meditating, and just generally trying to make myself a better person and see the best in others too. I really don't know what's going on with me and Jack right now, but there are definitely still feelings there.

Men aside, I know that most of all I need to face up to the problems I've got buried in my past about my mum. But I find it so hard to talk about how much the lies back then hurt me – even now. When all that stuff happened between us I felt like a little part of me had been killed off. After everything I'd given up for her, everything I'd done to look after her, she'd chosen something filthy and dirty instead of me. And to have to accept that? I just don't feel equipped to deal with the emotion of it. To this day I still have the fear that Mum might go back on the drugs, and it's going to stay with me for ever. And it really bothers my mum to know I don't trust her. Whenever she's on her own for too long now I worry about who she's been with. If she doesn't answer her phone all day, my head kicks into, what's she doing? Where is she? But I have to cling to the knowledge that once she decides something, that's it, which means now, as far as she's concerned, she's done with drugs.

In a way *Big Brother* saved my mum. Because when I

first entered the house in 2002 and she was faced with having a daughter who was a 'celebrity' she had no choice but to focus on what was going on and to field questions from the press and other people who were suddenly interested in our lives.

The memories are still there, though. And they're still raw. We had an argument the other day and I ended up shouting at her, 'My rage, my anger, it stems from you lying to me, Mum! That's why I'm like I am!'

She broke down in tears. 'Do you think I don't know that, Jade? Do you think I don't look at you and know it's my fault you get so angry at the world?'

Our relationship is so volatile because there's so much between us; there's much more to us than any normal mother-and-daughter relationship.

I also worry about her growing older on her own. She was seeing a woman recently and it got so serious that Mum moved in with her – in Yorkshire! She loved it at first, but, while I was pleased that my mum was settled and happy, it was strange not having her nearby. I'm always ringing her up to come over and help me with things to do with the kids. 'There's poo in the bath! What do I do?' But I was glad she was somewhere clean, away from all the bad influences of London, and if she'd chosen to stay for good I would've accepted that. They finished in the end, though – my mum's not the easiest person to live with. She says she's fine on her own, but I do still worry. I'm a bit of a romantic at heart and want happy endings for everyone. When I watch things like *My Best Mate's Wedding* (or whatever it's called) I sob my guts out because it's such a nice story. And if I see old people holding hands together and looking all sweet, I think,

That's so beautiful. My mum's got a lot of front, but I know she wants to settle down one day. Whoever gets her will have their hands full, though!

As for my own role as a mum, my boys give me more pleasure every day. They're growing up so quickly it's unbelievable. And I want to savour every bit of time I have with them before they're old enough to start being mouthy to me!

Ultimately, one thing that being in The Priory taught me was that I shouldn't be embarrassed to ask for help or talk about my problems. I shouldn't be embarrassed about doing things that will make me feel better. So I'm getting into meditation now. Jeff introduced me to the idea. He's been doing it for a while. (I always wondered how he managed to stay so calm in situations and look on the bright side of things.) We actually really like each other again too. It has taken a long, long while for us to get like this, but he's happy in his relationship with his girlfriend and I'm happy in myself, so we can finally get on. We're not just amicable; we're actually friends, which is great for the boys. We've been through a lot together and we have to accept we're going to be part of each other's life for ever so we might as well learn to deal with it. Thank God we've finally grown up, eh? A few months ago Jeff gave me this book called *The Secret*, saying, 'You should read this.' It's all about rethinking things and retuning your brain. And it must have worked with Jeff. No matter what he's been through, or where he is financially, he never seems to have any issues or stress. Give me some of that, I've often thought. I'm stressed the entire time!

I've only read a bit of it so far but I intend to finish it

and learn something about myself. God knows I still need to (or Buddha knows, should I say).

Buddhism has always interested me. After what happened in the *Celebrity Big Brother* house I was sent a book by one of my friends in the magazine world because she was worried about my state of mind. It's called *The Buddha in Your Mirror* and it's really interesting (well, the bits I understood anyway – I only got a few pages in before it told you the words to say when you're chanting and I couldn't read how you were meant to say them, it looked a bit complicated). But I've always wanted to go and spend a week with a Buddhist – you know, go and dress up in orange and meditate with them. Maybe it's something I'll do in the future because I do hope that one day I can find peace in myself. I don't want to be hung up about lies, or about men who I think are going to run out on me. I hope I find that contentment.

At the end of my last book I said, 'The day before I left the *Big Brother* house I went into the diary room and was asked how I'd like to be remembered. I said, "As the person who let everybody see every single side of her, and they either liked her or they didn't."'

Well, once again I've managed to do that. Even if most people were of the 'didn't' camp following my second visit to the *Big Brother* house. All I can say is that my life has continued to be one huge learning curve. Here are some of the things I've learnt this time:

Never attempt to run the Marathon when you've only done 20 minutes of training on the treadmill.

Try to control your temper and treat others how you want to be treated.

Check your boyfriend's age before you start dating him. Never take slimming pills.

Ban your mum from talking to reporters unless you want to see a front-page headline saying your face was washed in wee.

Afterword

Just before I went to India to go on their version of *Celebrity Big Brother*, (more about the madness of that later) I had another bad experience of blood loss and was rushed to hospital again for a load more tests. I was at home on my own at the time and for a couple of days I had been getting really bad pains in my tummy. I kept getting these really horrible cramps as I sat on the sofa, so I stood up to try and bend over in the hope that it would take the pain away and straight away I knew something was really wrong. As soon as I got up I could feel the blood pouring out of me (sorry to be so graphic, but that's what happened), so I made my way to the toilet as fast as I could. When I got there it was the same old story as before – blood clots, the lot. And I was feeling so faint, when I saw all the blood pouring out, I fell on the floor and bumped my head. Thank God I didn't knock myself unconscious, because there was no one there to help me. Somehow I managed to crawl to where my phone was and ring for an ambulance.

As I was waiting for the ambulance to arrive I rang my mate Danielle, but there was no answer, so I instinctively rang Jack. He was amazing and rushed straight over. He got there just as I was being taken away, so he and his mate followed me to the hospital to check I was OK.

Well, I wasn't. And it was nothing to do with the blood loss. In the ambulance the paramedics had given me morphine to stop the cramping pain, and it subsequently turned out that I was allergic to it. It was the worst feeling ever. I was sweating, my lips turned blue and I couldn't see a thing – it felt like something out of a horror film. I could hear people shouting my name, but I couldn't breathe and was slipping in and out of consciousness. I also remember this horrible feeling in my skin – it felt like there were worms crawling around underneath it.

It took 24 hours for it to work its way out of my system, so I had to stay in for longer than expected for tests. Once the doctors could do tests they said they thought the blood loss was a miscarriage. I said, if that was the case, I should change my name to Mary because I definitely hadn't had sex with anyone! So I had more and more tests and they were still unclear about what it could be.

Then I was taken to have a smear test and they burnt off more dodgy cells on my cervix. I think they thought, Now we've finally got her in here lets get it over with. So, just like that, I was whisked off to have more cells removed.

Afterwards the doctor told me that I was fine and could go home. They gave me a load of painkillers and told me to take them as and when I needed them.

Jack has really amazed me with how good he's been when I've needed him. When I was in hospital he took all my washing to my mum's house and made sure everything was fresh and clean for when I got home. I didn't even have to drop any hints! And he also picked Freddy up from my mum's and stayed with him until I got out because he knew he just wanted to be back home. I guess he's *finally* growing up!

I got another massive shock – the shock of my life – while I was in hospital. But this was a good shock. I can remember it really clearly. It was about five past eight in the evening on 8 August 2008 (08.08.08 – spooky, eh? And apparently good luck too!) and I had just been told that I could go home, when I got a call from my agent:

'You OK Jade? How are you feeling?'

'Fine now, thank you. Much better.'

'Good. I have a bit of a proposal for you ...' (He started laughing.)

'What is it?'

'Endemol in India have been on the phone.'

'What?'

'The makers of *Big Brother* in India.'

'What did they want?!'

'They want you to be the star booking to go into their *Celebrity Big Brother* house.'

'Really? Oh my God!'

'You need to fly out in a few days and, if it all goes well, you could end up being in there for three months.'

'Oh my God. You know what, I'd love nothing more.'

It felt like now I'd really have a chance to prove myself. And, as long as I kept my head together, which I hoped as a result of my life coaching I'd be able to do, I could really make amends. And who knows, if they liked me, I might end up in a Bollywood movie!

'Jade, there's one more thing,' my agent said.

'What's that?

'Shilpa Shetty is the host!'

I was flown to India for the show within a matter of days of getting the call. As I stood on the stage being interviewed by Shilpa (who hugged me and was really nice) I thought things could finally be turning around for the better. The crowd was cheering me on and I actually felt *liked*. Although I was shitting myself, it felt so good. Of course, no attempt to be dignified ever works for me and even though I managed to get my words out and say the right things about why I wanted to go into the house, just as I said 'See you later' to Shilpa, I tripped over. Typical.

Big Boss is India's celebrity version of *Big Brother*. Of course, I didn't know who any of the housemates were because I hadn't watched Indian TV, but they were all well known in their country. There were dancers, actors and actresses, an MP and a chef. And they were all absolutely lovely. I got on with everyone in there – it was just brilliant.

I had the best time and I did all sorts of exciting things in the few days I was in the house: I learnt how to say my name and where I lived in Indian, I was taught a bit of Bollywood dancing and I ate lots of amazing food – it was out of this world! When I first got there I announced – possibly rudely, but I didn't mean it like that – 'I ain't eating curry in the morning. I can't handle it for breakfast!' But the housemates insisted I try what they'd made, and I'm glad I did. One of the housemates owned his own restaurant and he cooked me this sort of scrambled curried egg dish. I could've eaten a whole house full. It was yum.

Luckily for them I didn't insist on them trying any of my dishes. For some reason I decided to take on a slightly less glamorous role in the house – the bog cleaner. I couldn't stand the idea of the toilet getting filthy, so there I was scrubbing and bleaching on my hands and knees every night. Well, for the short time I was there that is.

As it turned out I was only in there for three days.

On the third day I was called into the diary room for what I thought was just a chat about how I was getting on in the house. But, as soon as I opened the door and saw one of the producers stood in there, I knew something was wrong. My instant reaction was that the Indian public wanted me out because they hated me and that they'd had enough of me being in there. But the man looked at me and said, 'A doctor keeps calling and trying to talk to you – we think this might be a hoax.'

'Of course it's a hoax!' was my response. 'It's probably a journalist or something from back home.'

What else was I supposed to think? As far as I was concerned I had left hospital believing everything was all fine. Otherwise, I assumed, the doctors wouldn't have let me go to India.

I was then asked if I would permit the doctor to speak to me on loudspeaker – as that's how all conversations in the house were conducted. I said yes. Then, there, crouched in the familiar surroundings of a diary room chair, I heard the doctor's voice:

'Jade, just to let you know, we've had a look at the tests again and it has come to our attention that there's something severely wrong.'

'What do you mean severely wrong?'

'Jade, we need you to come home immediately.'

'Why do I have to come home? What's wrong with me?'

They told me I had severe 1b or 1 something Cancer. Whatever that means. All I thought was, Cancer, chemo – dead.

'What? What does that mean? Am I going to die?'

'It's an emergency Jade – you need to come home.'

I was distraught. I asked to use a phone so that I could speak to my agent Mark. I had to give the doctor permission to tell him what he'd told me, and then I told Mark to phone my family straight away. I couldn't risk them seeing the news go out on air before they'd been told. I knew that as soon as I walked out of the diary room the housemates would see that I was upset and, although I could put them off for a certain amount of time, I wouldn't be able to hold off saying something forever. And I didn't want what I said in the house suddenly flashing up on Sky News at home for all my family and friends to see. Not before I'd told them anyway.

If you watch the footage, when I go out of the diary room I don't tell the housemates straight away – I don't tell them what's the matter. I'm sobbing but I say I can't tell them what it is yet as my family don't know. The housemates were all trying to comfort me and being lovely, but I was inconsolable. It was only about an hour-and-a-half later, when Mark said he'd told my mum and Jack, that I could let them in.

After that I was shipped out to a hotel room and told the plane home was booked. I couldn't stop crying. A million things were running through my head over and over again: How long has it been there? Why haven't they found it before? How can it be severe if no one knew it was there?

I had all these questions, but there was no one that I could ask. The show's producers had sent someone from Endemol to be with me, but I didn't want a stranger. I wanted a hug from someone I loved. I wanted someone to tell me it was all a horrible dream.

I just didn't know what to do with myself. I got to the hotel room and my phone was dead, so I couldn't even call anyone. I was like a lost soul. I had a bath and lay in there for ages – motionless, numb – what was going on? I just wanted to see my boys; that's all I could think about.

What was happening to me?

I fell asleep crying in the end and then was taken to get my flight first thing the next morning. There was a man assigned to be with me – not that we had anything to say to each other, but I guess it was better than being alone. The plane was delayed for an hour, so he helped me find a charger for my phone so I could get the numbers of my mum and Jack and call them. Mum didn't really know what to say – bless her, she never does really. She's not very good at stuff like that.

'You're going to be all right Jade,' she said.

'Why don't you understand?' I shrieked. I was angry. Why couldn't my mum be like a mum should be and tell me that she could help make everything better?

All I could do in the end was try and make a joke about

it – 'I'm going to be bald mum. You'll have to help me shave my head!' She laughed.

That was all I could do – try to make jokes.

My friends and family aren't used to me being down or upset, so the only way I know how to cope is to try and make people laugh. And in all honesty that did start to make me feel better.

I spoke to Jack next. He didn't really know what to say either – he's not very good with words. He's been there for me so much, which speaks volumes – he just doesn't know how to express himself.

He said, 'You'll be all right. They've said it's not severe ...'

But it's those words, that notion of 'everything being OK', that came to upset and frustrate me the most. When I got home afterwards I saw blogs, websites and chat rooms commenting on what I had, as if they all knew: 'Oh it's only pre-cancerous cells ... it's not serious' ... 'Oh she's making a big deal out of nothing for publicity' ... 'I've been through cervical cancer and I'm fine now. It's no big deal.'

Everyone thought they knew what my problem was, but they didn't. This was cancer. The real thing. I had had it for two years. It had gone into my womb and now it could be in my bloodstream. It's so frustrating when people say, 'Oh you'll be all right', and it's bloody well not all right.

Some people in the media were so horrible too. In the past I could take people calling me names, but I couldn't handle people calling me a liar about something as bad as this. I agreed to do an interview with the *Sun* because journalists were fighting to talk to me. But then I just got criticised for making it public! But what choice did I have?

AFTERWORD

I felt I needed to speak out to defend myself, and let people see that it was real and that I wasn't making it up.

Why would I make something like *this* up?!

This cancer, *my* cancer, has been there in my body for two years.

I flew back home with Virgin, first class, and they were all lovely. I felt like everyone knew – but they were very nice and caring. I fell asleep for most of the journey, and then I had a little cry to myself. I tried not to let anyone see, but I thought somehow that if I let it out then it would mean I could hold it together when I got off. But no, of course it didn't work out like that.

When I got off the plane and walked through the airport in London I felt like I was naked. I felt as if I was completely starkers with a big torchlight shining through me and that everyone could see every single part of me.

I knew there would be press when I arrived, but wasn't expecting anything like I saw. Press are allowed in the airport terminals and there were swarms everywhere – video cameras, photographers, reporters, all shouting: 'Jade, Jade – are you OK?'

I couldn't cope. It was just too much. I tried to keep my head down and keep walking, but as soon as people started asking questions I felt my lips quiver. I didn't know where to turn. In the end I just put my head in the air stewardess's arm and whispered, 'I can't take this. Please make them stop, please.'

In the end I was taken out of a side door and given a police escort because there were that many people running round trying to get pictures. It was unbelievable. I couldn't bear it.

After that I was driven straight home. The boys were with my mum – they'd been there anyway because I'd planned to be in the Indian *BB* house for three months. I'd been more organised than ever in my life before I went to India – I'd done a rota of who was to look after them; I'd recorded video messages to play to them each week; I'd made preparations for Freddy's birthday party – the lot. So at least that was one thing I didn't have to worry about. I couldn't tell them what was wrong with me anyway – they're too young. All I've said, even now, is that mummy's got something wrong with her belly and that I need to go to see the doctor to make it better. I can't go into explaining about cancer. It's too much. They don't need to know.

When I arrived outside the house, I rang Jack, who was in there waiting for me. But when I called his phone to ask him to unlock the electric gates he didn't hear it, which meant I had to get out of the car. There was about fifty people out there waiting – shouting questions, flashing their cameras – and it was the last thing I needed.

When I finally got in, I ran into the lounge and just sobbed into Jack's lap.

He had been sitting on the sofa for hours clutching a card that he'd bought for me. Problem is he's so rubbish with words that the only thing he'd written so far was, 'To Jade'. (It took him three days before he actually finished it because he just didn't know what to say. In the end it was quite a nice message – but it did take a while!)

He cuddled me as I cried quietly and then we sat up for a bit talking. We talked about anything and everything – anything but the cancer. I asked him what it was like at the V festival and we chatted about tons of other meaningless stuff. It was only when we finally lay in bed at about 2am that I finally mumbled, 'I've got to go to the doctor's tomorrow and I'm really scared. Will you come with me?'

When I got to the doctor's the next day I was told that rather than it being stage one cancer – it was nearer to a stage two or three. They said I needed to have an MRI scan. I found out afterwards that, when you're told you need an MRI scan, normally you have to wait for about a week for it, but when I got home that day, I got a phone call almost immediately: 'We've had a cancellation for an MRI – please come in this afternoon'.

Jack came with me to the hospital and we were taken into this room where I had to lay down while they put me underneath this big tube thing. I was crying the whole time thinking, What are they doing? What is it? The machine was making all these weird noises. The doctor told Jack that he could come in the room with me, so he sat there trying to talk to me and check I was OK. We didn't really say much to each other though – it wasn't really the time to chat about the weather – he just wiped the tears from my eyes because I couldn't move my hands.

When I came out of the hospital I spoke to my publicist Max Clifford. He said he'd spoken to his own doctor who told him that, in her opinion, we needed to act quickly. She felt it could have been fatal if I had stayed in the *BB* house in India for the full three months.

Max took it upon himself to pay for me to go and see her. Her name was Ann and I was booked in the next day. I couldn't afford it on my own, but he wanted me to get the best help I possibly could. It meant that I could get access to the very top doctors and specialists.

When I saw Ann she gave me another MRI scan – and this time it seemed a lot more intense. There were so many instructions – when to breathe in and out, not to move my toes.

The results came back the very next day and I went to see Ann immediately. She got straight to the point, and I liked that. But somehow she also made me laugh, which I desperately needed. First of all she showed me a picture of the tumour. It was horrible – all I could see was this big dark lump that made me feel sick. It looked really gross. Then she went into great detail explaining exactly what all of this meant.

She sat me down and told me in no uncertain terms that there was a possibility that it had gone into the bloodstream and that if that was the case I'd be having lots of chemotherapy. Maybe for as long as the next five years! She told me that if it's not in the bloodstream I'd need surgery to remove the entire womb. But if it has spread, then my insides would be left untouched. Instead they'd be blasted with chemo in the hope that that would get rid of the fucker.

Either way I will never be having children ever again.

I know I have two beautiful kids, but I can't help thinking that the only thing that makes me a woman and not a man is my insides – my ovaries and my womb. And to think that could all be gone makes me so sad.

Ever since I was told the news I've been going through a circle of emotions – from laughing, to crying, to going totally insane …

Jeff has been great through all this – he's rung me every other day wanting to know I'm OK and asking about the test results.

I've given up on the life coaching for now – I feel like it hasn't really done much for me – it didn't stop me having bloody cancer did it? Maybe I'll go back to it someday but, call me cynical, it just doesn't feel right at the moment.

I thought my 'friend' the Prince might've texted me, but he hasn't made any contact yet, which makes me a bit sad. I am upset another guy hasn't contacted me as well. I've known him for years, but he hasn't said a word to me since he stopped speaking to me earlier this year because I didn't go to his birthday party! I would've thought he might've at least texted to say, 'Are you OK?'

I guess at times like this you find out who your real friends are.

I now face a long, long time in and out of hospital. But somehow out of all of this I seem to have found a focus. When I sat on the plane coming back from India I wrote down a list of things that I wanted to do – the writing is so messy I have to squint to read my words now, but I couldn't stop the flow – it just poured out of me.

One of the first things I want to do is to make amends with my dad. I want to go and put flowers on his grave. He's dead for God's sake, so for me to have such hatred towards him still is ridiculous. I also want to make up with my half-brother, who I've slagged off pretty badly in the past. And finally, I want to take the boys to a poor country – just to let them know that what they have isn't normal. They're not spoilt at all, but they've got all the computer games and toys that any little boy could ever want and I want them to see how other kids have to live so that they really appreciate what they've got.

I don't want people to think I'm doing it for the sake of it, but I know they will. I just suddenly had this overwhelming feeling that I want to give something back. You might think I sound like a righteous idiot, but I can't help it. And I just keep thinking about the fact that I've been on all these amazing holidays – to all these great places – and what have I done when I got there? Sat browning my fat arse on a beach, that's what. From here on in it's going to be different. I want to take the kids camping, teach them to fish, take them climbing. I want to do all things I never would have bothered about doing before.

I'm only 27 and I would have liked to have a little girl. I know I have two beautiful boys, but that doesn't mean I don't want more. I would like to think I could freeze my eggs, but I think that makes things too complicated. Maybe I'll adopt one day (I might even end up going down the Angelina Jolie route after all – who'd of thought it eh John Noel?).

I don't like relying on other people and I always feel the need to come across as a strong person, but there have been times since I found out about the cancer that I've just completely broken down. Like the other night, the thought of never being able to have kids again, of having my womb removed, just got too much for me. I felt like I was being told I'm not going to be a woman anymore. You might think it's ridiculous, but, I even thought the other day, what's the point of sex anymore, if I can't have kids?

I've had some shit to deal with in the past – some my own fault, some not – but until now there's always been some sort of solution. This time I'm faced with dealing with something I know I have no control over. I just have to get on with it.

It annoys me when people say, 'You're strong. You'll be OK' – I'm fed up of always having to be the strong one. Why can't people just give me a cuddle? I want people to say it's all right to be weak and it's all right to cry (mind you, knowing me, if that happens then I'll feel weak and helpless and won't be able to cope with that either!).

Ultimately, through all of this, I know I just have to keep smiling. The boys make me laugh every day, which takes my mind off things and keeps me normal. I don't know what I would do without them. I'm also writing a diary about how I feel so I have something to look back on and so that I can be proud of what I've come through.

Prepare yourself for the fact that the next time you see me I could very well be bald from all the chemo. But please don't feel sorry for me. Losing my hair is just another hurdle I'll have to go through (or jump over – whatever you do with hurdles). And all I can say is – losing my barnet is nothing compared to having my perfume taken off the shelves! Just kidding, of course, but don't they say that laughing is half the battle?